HENRY IV
Part II

The RSC Shakespeare

Edited by Jonathan Bate and Eric Rasmussen

Chief Associate Editors: Héloïse Sénéchal and Jan Sewell

Associate Editors: Trey Jansen, Eleanor Lowe, Lucy Munro,
Dee Anna Phares

Henry IV Part II

Textual editing: Eric Rasmussen

Introduction and Shakespeare's Career in the Theater: Jonathan Bate

Commentary: Jan Sewell and Héloïse Sénéchal

Scene-by-Scene Analysis: Esme Miskimmin

In Performance: Karin Brown (RSC stagings), Jan Sewell (overview)

The Actor's Voice and the Director's Cut

(interviews by Jonathan Bate and Kevin Wright): Michael Pennington,
Adrian Noble, Michael Boyd

The RSC Shakespeare

William Shakespeare

HENRY IV
PART II

Edited by Jonathan Bate and Eric Rasmussen

Introduction by Jonathan Bate

The Modern Library
New York

CONTENTS

INTRODUCTION*

TRAGICAL-COMICAL-HISTORICAL-PASTORAL

Shakespeare's art of mingling comedy, history, and tragedy reached its peak in the two parts of *Henry IV*. As history, the plays paint a panorama of England, embracing a wider social range than any previous historical drama as the action moves from court to tavern, council chamber to battlefield, city to country, Archbishop and Lord Chief Justice to whore and thief. As comedy, they tell the story of a prodigal son's journey from youth to maturity and an old rogue's art of surviving by means of jokes, tall tales, and the art of being not only witty in himself, but the cause that wit is in other men. As tragedy, they reveal the slow decline of a king who cannot escape his past, the precipitate demise of an impetuous young warrior who embodies both the glory and the futility of military heroism, and the heartbreaking dismissal of a substitute father who has loved a prince with a warmth of which his true father is incapable.

The action of *Part I* had begun some time after the events that ended Shakespeare's earlier play, *Richard II*. Henry Bullingbrook has usurped the throne of King Richard, who has been murdered. But now the rebels who helped Henry to the throne have turned against him. Whereas *Richard II* conformed to the traditional structure of tragedy— the story of the fall of a powerful man—the *Henry IV* plays adopt a wider perspective. *Richard II* had been written entirely in verse, the medium of royal and aristocratic characters, whereas long stretches of the *Henry IV* plays are in prose, the medium of the common people. The scenes with Justice Shallow in his Gloucestershire orchard are the closest that Shakespeare ever came to a stage representation of the rural England of his own early life in Stratford-upon-Avon.

---

* Since the play is a continuation of *Henry IV Part I*, some sections of this introduction overlap with that to the companion edition of *Part I*. Readers who are unfamiliar with *Part I* may wish to begin by reading the synopsis of its plot on p. 3.

Though the language of King Henry IV as he approaches death is deeply tragic in tone, the deep structure of the two parts of *Henry IV* is that not of tragedy but of pastoral comedy. They were written around the same time as *Much Ado About Nothing* and *As You Like It*, when Shakespeare's comic muse was at its zenith. They are his most enjoyable history plays because they are his funniest—and in the figure of Sir John Falstaff they introduce his greatest comic charac-ter—but they also share with the comedies a technique of counter-pointing the intrigue of court and power politics against what has been called the "green" or "festive" world.

The traditional comic pattern turns on the successful effort of a young man to outwit an opponent and possess the girl of his choice. The girl's father, or some other authority figure of the older genera-tion, resists the match, but is outflanked, often thanks to an inge-nious scheme devised by a clever servant, perhaps involving disguise or flight (or both). The union of the lovers brings a renewed sense of social integration, expressed by some kind of festival at the climax of the play—a marriage, a dance, or a feast. All right-thinking people come over to the side of the lovers, but in Shakespearean comedy there is usually a party pooper, a figure who refuses to be assimilated into the harmony—Malvolio in *Twelfth Night*, Don John in *Much Ado About Nothing*, Jaques in *As You Like It*, Shylock in *The Merchant of Venice*. The key to the two parts of *Henry IV* is that they take the comic structure and apply it to Prince Harry—with the difference that instead of his courtship (which ends up being tacked on very briefly at the end of *Henry V*), the action turns on his maturation from wild youth to exemplary warrior prince and statesman. And, in a brilliant reversal, the figure who is isolated at the end is not the party pooper but the very embodiment of the festive spirit: Sir John Falstaff. Comedy is thus placed in opposition to the march of history. Beside the sense of waste and exhaustion in the figure of the dying king, the necessity to reject Falstaff in the name of historical destiny and social order is why the final resolution is tinged with the feeling of tragedy.

The distinctive feature of pastoral comedy is that the action devel-ops by means of a shift of location from the everyday world of work, business, politics, patriarchy, and power to a "green" or "festive" place of play, leisure, anarchy, feminine influence, and love—the wood in *A Midsummer Night's Dream*, Belmont in *The Merchant of Venice*, the Forest of Arden in *As You Like It*, rural Bohemia in *The Winter's Tale*. After the comic resolution is achieved, there has to be a return to the normative world, but recreative change has been effected by the values of the festive world. In *Henry IV Part I*, a tavern in Eastcheap has played the part of the festive world. In *Part II*, there is a reprise of that setting, but also a journey into a rural green world. As in the comedies, the shuttle between contrasting worlds and contradictory value systems creates the dialectic of the drama. But because of the calling of the prince to power, there can be no reconciliation between the value systems. As Prince Hal has announced in his first soliloquy back in *Part I*, his time of "playing holidays" and "loose behaviour" will be but an interlude before he takes upon himself the mantle of historical duty.

"THE PRINCE BUT STUDIES HIS COMPANIONS"?

Henry IV believes that one of the failings of his predecessor Richard II had been to seek to make himself popular, thus eroding the necessary distance that creates awe and gives mystique to the monarchy. But King Henry's own distance from public life—he is nearly always seen surrounded by an inner circle of courtiers or closeted alone in his chamber—causes power to ebb from him. His son, by contrast, comes to know the common people, developing a rapport that will enable him to inspire and lead his army in *Henry V*. The point is made through the very linguistic medium of the drama: all Shakespeare's other English kings speak entirely in verse, whereas Prince Hal has command of a flexible prose voice, with which he reduces himself to the level of his people, an Eastcheap trick that he repeats when he goes in disguise among his men on the night before the battle of Agincourt.

The king's trustiest follower, the Earl of Warwick, reassures him that Prince Hal's intention has always been to throw off his companions when the time is ripe:

The prince but studies his companions
Like a strange tongue, wherein, to gain the language,
'Tis needful that the most immodest word
Be looked upon and learned, which once attained,
Your highness knows, comes to no further use
But to be known and hated. So, like gross terms,
The prince will, in the perfectness of time,
Cast off his followers, and their memory
Shall as a pattern or a measure live,
By which his grace must mete the lives of others,
Turning past evils to advantages.

According to this account, the prince works according to the principle articulated by the cunning politician Ulysses in *Troilus and Cressida:* a man "Cannot make boast to have that which he hath, / Nor feels not what he owes, but by reflection, / As when his virtues shining upon others / Heat them and they retort that heat again / To the first giver." That is to say, we can only make value judgments through a process of comparison. In *Part I*, by temporarily ceding glory to Henry Hotspur, Prince Henry shows himself all the more glorious when he eventually triumphs over his adversary. His whole strategy is revealed in the imagery of his first soliloquy in *Part I*, "I know you all, and will awhile uphold / The unyoked humour of your idleness. / Yet herein will I imitate the sun . . .": the sun seems brighter after cloud and a jewel on a dull background will "show more goodly and attract more eyes / Than that which hath no foil to set it off." The offsetting of the prince against his various foils is the structural key to the progression of the two-part drama.

What is the basis of political rule? Orthodox Tudor theory propounded that kings and magistrates were God's representatives on earth, their authority sanctioned by divine law. But the Elizabethan stage had another possible answer. Christopher Marlowe's tragedy *The Jew of Malta*, written in about 1589 and well known to Shakespeare, has an extraordinary opening. The prologue is spoken by an actor pretending to be the Florentine political theorist Niccolò Machiavelli. He voices a series of deeply subversive suggestions about the nature of sovereignty. His riposte to political orthodoxy is that the only basis of effective government is raw power:

> I count religion but a childish toy,
> And hold there is no sin but ignorance . . .
> Many will talk of title to a crown:
> What right had Caesar to the empery?
> Might first made kings, and laws were then most sure
> When, like the Draco's, they were writ in blood.

Religion as an illusion; the idea that human knowledge does not require divine sanction; the notion that it is "might" not "right" that decides who rules; the proposition that the most effective laws are those based not on justice but on the severity exemplified by the ancient Greek lawgiver Draco (from whose name we get the word "draconian"). French and English thinkers of Shakespeare's time demonized Machiavelli for holding these views, but for Christopher Marlowe the act of thinking the unthinkable made Machiavelli a model for his own overreaching stage heroes.

Shakespeare's history plays are steeped in the influence of Marlowe, but politically he was much more cautious—he would never have risked suffering Marlowe's end, stabbed to death by a government spy while awaiting questioning in a heresy investigation. But that did not stop Shakespeare from recognizing the theatrical charisma of the Marlovian Machiavel. He created a string of such characters himself—Aaron the Moor in *Titus Andronicus*, Richard III, Iago in *Othello*, Edmund in *King Lear*. What attracted him to the type was not so much the subversive politics as the stage panache of the unapologetic villain. Political orthodoxy is staid and solemn. The Machiavel is nimble and witty. But is he necessarily brutal and irreligious?

Prince Harry is a man of the future; his father is haunted by the past. Both parts of *Henry IV* are suffused with the memory of the "by-paths and indirect crooked ways" by which Bullingbrook "met" (or rather took) the crown. The king is revealed at his most vulnerable halfway through *Part II*, in a scene that may have troubled the censor: sick and sleepless, he meditates on the cares of state, the fragility of office, and the weight of his past sin. A usurper himself, Henry IV has no ground on which to base his authority over the rebels who were once his allies. The only basis of his power is victory on the battlefield. In each part, this is achieved by means of a trick. At Shrewsbury in *Part I*, the device consists of dressing several different men as the king in order to confuse the enemy. Having slain one of the impersonators, Douglas assumes that he is addressing another of them: "What art thou, / That counterfeit'st the person of a king?" This time, however, it is the king, not a counterfeit—which beautifully dramatizes the point that the king *is* a counterfeit because of his usurpation. In *Part II*, the king is too sick to fight his own battle, so at Gaultree Forest the Machiavellian strategy of reneging upon the terms of a negotiated truce is carried out by his second son, Prince John of Lancaster. Does that make Prince Harry into the true follower of Machiavelli, who advised that the effective prince is one who gets someone else to do his dirty work for him?

At the beginning of *Part I*, the king says that he must postpone his Crusade to the Holy Land because of the new civil broils at home, the fresh wound upon the earth of England. His dream of expiating his sins by liberating Jerusalem from the heathen is never translated into action. The prophecy that he would end his life there is only realized ironically: he dies in the "Jerusalem chamber" of his own palace. Henry IV's fear, apparently borne out by the bad company that Prince Harry keeps, is that the sin of the father will be visited upon the reign of his son:

> For the fifth Harry from curbèd licence plucks
> The muzzle of restraint, and the wild dog
> Shall flesh his tooth in every innocent.
> O my poor kingdom, sick with civil blows!
> When that my care could not withhold thy riots,
> What wilt thou do when riot is thy care?
> O, thou wilt be a wilderness again,
> Peopled with wolves, thy old inhabitants!

He imagines that the "riot" of the wayward prince will be translated into civil disorder when he becomes king. That is also Falstaff's hope on hearing that his beloved Hal is now Henry V: "the laws of England are at my commandment . . . and woe unto my Lord Chief Justice!" But he is in for a shock: Hal immediately adopts Falstaff's adversary, the Lord Chief Justice, as his new surrogate father. As in *Part I* he had startled the rebels by transforming himself from tavern idler to armed warrior on horseback, so in *Part II* he will prove that he has learned the civic virtues as well as the military ones.

The prince's self-revelatory soliloquy early in *Part I* began with the words "I know you all." The newly crowned king's rejection of Falstaff late in *Part II* begins with the words "I know thee not, old man." The verbal echo is unmistakable: he has ceased to be Hal, he is now delivering on his promise that the time would come when he would throw off the companions and misleaders of his youth. As predicted in the soliloquy, Harry has succeeded in falsifying men's hopes. His reformation glitters over his fault. Falstaff and company suddenly seem to be no more than instruments in a princely conjuring trick, a theatrical act of self-transformation designed to impress a public audience.

Radically opposing interpretations thus become possible. By one account, the politic march of history stands in violent contrast to the humane virtues of friendship, loyalty, good humor, sociability, verbal inventiveness, self-mockery, loyalty, and love. Humanity gives way to what the Bastard in *King John* called "commodity." History is a Machiavellian nightmare of violence and self-interest. The alternative view is that Falstaff embodies the temptations of the flesh. He scores highly for at least three of the seven deadly sins—gluttony, lust, and sloth. He is the Vice figure of the old tradition of morality plays and his rejection is accordingly Hal's final step on the path toward political and moral redemption. So it is that Hal can be played equally persuasively as a young man going on a journey toward maturity but still enjoying his departures from the straight and narrow path, or as one of Shakespeare's Machiavellian manipulators—energetic and intellectually astute, a brilliant actor, but intensely self-conscious, emotionally reined in.

We may perhaps reconcile the opposing readings by supposing that, in the character of Prince Hal, Shakespeare—perhaps as his own riposte to Marlowe—set out to create a new and distinctive kind of "good Machiavel": a political realist who is prepared to take difficult, even brutal, decisions when it is necessary, but who, instead of being atheistic and self-interested, always tries to do what he takes to be God's will and so to serve the best interests of his nation and his people.

THE LANGUAGE OF TIME

The forms of Shakespeare's verse loosened and became more flexible as he matured as a writer. His early plays have a higher proportion of rhyme and a greater regularity in rhythm, the essential pattern being that of iambic pentameter (ten syllables, five stresses, the stress on every second syllable). In the early plays, lines are very frequently end-stopped: punctuation marks a pause at the line ending, meaning that the movement of the syntax (the grammatical construction) falls in with that of the meter (the rhythmical construction). In the later plays, there are far fewer rhyming couplets (sometimes rhyme only features as a marker to indicate that a scene is ending) and the rhythmic movement has far greater variety, freedom, and flow. Mature Shakespearean blank (unrhymed) verse is typically not end-stopped but "run on" (a feature known as "enjambment"): instead of pausing heavily at the line ending, the speaker hurries forward, the sense demanded by the grammar working in creative tension against the holding pattern of the meter. The heavier pauses migrate to the middle of the lines, where they are known as the "caesura" and where their placing varies. A single line of verse is shared between two speakers much more frequently than in the early plays. And the pentameter itself becomes a more subtle instrument: the iambic beat is broken up, there is often an extra ("redundant") unstressed eleventh syllable at the end of the line (this is known as a "feminine ending"). There are more modulations between verse and prose. Occasionally the verse is so loose that neither the original typesetters of the plays when they were first printed nor the modern editors of scholarly texts can be entirely certain whether verse or prose is intended.

Iambic pentameter is the ideal medium for dramatic poetry in English because its rhythm and duration seem to fall in naturally with the speech patterns of the language. In its capacity to combine the ordinary variety of speech with the heightened precision of poetry, the supple mature Shakespearean "loose pentameter" is perhaps the most expressive vocal instrument ever given to the actor. The development in the suppleness of Shakespearean verse is apparent if we compare the highly formalized language in which King Henry VI meditates on mortality in his play, written about 1591,

> . . . then to divide the times:
> So many hours must I tend my flock,
> So many hours must I take my rest,
> So many hours must I contemplate,
> So many hours must I sport myself,
> So many days my ewes have been with young,
> So many weeks ere the poor fools will ean,
> So many years ere I shall shear the fleece.
> So minutes, hours, days, months and years,
> Passed over to the end they were created,
> Would bring white hairs unto a quiet grave.

and the fluid idiom in which King Henry IV addresses a similar theme in his night scene, written seven or eight years later:

> . . . That one might read the book of fate,
> And see the revolution of the times
> Make mountains level, and the continent,
> Weary of solid firmness, melt itself
> Into the sea. And other times, to see
> The beachy girdle of the ocean
> Too wide for Neptune's hips; how chance's mocks
> And changes fill the cup of alteration
> With divers liquors! . . .

Whereas the early passage conveys the metronomic beat of the clock, the later one conveys a more complex sense of the movement of human time, and thus of history, in which the movement of the verse ebbs and flows like the ocean to which it is compared.

Perhaps the greatest difference between the two parts of *Henry IV* is the sense in which *Part II* is suffused with a pervasive consciousness of time, of age, and of mortality.

THE REFORMATION OF ENGLAND?

It is not known whether Shakespeare always intended *Henry IV* to be a two-part play or whether he discovered at some point in the writing or production of *Part I* that it would be dramatically unsatisfying to contain a double climax in a single play, to have Prince Harry prove himself a chivalric hero by defeating Hotspur on the battlefield and then immediately dissociate himself from Falstaff and the other thieves. Instead, the rejection of Falstaff is withheld until *Part II*, but anticipated in the play-within-the-play in *Part I*, where the prince's return to his father is pre-enacted in the tavern.

There is little historical warrant for the story of Henry V's riotous youth. A "prodigal son" narrative was attached to him in the Chronicles and the anonymous play *The Famous Victories of Henry the Fifth* in order to highlight the change he undergoes when he becomes king, submits to the rule of law, and so unifies and brings to order the nation that his father divided. The rejection of Falstaff and company is part and parcel of Harry's symbolically becoming a new person at the moment of his coronation. The notions of "reformation" and the washing away of past iniquities clearly have strong religious connotations. Each time the prince returns to the court, he speaks a language of "fall" and "pardon." When he fights well, his father tells him that "Thou hast redeemed thy lost opinion."

The rhythm of Prince Hal's life is that of providential history, leading to his "reformation" and his assumption of the roles that attracted Queen Elizabeth to him: unifier of the body politic, victor over a rival kingdom, heroic leader of a great and independent nation. The rhythm of Falstaff's life is that of the body and the seasons. In *Part II* he will journey into the deep England of Justice Shallow's Gloucestershire orchard. We learn from Shallow that Falstaff began his career as page to Thomas Mowbray, Duke of Norfolk. This appears to be a Shakespearean fancy without source: it is true of neither the historical Sir John Falstaff, who flees the battlefield in *Henry VI Part I*, nor the historical Sir John Oldcastle, of whom the character of Falstaff was originally an irreverent portrait. Why did Shakespeare give his fictional Falstaff a past that began in the service of Mowbray? At one level, it links him with opposition to the Lancastrian ascendancy represented by King Henry IV and his son. Mowbray was Henry IV's opponent when the latter was still Bullingbrook, back at the beginning of *Richard II*. Like father, like son: as Bullingbrook's accusation of treachery was instrumental in the banishment of Mowbray from the land, so Hal will banish Falstaff from his presence. Mowbray departs with a moving farewell to his native land and language; the effect of his words is to suggest that love of the English earth and the English word goes deeper than dynastic difference. We do not hear similar patriotic sentiments in the mouth of the self-interested Bullingbrook; he does nothing to bring back the old England idealized in the deathbed speech of his father, John of Gaunt (whose name and whose England will also be remembered by Shallow).

In Shakespeare's own time, those who suffered banishment because of ideological difference, but who claimed that they were nevertheless loyal to England, were predominantly Catholics. And this suggests another level to the allusion that binds Falstaff to the Duke of Norfolk. To an Elizabethan audience, the name of Norfolk— the only surviving dukedom in the land—was synonymous with overt or suspected Catholic sympathy. The old Catholic ways persisted in the country long after the official change of religion inaugurated by Henry VIII's break from Rome. The Catholic liturgy's integral relationship with the agricultural calendar and the cycles of human biology could not be shattered overnight. There may, then, be a sense in which Falstaff's journey into deep England is also a journey into the old religion of Shakespeare's father and maternal grandfather. One wonders if it is a coincidence that, in fleshing out the skeletal character of the prince's riotous companion which he inherited from the old play of *The Famous Victories of Henry the Fifth*, Shakespeare retained and made much of his own father's name, John. It is ironic that Falstaff's original surname, Oldcastle, had to be changed because the character was regarded as an insult to the memory of the proto-Protestant Lollard of that name: "for Oldcastle died a martyr," says the epilogue to *Part II*, "and this is not the man."

Indeed, it is not the man, for Falstaff is if anything an embodiment of those ancient Catholic rhythms that were suppressed in the name of Reformation. Vestiges of Oldcastle litter the text: "Falstaff sweats to death" suggests a martyr burning on a bonfire, and "if I become not a cart as well as another man" could suggest a religious dissident on the way to the stake as well as a criminal being taken to the gallows. Protestants, especially in the extreme form of puritans, were traditionally lean; fat monks were symbolic of the corruptions of Catholicism. By making Sir John fat and not calling him Oldcastle, Shakespeare raises the specter of Catholic as opposed to Protestant martyrdoms. Falstaff is Malvolio's opposite: he stands for cakes and ale, festival and holiday, all that was anathema to puritanism. At the beginning of *Henry V*, the Archbishop of Canterbury confirms that Prince Harry's transformation was completed with the rejection of Falstaff: "Never came reformation in a flood, / With such a heady currance, scouring faults." If there is a proto-Protestant or embryonic puritan in the plays, it is King Harry V, newly washed of his past, casting off his old companions, turning away England's former self.

Even as he uses Hal for his own advancement, Falstaff is always a truer father than the cold and politic King Henry IV can ever be. The point is made with beautiful clarity by the contrast between Falstaff's heated engagement in the scene in which he and Hal act out the prodigal prince's forthcoming interview with his father and the king's chilly detachment in the interview itself. The complexity and the pain of the end of *Part II* stem from the way in which, by casting himself as the prodigal son and coming home to his politic heritage, Hal tears into the heart of old England. According to Holinshed's *Chronicles*, King Henry V left no friendship unrewarded. This cannot be said of Shakespeare's version of history. "Master Shallow, I owe you a thousand pound," says Falstaff immediately after he has been publicly denounced by his "sweet boy," changing the subject in the way that people often do when they feel betrayed or bewildered. At this moment, the spectator who has attended carefully to both parts may remember an earlier exchange when Hal asks: "Sirrah, do I owe you a thousand pound?," and Falstaff replies: "A thousand pound, Hal? A million. Thy love is worth a million: thou ow'st me thy love."

In the epilogue, Shakespeare promises that "our humble author will continue the story, with Sir John in it, and make you merry with fair Katherine of France." Audience members attending *Henry V* on the basis of this promise might be justified in asking for their money back: we do not see Sir John Falstaff in the Agincourt play. His presence would raise too many awkward questions of the "reformed" king. We only hear—most comically and at the same time most movingly—of his death. The king has broken his heart.

Shakespeare endures through history. He illuminates later times as well as his own. He helps us to understand the human condition. But he cannot do this without a good text of the plays. Without editions there would be no Shakespeare. That is why every twenty years or so throughout the last three centuries there has been a major new edition of his complete works. One aspect of editing is the process of keeping the texts up to date—modernizing the spelling, punctuation, and typography (though not, of course, the actual words), providing explanatory notes in the light of changing educational practices (a generation ago, most of Shakespeare's classical and biblical allusions could be assumed to be generally understood, but now they can't).

But because Shakespeare did not personally oversee the publication of his plays, editors also have to make decisions about the relative authority of the early printed editions. Half of the sum of his plays only appeared posthumously, in the elaborately produced First Folio text of 1623, the original "Complete Works" prepared for the press by Shakespeare's fellow actors, the people who knew the plays better than anyone else. The other half had appeared in print in his lifetime, in the more compact and cheaper form of "Quarto" editions, some of which reproduced good quality texts, others of which were to a greater or lesser degree garbled and error-strewn. In the case of a few plays there are hundreds of differences between the Quarto and Folio editions, some of them far from trivial.

If you look at printers' handbooks from the age of Shakespeare, you quickly discover that one of the first rules was that, whenever possible, compositors were recommended to set their type from existing printed books rather than manuscripts. This was the age before mechanical typesetting, where each individual letter had to be picked out by hand from the compositor's case and placed on a stick (upside down and back to front) before being laid on the press. It was an age of murky rush-light and of manuscripts written in a secretary hand that had dozens of different, hard-to-decipher forms.

Printers' lives were a lot easier when they were reprinting existing books rather than struggling with handwritten copy. Easily the quickest way to have created the First Folio would have been simply to reprint those eighteen plays that had already appeared in Quarto and only work from manuscript on the other eighteen.

But that is not what happened. Whenever Quartos were used, playhouse "promptbooks" were also consulted and stage directions copied in from them. And in the case of several major plays where a reasonably well-printed Quarto was available, the Folio printers were instructed to work from an alternative, playhouse-derived manuscript. This meant that the whole process of producing the first complete Shakespeare took months, even years, longer than it might have done. But for the men overseeing the project, John Hemings and Henry Condell, friends and fellow actors who had been remembered in Shakespeare's will, the additional labor and cost were worth the effort for the sake of producing an edition that was close to the practice of the theater. They wanted all the plays in print so that people could, as they wrote in their prefatory address to the reader, "read him and again and again," but they also wanted "the great variety of readers" to work from texts that were close to the theater-life for which Shakespeare originally intended them. For this reason, the *RSC Shakespeare*, in both *Complete Works* and individual volumes, uses the Folio as base text wherever possible. Significant Quarto variants are, however, noted in the Textual Notes.

Henry IV Part II is one of the plays where the Folio text was printed from a manuscript that shows strong signs of theatrical influence, not from an available printed Quarto. It contains eight significant passages that are absent—perhaps because of political censorship—from the Quarto. But the Folio text has signs of its own theatrical censorship of a different kind: a large number of oaths have been removed in accordance with the 1606 Parliamentary "Act to Restrain the Abuses of Players," whereby theater companies were prohibited from taking God's name in vain. Most modern editors use the Quarto of 1600 as their copy text but import the eight additional passages from the Folio. Our Folio-led editorial practice follows the reverse procedure: we use Folio as copy text, but deploy the First Quarto as a "control text" that offers assistance in the correction and identification of manifest compositors' errors in the Folio. In order to respect the integrity of the Folio text, we have not reinserted the Quarto oaths that were removed from the stage version that lies behind it. The Quarto oaths are, however, listed at the end of the text and we recommend classroom discussion of the effect of their removal and rehearsal room reinsertion of them for the purposes of contemporary performance.

The following notes highlight various aspects of the editorial process and indicate conventions used in the text of this edition:

Lists of Parts are supplied in the First Folio for only six plays, one of which is *Henry IV Part II*, so the list at the beginning of the play is adapted from that in the First Folio. Capitals indicate that part of the name which is used for speech headings in the script (thus "Prince John of LANCASTER").

Locations are provided by the Folio for only two plays. Eighteenth-century editors, working in an age of elaborately realistic stage sets, were the first to provide detailed locations. Given that Shakespeare wrote for a bare stage and often an imprecise sense of place, we have relegated locations to the explanatory notes at the foot of the page, where they are given at the beginning of each scene where the imaginary location is different from the one before.

Act and Scene Divisions were provided in the Folio in a much more thoroughgoing way than in the Quartos. Sometimes, however, they were erroneous or omitted; corrections and additions supplied by editorial tradition are indicated by square brackets. Five-act division is based on a classical model, and act breaks provided the opportunity to replace the candles in the indoor Blackfriars playhouse which the King's Men used after 1608, but Shakespeare did not necessarily think in terms of a five-part structure of dramatic composition. The Folio convention is that a scene ends when the stage is empty. Nowadays, partly under the influence of film, we tend to consider a scene to be a dramatic unit that ends with either a change of imaginary location or a significant passage of time within the narrative. Shakespeare's fluidity of composition accords well with this convention, so in addition to act and scene numbers we provide a *running scene* count in the right margin at the beginning of each new scene, in the typeface used for editorial directions. Where there is a scene break caused by a momentary bare stage, but the location does not change and extra time does not pass, we use the convention *running scene continues*. There is inevitably a degree of editorial judgment in making such calls, but the system is very valuable in suggesting the pace of the plays.

Speakers' Names are often inconsistent in Folio. We have regularized speech headings, but retained an element of deliberate inconsistency in entry directions, in order to give the flavor of Folio.

Verse is indicated by lines that do not run to the right margin and by capitalization of each line. The Folio printers sometimes set verse as prose, and vice versa (either out of misunderstanding or for reasons of space). We have silently corrected in such cases, although in some instances there is ambiguity, in which case we have leaned toward the preservation of Folio layout. Folio sometimes uses contraction ("turnd" rather than "turned") to indicate whether or not the final "-ed" of a past participle is sounded, an area where there is variation for the sake of the five-beat iambic pentameter rhythm. We use the convention of a grave accent to indicate sounding (thus "turnèd" would be two syllables), but would urge actors not to overstress. In cases where one speaker ends with a verse half line and the next begins with the other half of the pentameter, editors since the late eighteenth century have indented the second line. We have abandoned this convention, since the Folio does not use it, nor did actors' cues in the Shakespearean theater. An exception is made when the second speaker actively interrupts or completes the first speaker's sentence.

Spelling is modernized, but older forms are occasionally maintained where necessary for rhythm or aural effect.

Punctuation in Shakespeare's time was as much rhetorical as grammatical. "Colon" was originally a term for a unit of thought in an argument. The semicolon was a new unit of punctuation (some of the Quartos lack them altogether). We have modernized punctuation throughout, but have given more weight to Folio punctuation than many editors, since, though not Shakespearean, it reflects the usage of his period. In particular, we have used the colon far more than many editors: it is exceptionally useful as a way of indicating how many Shakespearean speeches unfold clause by clause in a developing argument that gives the illusion of enacting the process of thinking in the moment. We have also kept in mind the origin of punctuation in classical times as a way of assisting the actor and orator: the comma suggests the briefest of pauses for breath, the colon a middling one, and a full stop or period a longer pause. Semicolons, by contrast, belong to an era of punctuation that was only just coming in during Shakespeare's time and that is coming to an end now: we have accordingly used them only where they occur in our copy texts (and not always then). Dashes are sometimes used for parenthetical interjections where the Folio has brackets. They are also used for interruptions and changes in train of thought. Where a change of addressee occurs within a speech, we have used a dash preceded by a full stop (or occasionally another form of punctuation). Often the identity of the respective addressees is obvious from the context. When it is not, this has been indicated in a marginal stage direction.

Entrances and Exits are fairly thorough in Folio, which has accordingly been followed as faithfully as possible. Where characters are omitted or corrections are necessary, this is indicated by square brackets (e.g. "[*and Attendants*]"). *Exit* is sometimes silently normalized to *Exeunt* and *Manet* anglicized to "remains." We trust Folio positioning of entrances and exits to a greater degree than most editors.

Editorial Stage Directions such as stage business, asides, indications of addressee and of characters' position on the gallery stage are used only sparingly in Folio. Other editions mingle directions of this kind with original Folio and Quarto directions, sometimes marking them by means of square brackets. We have sought to distinguish what could be described as *directorial* interventions of this kind from Folio-style directions (either original or supplied) by placing them in the right margin in a different typeface. There is a degree of subjectivity about which directions are of which kind, but the procedure is intended as a reminder to the reader and the actor that Shakespearean stage directions are often dependent upon editorial inference alone and are not set in stone. We also depart from editorial tradition in sometimes admitting uncertainty and thus printing permissive stage directions, such as an *Aside?* (often a line may be equally effective as an aside or as a direct address—it is for each production or reading to make its own decision) or a *may exit* or a piece of business placed between arrows to indicate that it may occur at various different moments within a scene.

Line Numbers in the left margin are editorial, for reference and to key the explanatory and textual notes.

Explanatory Notes at the foot of each page explain allusions and gloss obsolete and difficult words, confusing phraseology, occasional major textual cruces, and so on. Particular attention is given to nonstandard usage, bawdy innuendo, and technical terms (e.g. legal and military language). Where more than one sense is given, commas indicate shades of related meaning, slashes alternative or double meanings.

Textual Notes at the end of the play indicate major departures from the Folio. They take the following form: the reading of our text is given in bold and its source given after an equals sign, with "Q" indicating that it derives from the First Quarto of 1600, "F" from the First Folio of 1623, "F2" a reading from the Second Folio of 1632, and "Ed" one that derives from the subsequent editorial tradition. The rejected Folio ("F") reading is then given. Thus, for example, "**2.4.132 With** = Q. F = where" indicates that at Act 2 Scene 4 line 132, we have restored the Quarto reading "with" because we judge the Folio reading "where" to be a printer's error.

MAJOR PARTS: (*with percentage of lines/number of speeches/scenes on stage*) Falstaff (20%/184/8), Prince Henry (9%/60/5), King Henry IV (9%/34/4), Shallow (6%/77/4), Lord Chief Justice (5%/56/4), Hostess Quickly (5%/49/3), Archbishop Scroop (5%/25/3), Prince John of Lancaster (3%/26/5), Westmorland (3%/21/4), Lord Bardolph (3%/18/2), Northumberland (3%/17/2), Pistol (2%/31/3), Doll Tearsheet (2%/31/2), Bardolph (2%/30/6), Poins (2%/28/2), Warwick (2%/26/4), Mowbray (2%/18/3), Hastings (2%/17/3), Morton (2%/6/1).

LINGUISTIC MEDIUM: 50% verse, 50% prose.

DATE: Around 1597–98. Must have been written after *The First Part* (1596–97) and before *Henry V* (early 1599); registered for publication August 1600. Vestiges of the name "Oldcastle" for "Falstaff" suggest that drafting may have begun before Lord Cobham's objections led to the name change in *The First Part*, but the play was probably not acted before this. The double epilogue (see "Text," below) suggests different stages of production.

SOURCES: Based on the account of the reign of Henry IV in the 1587 edition of Holinshed's *Chronicles*, with some use of Samuel Daniel's epic poem *The First Four Books of the Civil Wars* (1595). The intermingling of historical materials and comedy, in the context of the Prince's riotous youth, is developed from the anonymous Queen's Men play, *The Famous Victories of Henry the Fifth* (performed late 1580s), which included characters who may be regarded as crude prototypes of Falstaff and company, a scene in "which a labouring man is press-ganged into the army, and a well-known encounter where the prince boxes the Lord Chief Justice on the ears."

TEXT: Quarto 1600, in two different issues, one of which omits Act 3 Scene 1 (showing the sick and sleepless king): scholars debate whether the scene was a late Shakespearean addition to his original draft or an omission because of its politically sensitive references back to the deposition of Richard II. The Quartos are usually thought to have been printed from Shakespeare's working manuscript. The 1623 Folio contains eight significant passages that are not in the Quarto, some relating to either the Archbishop's insurrection or the deposition of Richard II. These are more likely to be Quarto cuts (some for reasons of censorship, others for dramatic compression) than Folio additions. The Folio text shows some signs of consultation of a theatrical manuscript, probably sometime after the 1606 "Act to Restrain the Abuses of Players" (profanity has been toned down). The most plausible explanation of the complex textual history is that Folio was typeset from a carefully prepared manuscript based on a post-1606 promptbook, perhaps collated with the first issue of the Quarto. A further complication is that the Epilogue is printed in different ways in Quarto and Folio, and seems to combine two different speeches, probably one written for public performance and the other for a staging at court in the presence of Queen Elizabeth. Most editions are based on Quarto, with the Folio-only passages inserted, whereas we respect Folio as an autonomous text, though use Quarto for the correction of manifest printer's errors.

THE SECOND PART OF HENRY THE FOURTH,

Containing His Death and the Coronation of King Henry the Fifth

SYNOPSIS OF
HENRY IV PART I

After deposing King Richard II, Henry Bullingbrook has ascended the throne as Henry IV. Guilt about the deposition troubles his conscience, and the stability of his reign is threatened by growing opposition from some of the nobles who helped him to the throne. His son, Prince Henry (also known as Harry and, by Falstaff, as Hal), is living a dissolute life, frequenting the taverns of Eastcheap in the company of Sir John Falstaff and other disreputable characters with whom he participates in a highway robbery. Opposition to the king becomes open rebellion, led by the Earl of Northumberland's son, Henry Percy, known, for his courage and impetuous nature, as "Hotspur." The Percy family support the claim to the throne of Hotspur's brother-in-law, Edmund Mortimer. The rebellion brings Hal back to his father's side, while Falstaff musters a ragged troop of soldiers. The king's army defeats the rebels at the battle of Shrewsbury, where Hal kills Hotspur. Falstaff lives to die another day.

LIST OF PARTS

RUMOUR, the presenter

KING HENRY IV

PRINCE HENRY, later King Henry V, also known as Hal or Harry Monmouth

Prince John of LANCASTER, brother to the prince

Humphrey, Duke of GLOUCESTER, a younger brother

Thomas, Duke of CLARENCE, a younger brother

Earl of NORTHUMBERLAND

Scroop, ARCHBISHOP OF YORK

MOWBRAY

Lord HASTINGS

Lord BARDOLPH

Sir John COLEVILLE

TRAVERS

MORTON

} opposites against King Henry the Fourth

LADY NORTHUMBERLAND, Northumberland's wife

LADY PERCY, Northumberland's daughter-in-law, widow of Henry Percy known as Hotspur

Northumberland's PORTER

Earl of WARWICK

Earl of SURREY

Earl of WESTMORLAND

HARCOURT

Sir John BLUNT

GOWER

} of the king's party

LORD CHIEF JUSTICE and his SERVANT

Sir John FALSTAFF

BARDOLPH

PISTOL

Edward or Ned POINS

PETO

Sir John's PAGE

} irregular humorists

HOSTESS QUICKLY, landlady of a tavern

DOLL TEARSHEET

FRANCIS, a drawer

WILLIAM, a drawer

SECOND DRAWER

SHALLOW, a country Justice of the Peace

SILENCE, his kinsman, another Justice of the Peace

List of parts   **irregular humorists** lawless/disorderly men with wayward temperaments

DAVY, servant to Shallow

RALPH MOULDY

SIMON SHADOW

THOMAS WART   } country soldiers

FRANCIS FEEBLE

PETER BULLCALF

FANG, a constable

SNARE, his yeoman or assistant

Page to the King, Messengers, Servants, Musicians, Grooms, Beadles, Soldiers, Attendants

Speaker of the EPILOGUE

Induction

Enter Rumour

RUMOUR   Open your ears, for which of you will stop
The vent of hearing when loud Rumour speaks?
I, from the orient to the drooping west,
Making the wind my post-horse, still unfold
5   The acts commencèd on this ball of earth.
Upon my tongue continual slanders ride,
The which in every language I pronounce,
Stuffing the ears of them with false reports.
I speak of peace, while covert enmity
10   Under the smile of safety wounds the world.
And who but Rumour, who but only I,
Make fearful musters and prepared defence
Whilst the big year, swoll'n with some other griefs,
Is thought with child by the stern tyrant war,
15   And no such matter? Rumour is a pipe
Blown by surmises, jealousies, conjectures
And of so easy and so plain a stop
That the blunt monster with uncounted heads,
The still-discordant wavering multitude,
20   Can play upon it. But what need I thus
My well-known body to anatomize
Among my household? Why is Rumour here?
I run before King Harry's victory,
Who in a bloody field by Shrewsbury

Induction prologue. *The Second Part of Henry the Fourth* is continuous with *The First Part*, taking place immediately after the battle of Shrewsbury   *Rumour* allegorical figure traditionally covered in painted tongues   **2 vent of hearing** i.e. ear   **3 orient** east   **drooping** declining, where the sun sets   **4 post-horse** horse kept at a post-house or inn for the use of messengers or travelers   **still** always, continually   **unfold** reveal   **5 acts** actions, events/divisions of a play   **12 fearful . . . defence** enrollment of troops and preparations for defense inspired by fear   **13 big** pregnant   **griefs** suffering, hardship   **15 And . . . matter** which is not the case   **pipe** small wind instrument, recorder   **16 jealousies** suspicions   **17 of . . . stop** so easy and straightforward to play   **stop** finger-hole of a wind instrument   **18 blunt** stupid, dull   **19 still-discordant** constantly quarreling   **21 anatomize** dissect, analyze   **22 household** domestic intimates, i.e. audience   **23 King Harry's victory** Henry IV's troops defeated Hotspur and the other rebels at the Battle of Shrewsbury (dramatized in *1 Henry IV*)   **24 field** battlefield   **Shrewsbury** town on the Welsh-English border

25   Hath beaten down young Hotspur and his troops,
Quenching the flame of bold rebellion
Even with the rebels' blood. But what mean I
To speak so true at first? My office is
To noise abroad that Harry Monmouth fell
30   Under the wrath of noble Hotspur's sword,
And that the king before the Douglas' rage
Stooped his anointed head as low as death.
This have I rumoured through the peasant towns
Between the royal field of Shrewsbury
35   And this worm-eaten hold of ragged stone,
Where Hotspur's father, old Northumberland,
Lies crafty-sick. The posts come tiring on,
And not a man of them brings other news
Than they have learned of me. From Rumour's tongues
40   They bring smooth comforts false, worse than true
wrongs.   *Exit*

Act 1 Scene [1]   *running scene 1*

Enter Lord Bardolph and the Porter [separately]

LORD BARDOLPH   Who keeps the gate here, ho? Where is the
earl?
PORTER   What shall I say you are?
LORD BARDOLPH   Tell thou the earl
That the lord Bardolph doth attend him here.
5   PORTER   His lordship is walked forth into the orchard.

---

25 **Hotspur** Sir Henry (or Harry) Percy, the Earl of Northumberland's son   28 **office** duty, task
29 **Harry Monmouth** Prince Henry (or Harry, or Hal), named after the town on the Welsh-
English border where he was born   31 **the Douglas** Archibald, Earl of Douglas; the signifies
the head of a Scottish clan   32 **anointed** i.e. royal, legitimate (having been marked with holy
oil as part of the coronation ceremony)   33 **peasant** country, rustic (with connotations of
"unsophisticated, credulous")   35 **hold** fortress; Warkworth Castle was the Earl of
Northumberland's residence   **ragged** rough, eroded   37 **crafty-sick** feigning illness   **posts**
messengers on horseback   **tiring on** in tearing haste/exhausting themselves and their horses
39 **Than** except what   40 **true wrongs** the painful truth   **1.1** *Location: Warkworth
Castle (residence of the Earl of Northumberland)*   **Porter** gatekeeper   1 **keeps** guards
3 **What** who   4 **attend** wait for/wait upon   5 **is** has   **orchard** garden

Please it your honour, knock but at the gate,
And he himself will answer.

Enter Northumberland

LORD BARDOLPH Here comes the earl.   [*Exit Porter*]

NORTHUMBERLAND What news, Lord Bardolph? Every minute now
10   Should be the father of some stratagem;
        The times are wild: contention, like a horse
        Full of high feeding, madly hath broke loose
        And bears down all before him.

LORD BARDOLPH Noble earl,
15   I bring you certain news from Shrewsbury.

NORTHUMBERLAND Good, an heaven will!

LORD BARDOLPH As good as heart can wish:
        The king is almost wounded to the death
        And, in the fortune of my lord your son,
20   Prince Harry slain outright, and both the Blunts
        Killed by the hand of Douglas, young Prince John
        And Westmorland and Stafford fled the field,
        And Harry Monmouth's brawn, the hulk Sir John,
        Is prisoner to your son. O, such a day,
25   So fought, so followed and so fairly won,
        Came not till now to dignify the times
        Since Caesar's fortunes!

NORTHUMBERLAND How is this derived?
        Saw you the field? Came you from Shrewsbury?

30   LORD BARDOLPH I spake with one, my lord, that came from thence,
        A gentleman well bred and of good name,
        That freely rendered me these news for true.

---

6 **Please it** if it please   10 **stratagem** violent deed/scheme, plot   11 **wild** savage, rebellious,
unruly   12 **high feeding** overly rich food   13 **bears down** tramples   15 **certain** definite
16 **an** if   **will** is willing, wishes it   19 **your son** Sir Henry Percy (Hotspur)   20 **Blunts** Sir
Walter Blunt was killed by **Douglas** in *1 Henry IV*, Act 5 Scene 1; another Blunt is only
mentioned in one of the play's sources   21 **Prince John** Prince Henry's younger brother
22 **Westmorland** Ralph Neville, a kinsman of the king's   **Stafford** in *1 Henry IV*, Act 5
Scene 1, the Earl of Stafford is said to have been killed in the battle   23 **brawn** lump of flesh/
fattened boar or pig   **hulk** big, unwieldy person (literally, large ship)   **Sir John** i.e. Falstaff
25 **followed** supported by loyal troops   27 **fortunes** successes   28 **How . . . derived?** What is
the source of your information?   32 **rendered** gave, related

NORTHUMBERLAND Here comes my servant Travers, whom I sent
    On Tuesday last to listen after news.

Enter Travers

35 **LORD BARDOLPH** My lord, I over-rode him on the way,
    And he is furnished with no certainties
    More than he haply may retail from me.

NORTHUMBERLAND Now, Travers, what good tidings comes from
    you?

TRAVERS   My lord, Sir John Umfrevile turned me back
40 With joyful tidings; and, being better horsed,
    Outrode me. After him came spurring hard
    A gentleman, almost forspent with speed,
    That stopped by me to breathe his bloodied horse.
    He asked the way to Chester, and of him
45 I did demand what news from Shrewsbury:
    He told me that rebellion had ill luck
    And that young Harry Percy's spur was cold.
    With that, he gave his able horse the head,
    And bending forwards struck his able heels
50 Against the panting sides of his poor jade
    Up to the rowel-head, and starting so
    He seemed in running to devour the way,
    Staying no longer question.

NORTHUMBERLAND Ha? Again:
55 Said he young Harry Percy's spur was cold?
    Of Hotspur Coldspur? That rebellion
    Had met ill luck?

LORD BARDOLPH My lord, I'll tell you what:
    If my young lord your son have not the day,

---

33 Travers his name suggests his function to contradict Lord Bardolph   **35 over-rode** overtook   **37 haply** perhaps   **retail** recount   **39 Sir John Umfrevile** either the name originally given to Lord Bardolph's character in an earlier version of the scene, or the **gentleman** who also gave Bardolph good news of the battle   **41 Outrode** rode faster than, left behind   **42 forspent** exhausted   **43 breathe** allow to rest and recover breath   **bloodied** i.e. from the constant digging of spurs   **44 Chester** town in the northwest of England   **48 gave . . . head** let him go freely, without restraint of the bridle   **able** recovered/strong/ easy to handle   **49 able** capable/powerful   **50 jade** worn-out horse   **51 rowel-head** spiked wheel at the end of a spur   **52 devour the way** eat up the road   **53 Staying** waiting for   **59 have . . . day** has not won the battle

60   Upon mine honour, for a silken point
      I'll give my barony. Never talk of it.
      NORTHUMBERLAND   Why should the gentleman that rode by
          Travers
      Give then such instances of loss?
      LORD BARDOLPH   Who, he?
65   He was some hilding fellow that had stolen
      The horse he rode on, and, upon my life,
      Spoke at a venture. Look, here comes more news.

Enter Morton

      NORTHUMBERLAND   Yea, this man's brow, like to a title-leaf,
      Foretells the nature of a tragic volume:
70   So looks the strand when the imperious flood
      Hath left a witnessed usurpation.—
      Say, Morton, didst thou come from Shrewsbury?
      MORTON   I ran from Shrewsbury, my noble lord,
      Where hateful death put on his ugliest mask
75   To fright our party.
      NORTHUMBERLAND   How doth my son and brother?
      Thou trembl'st; and the whiteness in thy cheek
      Is apter than thy tongue to tell thy errand.
      Even such a man, so faint, so spiritless,
80   So dull, so dead in look, so woe-begone,
      Drew Priam's curtain in the dead of night,
      And would have told him half his Troy was burned.
      But Priam found the fire ere he his tongue,
      And I my Percy's death ere thou report'st it.
85   This thou wouldst say, 'Your son did thus and thus.
      Your brother thus. So fought the noble Douglas',
      Stopping my greedy ear with their bold deeds.

---

60 point lace for fastening clothing, i.e. something of small value   **61 barony** land held by
a baron   **63 instances** evidence   **65 hilding** worthless   **67 at a venture** without due
consideration/in a speculative manner   *Morton* another servant of Northumberland's; his
name suggests death   **68 title-leaf** title page of a book describing the contents   **70 strand**
shore, beach   **flood** sea   **71 witnessed usurpation** visible signs of its invasion (left by the
retreating tide)   **78 apter** more likely/more suitable   **79 Even** just   **81 Drew** drew aside,
opened   **Priam** King of Troy, killed in the Trojan war against the Greeks   **curtain** i.e. of his
bed   **83 ere** before   **87 Stopping** filling

But in the end, to stop mine ear indeed,
Thou hast a sigh to blow away this praise,
90   Ending with 'Brother, son, and all are dead.'

MORTON   Douglas is living, and your brother, yet.
But, for my lord your son—

NORTHUMBERLAND   Why, he is dead.
See what a ready tongue suspicion hath!
95   He that but fears the thing he would not know
Hath by instinct knowledge from others' eyes
That what he feared is chanced. Yet speak, Morton—
Tell thou thy earl his divination lies,
And I will take it as a sweet disgrace
100   And make thee rich for doing me such wrong.

MORTON   You are too great to be by me gainsaid:
Your spirit is too true, your fears too certain.

NORTHUMBERLAND   Yet, for all this, say not that Percy's dead.
I see a strange confession in thine eye:
105   Thou shak'st thy head and hold'st it fear or sin
To speak a truth. If he be slain, say so:
The tongue offends not that reports his death.
And he doth sin that doth belie the dead,
Not he which says the dead is not alive.
110   Yet the first bringer of unwelcome news
Hath but a losing office, and his tongue
Sounds ever after as a sullen bell,
Rememb'red knolling a departing friend.

LORD BARDOLPH   I cannot think, my lord, your son is dead.

115   MORTON   I am sorry I should force you to believe
That which I would to heaven I had not seen.
But these mine eyes saw him in bloody state,
Rend'ring faint quittance, wearied and out-breathed,

88 stop . . . indeed prevent me from ever hearing anything again, i.e. kill me   97 is chanced
has happened   98 divination prophecy, intuition   100 doing . . . wrong i.e. by telling me
that I'm mistaken (a servant should not contradict his master)   101 gainsaid contradicted
102 spirit instinct, intelligence   105 hold'st maintain, believe   108 belie slander
111 losing office profitless task   112 sullen mournful   113 knolling ringing the funeral bell
for   116 would wish   118 quittance repayment (of blows)   out-breathed breathless

To Henry Monmouth, whose swift wrath beat down
120 The never-daunted Percy to the earth,
From whence with life he never more sprung up.
In few, his death, whose spirit lent a fire
Even to the dullest peasant in his camp,
Being bruited once, took fire and heat away
125 From the best tempered courage in his troops,
For from his mettle was his party steeled;
Which once in him abated, all the rest
Turned on themselves, like dull and heavy lead.
And as the thing that's heavy in itself,
130 Upon enforcement flies with greatest speed,
So did our men, heavy in Hotspur's loss,
Lend to this weight such lightness with their fear
That arrows fled not swifter toward their aim
Than did our soldiers, aiming at their safety,
135 Fly from the field. Then was the noble Worcester
Too soon ta'en prisoner. And that furious Scot,
The bloody Douglas, whose well-labouring sword
Had three times slain th'appearance of the king,
'Gan vail his stomach and did grace the shame
140 Of those that turned their backs, and in his flight,
Stumbling in fear, was took. The sum of all
Is that the king hath won, and hath sent out
A speedy power to encounter you, my lord,
Under the conduct of young Lancaster
145 And Westmorland. This is the news at full.

---

120 never-daunted never overcome with fear   **122 In few** in short   **124 bruited** reported
125 best tempered of finest quality, most hardened (literally refers to the treating of a sword to
give it strength and resilience)   **126 mettle** character, courage plays on "metal"   **steeled**
hardened, literally overlaid with steel   **127 abated** blunted/diminished   **130 Upon
enforcement** under compulsion, with force applied   **131 heavy in** weighed down/saddened by
132 Lend . . . fear i.e. despite the weight of their loss, fear made them light   **135 Worcester**
Thomas Percy, Earl of Worcester, Northumberland's brother   **137 well-labouring** hard-
working   **138 th'appearance . . . king** several men, including Sir Walter Blunt and the Earl of
Stafford, had been dressed like the king to act as decoys on the battlefield   **139 'Gan . . .
stomach** began to lessen his courage   **grace . . . backs** i.e. Douglas joined those fleeing the
battle   **grace** dignify, sanction   **143 power** armed force   **encounter** meet in battle
144 Lancaster Prince John (so called because he was born in Lancaster)   **145 at** in

NORTHUMBERLAND   For this I shall have time enough to mourn.
        In poison there is physic, and this news,
        Having been well, that would have made me sick,
        Being sick, have in some measure made me well.
150   And as the wretch, whose fever-weakened joints,
        Like strengthless hinges, buckle under life,
        Impatient of his fit, breaks like a fire
        Out of his keeper's arms, even so my limbs,
        Weakened with grief, being now enraged with grief,
155   Are thrice themselves. Hence, therefore, thou   *Throws down*
            nice crutch!   *his crutch*
        A scaly gauntlet now with joints of steel
        Must glove this hand. And hence, thou sickly coif!   *Throws down*
        Thou art a guard too wanton for the head   *his nightcap*
        Which princes, fleshed with conquest, aim to hit.
160   Now bind my brows with iron, and approach
        The ragged'st hour that time and spite dare bring
        To frown upon th'enraged Northumberland!
        Let heaven kiss earth! Now let not Nature's hand
        Keep the wild flood confined! Let order die!
165   And let the world no longer be a stage
        To feed contention in a ling'ring act,
        But let one spirit of the first-born Cain
        Reign in all bosoms, that, each heart being set
        On bloody courses, the rude scene may end,
170   And darkness be the burier of the dead!
    LORD BARDOLPH   Sweet earl, divorce not wisdom from your
            honour.
    MORTON   The lives of all your loving complices

---

147 **physic** medicine   148 **Having . . . well** i.e. had I been healthy this bad news would have
made me ill; being ill, it has gone some way toward giving me strength   152 **Impatient . . . fit**
unable to endure his attack of fever   153 **keeper** nurse   154 **Weakened** "weak'ned" in Folio,
perhaps playing on "weak-kneed"   155 **nice** effeminate, unmanly   156 **scaly gauntlet**
armored glove covered with plates of steel, giving it the appearance of scales   157 **coif**
nightcap   158 **wanton** self-indulgent, effeminate   159 **fleshed** made eager after having their
appetites whetted (as hunting dogs are fed raw meat to excite them)   161 **ragged'st** roughest,
harshest   166 **contention** strife   **ling'ring act** painfully protracted struggle/drawn-out part
of a play   167 **Cain** son of Adam and Eve who in killing his brother Abel became the world's
first murderer   169 **rude** violent/unpolished   172 **complices** confederates, supporters

Lean on your health, the which, if you give o'er
To stormy passion, must perforce decay.
175 You cast th'event of war, my noble lord,
And summed the account of chance, before you said
'Let us make head.' It was your presurmise
That in the dole of blows, your son might drop.
You knew he walked o'er perils on an edge,
180 More likely to fall in than to get o'er:
You were advised his flesh was capable
Of wounds and scars and that his forward spirit
Would lift him where most trade of danger ranged:
Yet did you say 'Go forth', and none of this,
185 Though strongly apprehended, could restrain
The stiff-borne action. What hath then befallen,
Or what hath this bold enterprise brought forth,
More than that being which was like to be?
LORD BARDOLPH   We all that are engagèd to this loss
190 Knew that we ventured on such dangerous seas
That if we wrought our life was ten to one.
And yet we ventured, for the gain proposed
Choked the respect of likely peril feared.
And since we are o'erset, venture again.
195 Come, we will all put forth, body and goods.
MORTON   'Tis more than time. And, my most noble lord,
I hear for certain, and do speak the truth:
The gentle Archbishop of York is up
With well-appointed powers. He is a man
200 Who with a double surety binds his followers.

---

173 give o'er give way, give in   174 passion outburst of emotion   perforce necessarily
175 cast th'event calculated the likely outcome   176 summed added up   177 make head
raise an army   presurmise suspicion beforehand   178 dole dealing out (may play on "dole,"
i.e. sorrow)   drop fall, die   179 edge i.e. narrow bridge/sword-edge   181 advised aware
capable Of susceptible to   182 forward eager, adventurous, rash   183 trade of trafficking in
ranged was positioned   185 apprehended anticipated/feared   186 stiff-borne proudly,
stubbornly carried   188 like likely   189 engagèd to involved in   191 if . . . one the odds of
coming out alive were ten to one   193 respect consideration   194 o'erset overcome
195 all put forth all set out (as if going to sea)/stake everything   196 'Tis . . . time i.e. we
shouldn't delay   198 gentle wellborn   up prepared for battle   199 well-appointed powers
well-equipped forces   200 double surety i.e. as he has both spiritual and temporal authority

My lord your son had only but the corpse,
But shadows and the shows of men, to fight,
For that same word, rebellion, did divide
The action of their bodies from their souls,
205   And they did fight with queasiness, constrained,
As men drink potions, that their weapons only
Seemed on our side. But, for their spirits and souls,
This word, rebellion, it had froze them up,
As fish are in a pond. But now the bishop
210   Turns insurrection to religion.
Supposed sincere and holy in his thoughts,
He's followed both with body and with mind,
And doth enlarge his rising with the blood
Of fair King Richard, scraped from Pomfret stones:
215   Derives from heaven his quarrel and his cause:
Tells them he doth bestride a bleeding land,
Gasping for life under great Bullingbrook:
And more and less do flock to follow him.

NORTHUMBERLAND   I knew of this before. But, to speak truth,
220   This present grief had wiped it from my mind.
Go in with me, and counsel every man
The aptest way for safety and revenge.
Get posts and letters, and make friends with speed.
Never so few, nor never yet more need.   *Exeunt*

Act 1 Scene [2]   *running scene 2*

Enter Falstaff and Page

FALSTAFF   Sirrah, you giant, what says the doctor to my water?

PAGE   He said, sir, the water itself was a good healthy

201 **corpse** bodies (not the souls)   202 **But** mere   205 **queasiness** uncertainty, reluctance
206 **As . . . potions** like men who drink medicine   210 **religion** i.e. a religious cause
211 **Supposed** known to be   213 **enlarge his rising** fortify, justify his uprising   **with . . . stones**
by recalling the murder of Richard II at Pomfret (Pontefract) Castle; Richard had been usurped
by his cousin, Henry Bullingbrook, now Henry IV   216 **bestride** stand over   217 **Bullingbrook**
i.e. Henry IV   218 **more and less** those of both high and low rank   222 **aptest** best, readiest
223 **posts** messengers   **1.2**   *Location: in London, but unspecified, probably a street*
1 **Sirrah** sir (used to social inferiors)   **giant** ironic since the Page is a boy   2 **water** urine

water, but, for the party that owed it, he might have more
diseases than he knew for.

5   FALSTAFF   Men of all sorts take a pride to gird at me. The brain
of this foolish-compounded clay, man, is not able to invent
anything that tends to laughter, more than I invent or is
invented on me. I am not only witty in myself, but the cause
that wit is in other men. I do here walk before thee like a sow
10   that hath o'erwhelmed all her litter but one. If the prince put
thee into my service for any other reason than to set me off,
why then I have no judgement. Thou whoreson mandrake,
thou art fitter to be worn in my cap than to wait at my heels.
I was never manned with an agate till now: but I will set you
15   neither in gold nor silver, but in vile apparel, and send you
back again to your master, for a jewel—the juvenal, the
prince your master, whose chin is not yet fledged. I will
sooner have a beard grow in the palm of my hand than he
shall get one on his cheek, yet he will not stick to say his face
20   is a face-royal. Heaven may finish it when he will, it is not a
hair amiss yet. He may keep it still at a face-royal, for a barber
shall never earn sixpence out of it; and yet he will be crowing
as if he had writ man ever since his father was a bachelor. He
may keep his own grace, but he is almost out of mine, I can
25   assure him. What said Master Dombledon about the satin for
my short cloak and slops?

PAGE   He said, sir, you should procure him better assurance
than Bardolph: he would not take his bond and yours. He
liked not the security.

---

3 owed owned   **4 knew for** was aware of   **5 gird at** taunt   **6 foolish-compounded** made up of
folly   **10 o'erwhelmed** squashed with her bulk   **11 set me off** display me to my best advantage;
perhaps plays on "make me appear ridiculous"   **12 whoreson** bastard (son of a whore)
mandrake poisonous plant whose forked root made it resemble the human form   **14 manned**
with attended by   **agate** diminutive person, an allusion to the tiny figures cut in the agate stones
that appeared in rings   **15 send . . . jewel** Falstaff jokingly threatens to return the page to the
prince as an ornament   **16 juvenal** youth (puns on first syllable of "jewel")   **17 fledged** covered
with down, i.e. he hasn't got a beard   **19 stick** hesitate   **20 face-royal** majestic face (**royal**
plays on the sense of "coin with the king's face on it")   **21 amiss** out of place   **a barber . . . it**
no barber could charge sixpence to shave a beardless face   **23 writ** called himself   **24 grace**
term of address to a prince/favor   **25 Dombledon** a name probably derived from "dommel"
or "dummel," i.e. dummy, stupid   **26 slops** loose baggy breeches   **27 assurance** financial
guarantee   **28 Bardolph** Falstaff's follower is unrelated to the rebel lord of the same name

30   FALSTAFF   Let him be damned, like the glutton! May his tongue be hotter! A whoreson Achitophel! A rascally yea-forsooth knave, to bear a gentleman in hand, and then stand upon security! The whoreson smooth-pates do now wear nothing but high shoes, and bunches of keys at their girdles. And if a

35   man is through with them in honest taking up, then they must stand upon security. I had as lief they would put ratsbane in my mouth as offer to stop it with security. I looked he should have sent me two and twenty yards of satin, as I am true knight, and he sends me security. Well, he

40   may sleep in security, for he hath the horn of abundance, and the lightness of his wife shines through it, and yet cannot he see, though he have his own lanthorn to light him. Where's Bardolph?

    PAGE   He's gone into Smithfield to buy your worship a

45   horse.

    FALSTAFF   I bought him in Paul's, and he'll buy me a horse in Smithfield. If I could get me a wife in the stews, I were manned, horsed, and wived.

Enter Chief Justice and Servant

    PAGE   Sir, here comes the nobleman that committed the

50   prince for striking him about Bardolph.

---

30 Let . . . hotter! refers to the biblical parable of Dives and Lazarus in which the rich Dives refused food to the poor leper Lazarus, and was condemned to hell where he begged for water to cool his tongue; gluttony is one of the seven deadly sins   **31 Achitophel** an adviser to King David who betrayed him; Old Testament equivalent to Judas Iscariot   **yea-forsooth** obsequious, like a tradesman who affects propriety by using mild oaths   **32 bear . . . hand** lead a man on   **stand** insist   **33 smooth-pates** men with short hair, an image associated with puritan tradesmen   **34 high** high-heeled, suggestive of pride   **girdles** belts; the **keys** signify the men's showy self-importance   **35 through . . . up** has agreed an honest and straightforward purchase with them   **36 lief** soon, willingly   **37 ratsbane** rat poison   **38 looked** expected   **40 horn of abundance** cornucopia or horn of plenty, i.e. lots of wealth (plays on the notion of the horns supposedly sprouted by cuckolds, i.e. men with unfaithful wives)   **41 lightness** light/sexual promiscuity   **42 lanthorn** lantern (continues play on "horn")   **44 Smithfield** area in the City of London with a horse and cattle market; of poor reputation   **46 Paul's** St. Paul's Cathedral; the aisle served as a place for servants to seek new masters   **47 stews** brothels   **49 nobleman . . . Bardolph** according to an apocryphal tale, the prince was expelled from the King's Privy Council for hitting the Lord Chief Justice, an episode also referred to in *1 Henry IV*, Act 3 Scene 2   **committed** imprisoned

FALSTAFF   Wait, close. I will not see him.   *Tries to sneak away*

LORD CHIEF JUSTICE   What's he that goes there?

SERVANT   Falstaff, an't please your lordship.

LORD CHIEF JUSTICE   He that was in question for the robbery?

55 SERVANT   He, my lord. But he hath since done good service at
        Shrewsbury, and, as I hear, is now going with some charge to
        the lord John of Lancaster.

LORD CHIEF JUSTICE   What, to York? Call him back again.

SERVANT   Sir John Falstaff!

60 FALSTAFF   Boy, tell him I am deaf.

PAGE   You must speak louder: my master is deaf.

LORD CHIEF JUSTICE   I am sure he is, to the hearing of anything
        good. Go, pluck him by the elbow, I must speak with him.

SERVANT   Sir John!

65 FALSTAFF   What? A young knave, and beg? Is there not wars?
        Is there not employment? Doth not the king lack subjects?
        Do not the rebels want soldiers? Though it be a shame to be
        on any side but one, it is worse shame to beg than to be on
        the worst side, were it worse than the name of rebellion can
70   tell how to make it.

SERVANT   You mistake me, sir.

FALSTAFF   Why, sir, did I say you were an honest man? Setting
        my knighthood and my soldiership aside, I had lied in my
        throat, if I had said so.

75 SERVANT   I pray you, sir, then set your knighthood and your
        soldiership aside, and give me leave to tell you, you lie in your
        throat if you say I am any other than an honest man.

FALSTAFF   I give thee leave to tell me so? I lay aside that which
        grows to me? If thou gett'st any leave of me, hang me: if

---

51 close stay close/stay out of sight   **not see him** avoid him/pretend I have not seen him
53 an't if it   **54 in question for** suspected of/was questioned about   **55 good service** in
1 Henry IV Falstaff claimed the credit for killing Hotspur, although Prince Henry had in fact
done so   **56 charge** military command   **65 A . . . wars?** Falstaff pretends to think the
servant is begging rather than undertaking proper employment   **67 want** lack   **69 were . . .
make it** although it's hard to say what could be worse than rebellion   **72 Setting . . . aside**
disregarding my honor as a knight and soldier (which signifies I couldn't lie)   **73 in my throat**
outrageously   **79 grows to** belongs to, is an integral part of

80   thou tak'st leave, thou wert better be hanged. You hunt
        counter, hence! Avaunt!

SERVANT   Sir, my lord would speak with you.

LORD CHIEF JUSTICE   Sir John Falstaff, a word with you.

FALSTAFF   My good lord! Give your lordship good time of the
85   day. I am glad to see your lordship abroad. I heard say your
        lordship was sick. I hope your lordship goes abroad by
        advice. Your lordship, though not clean past your youth,
        hath yet some smack of age in you, some relish of the
        saltness of time, and I most humbly beseech your lordship to
90   have a reverend care of your health.

LORD CHIEF JUSTICE   Sir John, I sent for you before your expedition
        to Shrewsbury.

FALSTAFF   If it please your lordship, I hear his majesty is
        returned with some discomfort from Wales.

95 LORD CHIEF JUSTICE   I talk not of his majesty: you would not come
        when I sent for you.

FALSTAFF   And I hear, moreover, his highness is fallen into this
        same whoreson apoplexy.

LORD CHIEF JUSTICE   Well, heaven mend him! I pray, let me speak
100   with you.

FALSTAFF   This apoplexy is, as I take it, a kind of lethargy, a
        sleeping of the blood, a whoreson tingling.

LORD CHIEF JUSTICE   What tell you me of it? Be it as it is.

FALSTAFF   It hath it original from much grief, from study and
105   perturbation of the brain. I have read the cause of his effects
        in Galen: it is a kind of deafness.

LORD CHIEF JUSTICE   I think you are fallen into the disease, for you
        hear not what I say to you.

FALSTAFF   Very well, my lord, very well. Rather, an't please

---

80 hunt counter one on the wrong track (hunting term: following the wrong scent);
conceivably "one asking to go to prison (the counter)"   81 Avaunt! Be off!   85 abroad out of
doors   86 by advice with the doctor's permission   88 smack hint, taste   relish flavor, taste
89 saltness artificially preserved vitality of youth (salt is used to preserve meat)   90 reverend
respectful   98 apoplexy illness causing paralysis   103 What why   104 it original its origin
106 Galen famous second-century Greek physician

110   you, it is the disease of not listening, the malady of not
       marking, that I am troubled withal.

LORD CHIEF JUSTICE   To punish you by the heels would amend the
       attention of your ears, and I care not if I be your physician.

FALSTAFF   I am as poor as Job, my lord, but not so patient: your
115   lordship may minister the potion of imprisonment to me
       in respect of poverty, but how I should be your patient to
       follow your prescriptions, the wise may make some dram of
       a scruple, or indeed a scruple itself.

LORD CHIEF JUSTICE   I sent for you, when there were matters
120   against you for your life, to come speak with me.

FALSTAFF   As I was then advised by my learned counsel in the
       laws of this land-service, I did not come.

LORD CHIEF JUSTICE   Well, the truth is, Sir John, you live in great
       infamy.

125   FALSTAFF   He that buckles him in my belt cannot live in less.

LORD CHIEF JUSTICE   Your means is very slender, and your waste
       great.

FALSTAFF   I would it were otherwise: I would my means were
       greater, and my waist slenderer.

130   LORD CHIEF JUSTICE   You have misled the youthful prince.

FALSTAFF   The young prince hath misled me. I am the fellow
       with the great belly, and he my dog.

LORD CHIEF JUSTICE   Well, I am loath to gall a new-healed wound:
       your day's service at Shrewsbury hath a little gilded over

---

111 **marking** paying attention   **withal** with   112 **punish . . . heels** i.e. shackle your ankles, or
put you in the stocks   114 **Job** biblical character who lost all his wealth but bore his ill luck
with patience   116 **in . . . poverty** i.e. because I am too poor to pay a fine   **how** why, in what
way   117 **wise . . . itself** a wise person might question   **dram** unit of weight/small measure
of medicine   118 **scruple** third of a dram/doubt   119 **matters . . . life** charges laid against
you that are punishable by the death penalty   122 **land-service** military service, which
meant one could not be summoned to answer a civil charge; also a euphemistic way of
referring to the robbery Falstaff carried out at Gad's Hill (in *1 Henry IV*)   125 **He . . . less** i.e.
one of my large girth cannot be anything but **great**   126 **means** financial resources, income
waste expenditure (puns on "waist")   131 **I . . . dog** presumably a joke about a fat man being
led by his dog; possibly alludes to the full moon, popularly supposed to be inhabited by a man
with a dog   133 **gall** irritate

135   your night's exploit on Gad's Hill. You may thank the
       unquiet time for your quiet o'er-posting that action.

FALSTAFF   My lord?

LORD CHIEF JUSTICE   But since all is well, keep it so: wake not a
       sleeping wolf.

140 FALSTAFF   To wake a wolf is as bad as to smell a fox.

LORD CHIEF JUSTICE   What? You are as a candle, the better part
       burnt out.

FALSTAFF   A wassail candle, my lord, all tallow: if I did say of
       wax, my growth would approve the truth.

145 LORD CHIEF JUSTICE   There is not a white hair on your face but
       should have his effect of gravity.

FALSTAFF   His effect of gravy, gravy, gravy.

LORD CHIEF JUSTICE   You follow the young prince up and down,
       like his evil angel.

150 FALSTAFF   Not so, my lord, your ill angel is light: but I hope he
       that looks upon me will take me without weighing. And yet,
       in some respects, I grant, I cannot go: I cannot tell. Virtue is
       of so little regard in these costermongers that true valour is
       turned bear-herd: pregnancy is made a tapster, and hath his
155   quick wit wasted in giving reckonings: all the other gifts
       appertinent to man—as the malice of this age shapes
       them—are not worth a gooseberry. You that are old consider
       not the capacities of us that are young. You measure the
       heat of our livers with the bitterness of your galls. And

---

135 exploit . . . Hill i.e. the robbery at Gad's Hill in Kent in which Falstaff was involved in
1 Henry IV   136 unquiet disturbed by war   your . . . action having that offense quietly
passed over   140 smell a fox be suspicious   141 better greater, most useful/more virtuous
143 wassail candle fat candle used at a feast   tallow animal fat (used in candle making)
144 wax beeswax (used for high-quality candles; plays on the sense of "growth")   approve
demonstrate, prove   146 his its   147 gravy grease, sweat   149 angel attendant spirit
(Falstaff plays on the sense of "gold coin")   150 light slim, underweight/counterfeit or
fraudulently filed/satanic (the devil was originally Lucifer, the angel of light)   151 weighing
considering, judging/determining physical weight   152 go pass as currency/walk/
perform sexually   cannot tell do not know/cannot be counted as a legitimate coin
153 costermongers barrow-boys, street salesmen; originally sellers of costard apples
154 bear-herd keeper of a performing bear   pregnancy cleverness, quick-wittedness
tapster innkeeper, barman   155 reckonings tavern bills   156 appertinent belonging
159 livers considered the seat of the passions   galls the source of bitterness and anger

160   we that are in the vaward of our youth, I must confess, are
wags too.

LORD CHIEF JUSTICE   Do you set down your name in the scroll of
youth, that are written down old with all the characters of
age? Have you not a moist eye? A dry hand? A yellow cheek?
165   A white beard? A decreasing leg? An increasing belly? Is not
your voice broken? Your wind short? Your wit single? And
every part about you blasted with antiquity? And will you
call yourself young? Fie, fie, fie, Sir John.

FALSTAFF   My lord, I was born with a white head and
170   something a round belly. For my voice, I have lost it with
halloing and singing of anthems. To approve my youth
further, I will not. The truth is, I am only old in judgement
and understanding, and he that will caper with me for a
thousand marks, let him lend me the money, and have at
175   him! For the box of th'ear that the prince gave you, he gave it
like a rude prince, and you took it like a sensible lord. I have
checked him for it, and the young lion repents; marry, not in
ashes and sackcloth, but in new silk and old sack.

LORD CHIEF JUSTICE   Well, heaven send the prince a better
180   companion!

FALSTAFF   Heaven send the companion a better prince! I
cannot rid my hands of him.

LORD CHIEF JUSTICE   Well, the king hath severed you and Prince
Harry. I hear you are going with Lord John of Lancaster
185   against the archbishop and the Earl of Northumberland.

FALSTAFF   Yes, I thank your pretty sweet wit for it. But look
you pray—all you that kiss my lady Peace at home—that our

---

160 vaward vanguard, forefront, early part   **161 wags** mischievous fellows   **163 characters**
letters/characteristics   **164 moist** watery, rheumy   **166 broken** cracked, weak   **single**
weak, poor   **167 blasted** blighted   **168 Fie** expression of shame and indignation
171 halloing shouting/calling to hunting dogs   **approve** prove/commend   **173 caper with**
dance with/compete in dancing with   **174 marks** a mark was worth two thirds of a pound
have at him expression of defiance: so much for him/let's go for it   **175 For** as for   **176 rude**
violent, unmannerly   **sensible** reasonable/capable of physical sensation   **177 checked**
rebuked   **marry** by the Virgin Mary   **178 ashes and sackcloth** symbols of repentance
sack Spanish white wine   **186 I . . . it** either a sarcastic "thank you for reminding me" or
implies that the Lord Chief Justice is responsible for the separation   **look you** be sure to

armies join not in a hot day, for if I take but two shirts out
with me, and I mean not to sweat extraordinarily: if it be a
190   hot day, if I brandish anything but my bottle, would I might
never spit white again. There is not a dangerous action can
peep out his head but I am thrust upon it. Well, I cannot last
ever.

LORD CHIEF JUSTICE Well, be honest, be honest, and heaven bless
195   your expedition.

FALSTAFF   Will your lordship lend me a thousand pound to
furnish me forth?

LORD CHIEF JUSTICE Not a penny, not a penny. You are too
impatient to bear crosses. Fare you well. Commend me to my
200   cousin Westmorland.   [*Exeunt Lord Chief Justice and Servant*]

FALSTAFF   If I do, fillip me with a three-man beetle. A man can
no more separate age and covetousness than he can part
young limbs and lechery: but the gout galls the one, and the
pox pinches the other; and so both the degrees prevent my
205   curses.—Boy!

PAGE   Sir?

FALSTAFF   What money is in my purse?

PAGE   Seven groats and two-pence.

FALSTAFF   I can get no remedy against this consumption of
210   the purse. Borrowing only lingers and lingers it out, but the
disease is incurable. Go bear this letter to my   *Gives letters*
lord of Lancaster, this to the prince, this to the Earl of
Westmorland, and this to old Mistress Ursula, whom I have
weekly sworn to marry since I perceived the first white hair on
215   my chin. About it: you know where to find me.   [*Exit Page*]
A pox of this gout, or a gout of this pox! For the one or

---

191 spit white i.e. be healthy (red spittle would result from illness or internal injury)   **action**
engagement with the enemy   **194 be honest** behave honorably   **197 furnish me forth** equip
me for the expedition   **199 bear crosses** sustain hardships/carry coins (stamped on one side
with a cross)   **201 fillip** strike   **three-man beetle** huge sledgehammer requiring three men to
lift it   **204 pox** venereal disease   **pinches** torments   **both the degrees** i.e. of age and youth
208 groats coins worth four old pence   **209 consumption** disease (specifically, tuberculosis,
which caused victims to waste slowly away)   **213 Mistress Ursula** not mentioned elsewhere;
either an error for Mistress Quickly (Nell) or perhaps Falstaff is involved with another woman
216 pox of plague on   **pox** syphilis

th'other plays the rogue with my great toe. It is no matter if
I do halt. I have the wars for my colour, and my pension shall
seem the more reasonable. A good wit will make use of
220   anything: I will turn diseases to commodity.   *Exit*

Act 1 Scene [3]   *running scene 3*

Enter Archbishop, Hastings, Mowbray and Lord Bardolph

ARCHBISHOP OF YORK   Thus have you heard our causes and know
     our means,
     And, my most noble friends, I pray you all
     Speak plainly your opinions of our hopes.
     And first, lord marshal, what say you to it?
5   MOWBRAY   I well allow the occasion of our arms,
     But gladly would be better satisfied
     How in our means we should advance ourselves
     To look with forehead bold and big enough
     Upon the power and puissance of the king.
10   HASTINGS   Our present musters grow upon the file
     To five and twenty thousand men of choice,
     And our supplies live largely in the hope
     Of great Northumberland, whose bosom burns
     With an incensèd fire of injuries.
15   LORD BARDOLPH   The question then, Lord Hastings, standeth thus:
     Whether our present five and twenty thousand
     May hold up head without Northumberland?
     HASTINGS   With him, we may.
     LORD BARDOLPH   Ay, marry, there's the point:
20   But if without him we be thought too feeble,

---

218 halt limp   **colour** excuse, pretext   **220 commodity** profit, advantage
1.3   *Location: presumably York, the Archbishop's palace*   **1 causes** concerns/
matters of legal dispute   **means** methods/resources   **4 lord marshal** i.e. Thomas Mowbray,
Duke of Norfolk, the son of the man banished by Richard II   **5 allow** grant   **occasion**
motive/necessity/opportunity   **arms** taking arms   **7 in** with   **advance ourselves** promote
our cause/be so ambitious/make military advances   **9 puissance** strength, influence
10 Our . . . file i.e. our current list of recruited soldiers grows   **11 men of choice** selected
troops   **12 supplies** reinforcements   **live . . . Of** rely chiefly on/are greatly increased by the
expectation of support from   **17 hold up head** form a sufficient army

My judgement is, we should not step too far
Till we had his assistance by the hand.
For in a theme so bloody-faced as this,
Conjecture, expectation and surmise
25   Of aids incertain should not be admitted.
ARCHBISHOP OF YORK   'Tis very true, Lord Bardolph, for indeed
It was young Hotspur's case at Shrewsbury.
LORD BARDOLPH   It was, my lord, who lined himself with hope,
Eating the air on promise of supply,
30   Flatt'ring himself with project of a power
Much smaller than the smallest of his thoughts,
And so, with great imagination
Proper to madmen, led his powers to death
And winking leaped into destruction.
35   HASTINGS   But, by your leave, it never yet did hurt
To lay down likelihoods and forms of hope.
LORD BARDOLPH   Yes, if this present quality of war—
Indeed the instant action, a cause on foot—
Lives so in hope as in an early spring
40   We see th'appearing buds, which to prove fruit,
Hope gives not so much warrant as despair
That frosts will bite them. When we mean to build,
We first survey the plot, then draw the model,
And when we see the figure of the house,
45   Then must we rate the cost of the erection,
Which if we find outweighs ability,
What do we then but draw anew the model
In fewer offices? Or at least desist

---

22 by the hand at hand, ready   23 theme cause   bloody-faced violent, bloody (perhaps
with additional sense of "shameful")   25 aids incertain uncertain support   admitted
entertained, treated as valid   27 case situation   28 lined fortified   29 Eating the air i.e.
feeding on false hopes   30 project the mental conception, prospect   power army   31 Much
smaller which turned out to be much smaller   34 winking with his eyes shut (to reality)
35 by your leave with your permission (to contradict)   37 Yes i.e. yes it can   hurt   quality
state, condition   38 instant present   cause on foot business that is already under way
39 Lives . . . them has as little chance of success as early spring buds that are likely to be killed
by frosts before they have borne fruit   41 warrant assurance, grounds for optimism
44 figure design   45 rate calculate   46 ability i.e. to pay   48 offices rooms   least worst

To build at all? Much more, in this great work—
50   Which is almost to pluck a kingdom down
And set another up—should we survey
The plot of situation and the model,
Consent upon a sure foundation,
Question surveyors, know our own estate,
55   How able such a work to undergo,
To weigh against his opposite. Or else
We fortify in paper and in figures,
Using the names of men instead of men,
Like one that draws the model of a house
60   Beyond his power to build it; who, half through,
Gives o'er and leaves his part-created cost
A naked subject to the weeping clouds
And waste for churlish winter's tyranny.

HASTINGS   Grant that our hopes, yet likely of fair birth,
65   Should be still-born, and that we now possessed
The utmost man of expectation,
I think we are a body strong enough,
Even as we are, to equal with the king.

LORD BARDOLPH   What, is the king but five and twenty thousand?

70   HASTINGS   To us no more, nay, not so much, Lord Bardolph.
For his divisions—as the times do brawl—
Are in three heads: one power against the French,
And one against Glendower, perforce a third
Must take up us. So is the unfirm king
75   In three divided, and his coffers sound
With hollow poverty and emptiness.

ARCHBISHOP OF YORK   That he should draw his several strengths
together

---

53 Consent agree   54 estate wealth, resources   55 able . . . undergo practical it is to
undertake the project   56 opposite adverse factors/the resources of the enemy   57 fortify
plays on sense of "strengthen structurally, build"   figures numbers/designs   61 o'er up
cost object of expense, i.e. the building   62 naked subject exposed, unprotected victim
63 churlish rough, unkind   65 now . . . expectation already have all the men we can expect
71 as . . . brawl given the present strife   73 Glendower leader of the Welsh rebels   perforce
of necessity   74 unfirm insecure/indecisive   75 coffers money chests, i.e. treasury

And come against us in full puissance
Need not be dreaded.

80   HASTINGS   If he should do so,
He leaves his back unarmed, the French and Welsh
Baying him at the heels: never fear that.

LORD BARDOLPH   Who is it like should lead his forces hither?

HASTINGS   The Duke of Lancaster and Westmorland:

85   Against the Welsh, himself and Harry Monmouth.
But who is substituted gainst the French,
I have no certain notice.

ARCHBISHOP OF YORK   Let us on,
And publish the occasion of our arms.

90   The commonwealth is sick of their own choice,
Their over-greedy love hath surfeited:
An habitation giddy and unsure
Hath he that buildeth on the vulgar heart.
O thou fond many, with what loud applause

95   Didst thou beat heaven with blessing Bullingbrook,
Before he was what thou wouldst have him be!
And being now trimmed in thine own desires,
Thou, beastly feeder, art so full of him
That thou provok'st thyself to cast him up.

100   So, so, thou common dog, didst thou disgorge
Thy glutton bosom of the royal Richard,
And now thou wouldst eat thy dead vomit up,
And howl'st to find it. What trust is in these times?
They that, when Richard lived, would have him die,

105   Are now become enamoured on his grave.
Thou, that threw'st dust upon his goodly head
When through proud London he came sighing on
After th'admirèd heels of Bullingbrook,

---

82 Baying hunting, barking at in pursuit like a pack of dogs   **83 like** likely   **86 substituted**
delegated   **87 notice** information   **89 publish the occasion** proclaim the cause
91 surfeited overindulged and become sick   **92 habitation** dwelling   **93 vulgar heart**
popular, public affection   **94 fond many** foolish multitude   **97 trimmed** furnished with,
adorned/strengthened   **98 Thou** i.e. the people   **99 cast** vomit   **100 So** in the same way
disgorge vomit up from   **102 eat . . . up** the idea that a **dog** eats its vomit is proverbial
(originating in Proverbs 26:11 and 2 Peter 2:22)

Criest now 'O earth, yield us that king again,
110   And take thou this.' O, thoughts of men accursed!
Past and to come seems best; things present worst.
MOWBRAY   Shall we go draw our numbers and set on?
HASTINGS   We are time's subjects, and time bids be gone.

[*Exeunt*]

Act 2 Scene 1   *running scene 4*

Enter Hostess [Quickly], with two officers: Fang and Snare

HOSTESS QUICKLY   Master Fang, have you entered the action?
FANG   It is entered.
HOSTESS QUICKLY   Where's your yeoman? Is it a lusty yeoman?
Will he stand to it?
5   FANG   Sirrah— Where's Snare?   *Looks around*
HOSTESS QUICKLY   Ay, ay, good Master Snare.
SNARE   Here, here.   *Comes forward*
FANG   Snare, we must arrest Sir John Falstaff.
HOSTESS QUICKLY   Ay, good Master Snare, I have entered him
10   and all.
SNARE   It may chance cost some of us our lives: he will stab.
HOSTESS QUICKLY   Alas the day. Take heed of him: he stabbed me
in mine own house, and that most beastly. He cares not what
mischief he doth, if his weapon be out. He will foin like any
15   devil, he will spare neither man, woman nor child.
FANG   If I can close with him, I care not for his thrust.
HOSTESS QUICKLY   No, nor I neither: I'll be at your elbow.
FANG   If I but fist him once, if he come but within my
vice—

112 draw add up/assemble   2.1   *Location: Eastcheap, London, near a tavern*
Hostess landlady of a tavern   1 **Master** Quickly errs in using an overly respectful title for a
mere constable   **entered the action** begun the lawsuit   3 **yeoman** police officer's assistant
lusty strong, vigorous/lustful   4 **stand to it** be up to the task/get an erection   9 **entered**
brought a lawsuit against   12 **stabbed** hurt (financially; plays on sense of "penetrated
sexually"   13 **house** inn (plays on sense of "vagina")   14 **weapon** with phallic connotations
foin lunge, thrust with a weapon (sexual connotations, continued in **thrust**)   16 **close**
grapple, fight (plays on sense of "embrace sexually")   18 **fist** punch (plays on the sense of
"masturbate")   **come** plays on sense of "have an orgasm"   19 **vice** grip

20 HOSTESS QUICKLY I am undone with his going. I warrant he is an
       infinitive thing upon my score. Good Master Fang, hold him
       sure: good Master Snare, let him not scape. He comes
       continuantly to Pie-corner—saving your manhoods—to
       buy a saddle, and he is indited to dinner to the Lubber's-head
25   in Lombard Street, to Master Smooth's the silkman. I pra'ye,
       since my exion is entered and my case so openly known to
       the world, let him be brought in to his answer. A hundred
       mark is a long one for a poor lone woman to bear, and I have
       borne, and borne, and borne, and have been fubbed off, and
30   fubbed off, from this day to that day, that it is a shame to be
       thought on. There is no honesty in such dealing, unless a
       woman should be made an ass and a beast, to bear every
       knave's wrong.

       Enter Falstaff [with his Page] and Bardolph

       Yonder he comes, and that arrant malmsey-nose Bardolph,
35   with him. Do your offices, do your offices: Master Fang and
       Master Snare, do me, do me, do me your offices.
   FALSTAFF   How now? Whose mare's dead? What's the matter?
   FANG   Sir John, I arrest you at the suit of Mistress Quickly.

---

20 undone ruined (financially/sexually, in terms of reputation)   **going** plays on the sense of
"sexual activity"   **warrant** assure you   **21 infinitive** malapropism for "infinite"   **thing** with
phallic connotations   **score** tavern bill, accounts   **22 sure** securely, firmly   **scape** escape
23 continuantly malapropism for "continually" or for "incontinently," i.e. immediately (plays
on "continently," i.e. chastely)   **Pie-corner** the corner of Giltspur Street and Cock Lane, in
Smithfield, London; famous for cooks' shops and saddlers, also known for prostitution (**pie** and
corner were both slang terms for the vagina)   **saving . . . manhoods** apologetic formula for
mentioning an indelicate subject (**manhoods** may have phallic connotations)   **24 saddle** with
slang sense of "whore"   **indited** malapropism for invited (to "indite" is to summon for trial)
Lubber's-head i.e. Libbard's or Leopard's Head, name of a public house; a lubber is a clumsy,
idle lout   **25 Lombard Street** London street running from Mansion House to Graçechurch
Street   **26 exion** i.e. action   **case** lawsuit (plays on sense of "vagina")   **27 A hundred mark**
equivalent to £66—a large sum; **mark** also means "score, reckoning," and has phallic
connotations   **28 long one** i.e. large bill (with phallic connotations)   **29 borne** endured
patiently (plays on the sense of "borne the weight of a man during sex")   **fubbed** fobbed
31 dealing plays on the sense of "having sex"   **33 wrong** assumes additional sense of
"(shaming) penis" or possibly "illegitimate child"   **34 arrant** notorious, downright
malmsey-nose red-nosed (from drink; **malmsey** is a sweet red wine)   **35 offices** official
duties/acts of bodily excretion   **36 do me** do (**me** is emphatic; plays on sense of "have sex
with me")   **37 Whose mare's dead?** What's the fuss?   **mare** plays on the sense of "whore"

FALSTAFF Away, varlets! Draw, Bardolph. Cut me   *They draw*
40   off the villain's head. Throw the quean in the channel.

HOSTESS QUICKLY Throw me in the channel? I'll throw thee there. Wilt thou? Wilt thou? Thou bastardly rogue! Murder, murder! O, thou honeysuckle villain, wilt thou kill God's officers and the king's? O, thou honey-seed rogue, thou art a
45   honey-seed, a man-queller, and a woman-queller.

FALSTAFF Keep them off, Bardolph.

FANG A rescue, a rescue!

HOSTESS QUICKLY Good people, bring a rescue.— Thou   *To Page*
wilt not? Thou wilt not? Do, do, thou rogue! Do, thou hemp-
50   seed!

PAGE   Away, you scullion, you rampallion, you   *To Fang*
fustilarian! I'll tuck your catastrophe.

Enter Chief Justice

LORD CHIEF JUSTICE What's the matter? Keep the peace here, ho!

HOSTESS QUICKLY Good my lord, be good to me. I beseech you
55   stand to me.

LORD CHIEF JUSTICE How now, Sir John? What are you brawling here? Doth this become your place, your time and business? You should have been well on your way to York. Stand from him, fellow; wherefore hang'st upon him?

60   **HOSTESS QUICKLY** O my most worshipful lord, an't please your grace, I am a poor widow of Eastcheap, and he is arrested at my suit.

LORD CHIEF JUSTICE For what sum?

HOSTESS QUICKLY It is more than for some, my lord, it is for all, all
65   I have. He hath eaten me out of house and home; he hath

---

39 varlets rogues, rascals   **40 quean** whore   **channel** gutter   **43 honeysuckle** malapropism for "homicidal"   **44 honey-seed** i.e. homicide (plays on sense of "sweet semen")   **45 man-queller** murderer, crusher of men (appropriate given Falstaff's size)   **woman-queller** with sexual connotations   **48 a rescue** i.e. help (or perhaps Quickly thinks a rescue is some type of weapon or restraining rope)   **49 hemp-seed** i.e. one fit for the hangman's rope (made of hemp); perhaps another malapropism for "homicide"   **51 scullion** most menial kitchen servant   **rampallion** scoundrel, ruffian   **52 fustilarian** unclear; perhaps derived from "fustilugs" (i.e. a fat, unkempt woman)   **tuck** punish (may pun on "fuck")   **catastrophe** arse   **54 Good my** my good   **55 stand to** support (plays on sense of "become erect for")   **57 become** befit, suit   **59 wherefore** why   **61 Eastcheap** London Street running from the junction of Cannon and Gracechurch streets to Great Tower Street

put all my substance into that fat belly of his. But I will have
some of it out again, or I will ride thee o'nights like the mare.

FALSTAFF   I think I am as like to ride the mare, if I have any
vantage of ground to get up.

70 LORD CHIEF JUSTICE   How comes this, Sir John? Fie, what a man of
good temper would endure this tempest of exclamation? Are
you not ashamed to enforce a poor widow to so rough a
course to come by her own?

FALSTAFF   What is the gross sum that I owe thee?

75 HOSTESS QUICKLY   Marry, if thou wert an honest man, thyself
and the money too. Thou didst swear to me upon a parcel-
gilt goblet, sitting in my Dolphin-chamber at the round table,
by a sea-coal fire, on Wednesday in Whitsun week, when the
prince broke thy head for lik'ning him to a singing-man of
80 Windsor; thou didst swear to me then, as I was washing thy
wound, to marry me and make me my lady thy wife. Canst
thou deny it? Did not goodwife Keech, the butcher's wife,
come in then and call me gossip Quickly, coming in to
borrow a mess of vinegar, telling us she had a good dish of
85 prawns, whereby thou didst desire to eat some, whereby I
told thee they were ill for a green wound? And didst not thou,
when she was gone downstairs, desire me to be no more
familiar with such poor people, saying that ere long they
should call me madam? And didst thou not kiss me and bid

---

67 **ride . . . mare** sit on you and suffocate you like the nightmare, a female spirit supposedly
responsible for bad dreams; with sexual connotations   **mare** plays on the sense of "whore"
69 **vantage of ground** superior position, favorable opportunity   **get up** with sexual
connotations   71 **temper** disposition   73 **come . . . own** get what is due to her (**come**
plays on the sense of "orgasm")   74 **gross** total (perhaps with play on "fat/lecherous")
75 **Marry** by the Virgin Mary (plays on the sense of "marriage")   76 **parcel-gilt** partly gilded
77 **Dolphin-chamber** a particular room in the inn (these were often individually named)
78 **sea-coal** superior type of coal transported by sea from the north of England   **Whitsun
week** seven weeks after Easter   79 **broke** hit, grazed   **singing-man of Windsor** chorister of
the royal chapel; possibly a reference to John Magdalen of the King's Chapel, who passed
himself off as Richard II in a plot to overthrow Henry IV   82 **goodwife** term of address for a
married woman   **Keech** lump of congealed fat, an appropriate name for a butcher
83 **gossip** familiar form of address for a female friend   84 **mess** small quantity   **dish**
perhaps with vaginal connotations   85 **whereby** whereupon   86 **green** fresh, unhealed
89 **madam** i.e. a suitable term of address for the wife of a knight

90   me fetch thee thirty shillings? I put thee now to thy book-
oath: deny it, if thou canst.

FALSTAFF   My lord, this is a poor mad soul, and she says up and
down the town that her eldest son is like you. She hath been
in good case, and the truth is, poverty hath distracted her.
95   But for these foolish officers, I beseech you I may have
redress against them.

LORD CHIEF JUSTICE   Sir John, Sir John, I am well acquainted with
your manner of wrenching the true cause the false way. It is
not a confident brow, nor the throng of words that come
100   with such more than impudent sauciness from you, can
thrust me from a level consideration. I know you ha'
practised upon the easy-yielding spirit of this woman.

HOSTESS QUICKLY   Yea, in troth, my lord.

LORD CHIEF JUSTICE   Prithee, peace.— Pay her the debt you owe
105   her, and unpay the villainy you have done her: the one you
may do with sterling money, and the other with current
repentance.

FALSTAFF   My lord, I will not undergo this sneap without reply.
You call honourable boldness 'impudent sauciness'. If a man
110   will curtsy and say nothing, he is virtuous. No, my lord—
your humble duty remembered—I will not be your suitor. I
say to you, I desire deliverance from these officers, being
upon hasty employment in the king's affairs.

LORD CHIEF JUSTICE   You speak as having power to do wrong. But
115   answer in the effect of your reputation, and satisfy the poor
woman.

FALSTAFF   Come hither, hostess.   *Takes Quickly aside*

---

90 **book-oath** oath on the Bible   93 **son . . . you** i.e. that you're his father   94 **in good case**
well-off (**case** plays on the sense of "vagina")   **distracted her** driven her mad   101 **level** fair,
balanced   102 **practised upon** worked craftily on, taken advantage of   **easy-yielding**
generous, soft-hearted/sexually pliant   103 **troth** truth (plays on the sense of "pledge of
marriage")   104 **Pay . . . debt** plays on the sense of "undertake your obligation of marital
sex"   105 **unpay** undo, make good   106 **current** present, immediate/genuine   108 **sneap**
snub, rebuke   110 **curtsy** bow   111 **your . . . remembered** not forgetting the respect due to
one in your position   **be your suitor** petition you for a favor   114 **power** authorization
115 **in . . . reputation** in accordance with the reputation you claim   **satisfy** financially
reimburse/sexually pleasure

Enter Master Gower

LORD CHIEF JUSTICE Now, Master Gower, what news?

GOWER The king, my lord, and Henry Prince of Wales

120 Are near at hand: the rest the paper tells. *Gives a paper*

FALSTAFF As I am a gentleman.

HOSTESS QUICKLY Nay, you said so before.

FALSTAFF As I am a gentleman. Come, no more words of it.

HOSTESS QUICKLY By this heavenly ground I tread on, I must be

125 fain to pawn both my plate and the tapestry of my dining
chambers.

FALSTAFF Glasses, glasses is the only drinking. And for thy
walls, a pretty slight drollery, or the story of the Prodigal, or
the German hunting in water-work is worth a thousand of

130 these bed-hangings and these fly-bitten tapestries. Let it be
ten pound, if thou canst. Come, if it were not for thy
humours, there is not a better wench in England. Go, wash
thy face, and draw thy action. Come, thou must not be in this
humour with me. Come, I know thou wast set on to this.

135 HOSTESS QUICKLY Prithee, Sir John, let it be but twenty nobles. I
loath to pawn my plate, in good earnest, la.

FALSTAFF Let it alone. I'll make other shift. You'll be a fool still.

HOSTESS QUICKLY Well, you shall have it, although I pawn my
gown. I hope you'll come to supper. You'll pay me all

140 together?

FALSTAFF Will I live?— Go, with her, with her— *To Bardolph*
hook on, hook on.

---

124 heavenly ground Quickly mixes religious and secular oaths: by this heavenly light/by the
ground I walk on **125 fain** content **plate** silver or gold tableware, presumably cups in view
of Falstaff's response **127 Glasses . . . drinking** in the late sixteenth century glassware was
becoming more fashionable than metal drinking vessels **128 drollery** comic picture or
drawing **Prodigal** biblical story of the wasteful prodigal son, a popular subject for wall
hangings **129 German hunting** hunting scenes of German origin **water-work** imitation
tapestry/watercolor **132 humours** moods **133 draw thy action** withdraw your lawsuit
134 set on put up **135 nobles** gold coins worth about a third of a pound I I am **136 la**
exclamation used for emphasis **137 shift** arrangements **still** always **141 Will I live?** i.e. as
sure as I live **142 hook on** hang on to her, don't let her out of sight

HOSTESS QUICKLY Will you have Doll Tearsheet meet you at supper?

145 **FALSTAFF** No more words. Let's have her.

[*Exeunt Quickly, Bardolph, Fang and others*]

LORD CHIEF JUSTICE I have heard bitter news.

FALSTAFF What's the news, my good lord?

LORD CHIEF JUSTICE Where lay the king last night?

GOWER At Basingstoke, my lord.

150 **FALSTAFF** I hope, my lord, all's well. What is the news, my lord?

LORD CHIEF JUSTICE Come all his forces back?

GOWER No. Fifteen hundred foot, five hundred horse,
Are marched up to my lord of Lancaster,
Against Northumberland and the Archbishop.

155 **FALSTAFF** Comes the king back from Wales, my noble lord?

LORD CHIEF JUSTICE You shall have letters of me presently. Come,
go along with me, good Master Gower.

FALSTAFF My lord!

LORD CHIEF JUSTICE What's the matter?

160 **FALSTAFF** Master Gower, shall I entreat you with me to dinner?

GOWER I must wait upon my good lord here. I thank you,
good Sir John.

LORD CHIEF JUSTICE Sir John, you loiter here too long, being you
are to take soldiers up in counties as you go.

165 **FALSTAFF** Will you sup with me, Master Gower?

LORD CHIEF JUSTICE What foolish master taught you these
manners, Sir John?

FALSTAFF Master Gower, if they become me not, he was a fool
that taught them me. This is the right fencing grace, my lord:
170 tap for tap, and so part fair.

LORD CHIEF JUSTICE Now the lord lighten thee! Thou art a great
fool.

Exeunt

---

143 **Doll** a common name for a prostitute   **Tearsheet** again suggestive of prostitution, evoking vigorous sexual activity sufficient to tear the bedsheets   145 **have** plays on the sense of "possess sexually"   149 **Basingstoke** a market town in Hampshire, forty-six miles southwest of London   156 **presently** immediately   163 **being** it being the case that   164 **take soldiers up** enlist soldiers   169 **grace** style   170 **tap for tap** tit for tat   **fair** on good terms   171 **lighten thee** enlighten you/reduce your weight   **great** considerable/fat

Act 2 Scene 2

Enter Prince Henry and Poins

PRINCE HENRY   Trust me, I am exceeding weary.

POINS   Is it come to that? I had thought weariness durst not have attached one of so high blood.

PRINCE HENRY   It doth me, though it discolours the complexion of
5   my greatness to acknowledge it. Doth it not show vilely in me to desire small beer?

POINS   Why, a prince should not be so loosely studied as to remember so weak a composition.

PRINCE HENRY   Belike then my appetite was not princely got, for,
10   in troth, I do now remember the poor creature, small beer. But indeed these humble considerations make me out of love with my greatness. What a disgrace is it to me to remember thy name? Or to know thy face tomorrow? Or to take note how many pair of silk stockings thou hast—*videlicet* these—
15   and those that were thy peach-coloured ones—or to bear the inventory of thy shirts, as one for superfluity, and one other for use? But that the tennis-court-keeper knows better than I, for it is a low ebb of linen with thee when thou kept'st not racket there, as thou hast not done a great while, because
20   the rest of thy Low Countries have made a shift to eat up thy Holland.

POINS   How ill it follows, after you have laboured so hard, you should talk so idly! Tell me, how many good young princes would do so, their fathers lying so sick as yours is?

25   **PRINCE HENRY**   Shall I tell thee one thing, Poins?

2.2   *Location: in London but unspecified—either the prince's apartments or the same street location as the previous scene*   **3 attached** arrested, taken into custody (legal term)   **4 discolours . . . greatness** makes me blush/tarnishes my princely status   **5 show vilely** appear base   **6 small beer** weak or thin beer/trivial occupations   **7 loosely studied** poorly educated/concerned with immoral matters   **8 composition** mixture, brew/invention   **9 Belike** perhaps, most likely   **got** begotten, created   **12 disgrace . . . name** a member of the royal family would not have been expected to have any kind of personal relationship with a commoner   **14 *videlicet*** "namely" (Latin)   **15 bear** be aware of   **16 for superfluity** as a spare   **18 low . . . racket** i.e. he doesn't play when he hasn't got a shirt to change into   **20 Low Countries** nether regions, i.e. his sexual appetite and brothel use   **made . . . Holland** contrived to use up the money that would have been spent on shirts (**Holland**, one of the **Low Countries**, was a source of fine linen)

POINS   Yes, and let it be an excellent good thing.

PRINCE HENRY It shall serve among wits of no higher breeding than thine.

30 POINS   Go to. I stand the push of your one thing that you'll tell.

PRINCE HENRY Why, I tell thee it is not meet that I should be sad now my father is sick—albeit I could tell to thee, as to one it pleases me, for fault of a better, to call my friend, I could be sad, and sad indeed too.

35 POINS   Very hardly upon such a subject.

PRINCE HENRY Thou think'st me as far in the devil's book as thou and Falstaff for obduracy and persistency. Let the end try the man. But I tell thee, my heart bleeds inwardly that my father is so sick: and keeping such vile company as thou art hath in 40 reason taken from me all ostentation of sorrow.

POINS   The reason?

PRINCE HENRY What wouldst thou think of me, if I should weep?

POINS   I would think thee a most princely hypocrite.

PRINCE HENRY It would be every man's thought, and thou art a 45 blessed fellow to think as every man thinks: never a man's thought in the world keeps the roadway better than thine: every man would think me an hypocrite indeed. And what accites your most worshipful thought to think so?

POINS   Why, because you have been so lewd and so much 50 engraffed to Falstaff.

PRINCE HENRY And to thee.

POINS   Nay, I am well spoken of. I can hear it with mine own ears: the worst that they can say of me is that I am a second brother and that I am a proper fellow of my hands. 55 And those two things, I confess, I cannot help. Look, look, here comes Bardolph.

---

29 **Go to** exclamation of dismissive impatience   **stand the push** withstand the thrust
31 **meet** fitting   32 **albeit** even though   33 **fault** lack   35 **Very hardly** with difficulty
37 **try** test, judge, determine   40 **ostentation** outward show   45 **never a** no   46 **keeps the roadway** sticks to the common path (of men's thoughts)   48 **accites** induces/summons (in legal sense)   49 **lewd** common, base   50 **engraffed** closely attached   54 **second brother** i.e. a younger son without an inheritance, dependent on his wits   **proper . . . hands** good in a fight

PRINCE HENRY   And the boy that I gave Falstaff. He had him from me Christian, and see if the fat villain have not transformed him ape.

Enter Bardolph [and Falstaff's Page]

60   BARDOLPH   Save your grace.

PRINCE HENRY   And yours, most noble Bardolph.

POINS   Come, you pernicious ass, you bashful   *To Bardolph* fool, must you be blushing? Wherefore blush you now? What a maidenly man-at-arms are you become! Is it such a matter
65   to get a pottle-pot's maidenhead?

PAGE   He called me even now, my lord, through a red lattice, and I could discern no part of his face from the window. At last I spied his eyes, and methought he had made two holes in the ale-wife's new petticoat and peeped
70   through.

PRINCE HENRY   Hath not the boy profited?   *To Poins*

BARDOLPH   Away, you whoreson upright rabbit, away!

PAGE   Away, you rascally Althaea's dream, away!

PRINCE HENRY   Instruct us, boy. What dream, boy?

75   PAGE   Marry, my lord, Althaea dreamed she was delivered of a fire-brand, and therefore I call him her dream.

PRINCE HENRY   A crown's worth of good interpretation.— There it is, boy.   *Gives Page money*

POINS   O, that this good blossom could be kept   *money*
80   from cankers!— Well, there is sixpence to preserve   *Gives Page* thee.   *money*

---

58 transformed him ape apparently Falstaff has dressed his page up in an elaborate outfit, like a performing monkey   **60 Save** God save   **your grace** respectful title, but Henry shifts the sense of grace to "virtue, honor"   **63 blushing** i.e. red-faced from drink   **65 get . . . maidenhead** i.e. drain a tankard of ale   **maidenhead** virginity   **66 red lattice** the lattice windows of alehouses were usually painted red; Bardolph's face is therefore indistinguishable from the background   **69 ale-wife's new petticoat** landlady's (red) skirt (not necessarily underwear); red clothing was associated with prostitution   **71 profited** benefited (from Falstaff's teaching)   **73 Althaea's dream** in classical mythology Althaea was told that her son would live until a burning brand was consumed; the Page confuses her with Hecuba, mother of Paris, who dreamed that she would give birth to a firebrand that would destroy Troy (as Paris' actions later did)   **76 fire-brand** burning log/mischief maker   **79 blossom** i.e. the Page **80 cankers** grubs that destroy plants   **sixpence** probably alludes to the cross on an Elizabethan sixpence

BARDOLPH   If you do not make him be hanged among you, the gallows shall be wronged.

PRINCE HENRY   And how doth thy master, Bardolph?

85   BARDOLPH   Well, my good lord. He heard of your grace's coming to town. There's a letter for you.   *Gives a letter*

POINS   Delivered with good respect. And how doth the martlemas, your master?

BARDOLPH   In bodily health, sir.

90   POINS   Marry, the immortal part needs a physician, but that moves not him: though that be sick, it dies not.

PRINCE HENRY   I do allow this wen to be as familiar with me as my dog, and he holds his place, for look you he writes.

POINS   *(Letter)*   *Reads*
'John Falstaff, knight.'—Every man must know that, as oft
95   as he hath occasion to name himself, even like those that are kin to the king, for they never prick their finger but they say, 'There is some of the king's blood spilt.' 'How comes that?' says he that takes upon him not to conceive. The answer is as ready as a borrower's cap, 'I am the king's poor cousin, sir.'

100   PRINCE HENRY   Nay, they will be kin to us, but they will fetch it from Japhet. But to the letter: 'Sir John Falstaff,   *Reads*
knight, to the son of the king, nearest his father, Harry Prince of Wales, greeting.'

POINS   Why, this is a certificate.

105   PRINCE HENRY   Peace! 'I will imitate the honourable   *Reads*
Romans in brevity.'

POINS   Sure he means brevity in breath,   *Takes the letter*
short-winded. 'I commend me to thee, I commend   *and reads*

---

82 **If ... among you** if your influence doesn't end up getting him hanged   87 **good respect** very properly, most ceremoniously (ironic given Bardolph's blunt delivery)   88 **martlemas** i.e. fattened beast; Martinmas, the feast of Saint Martin (11 November), was associated with the slaughter of cattle and pigs   92 **wen** wart, growth   93 **holds his place** insists on his rank   95 **as ... himself** since he continually reminds them whenever he mentions his name   **even like** in the same way as   98 **conceive** understand   99 **borrower's cap** i.e. readily removed in humble respect   100 **will be** are determined to be   **but ... Japhet** even if they have to derive their claim from as far back as Japhet, Noah's third son   104 **certificate** license issued to a subject by the king; in a letter the addressee's name should come first

thee, and I leave thee. Be not too familiar with Poins, for he
110   misuses thy favours so much, that he swears thou art to
marry his sister Nell. Repent at idle times as thou mayst, and
so farewell. Thine, by yea and no, which is as much as to say,
as thou usest him, Jack Falstaff with my familiars, John with
my brothers and sister, and Sir John with all Europe.' My
115   lord, I will steep this letter in sack and make him eat it.

PRINCE HENRY   That's to make him eat twenty of his words. But
do you use me thus, Ned? Must I marry your sister?

POINS   May the wench have no worse fortune! But I never
said so.

120   PRINCE HENRY   Well, thus we play the fools with the time, and the
spirits of the wise sit in the clouds and mock us.—   *To Bardolph*
Is your master here in London?

BARDOLPH   Yes, my lord.

PRINCE HENRY   Where sups he? Doth the old boar feed in the old
125   frank?

BARDOLPH   At the old place, my lord, in Eastcheap.

PRINCE HENRY   What company?

PAGE   Ephesians, my lord, of the old church.

PRINCE HENRY   Sup any women with him?

130   PAGE   None, my lord, but old Mistress Quickly and Mistress
Doll Tearsheet.

PRINCE HENRY   What pagan may that be?

PAGE   A proper gentlewoman, sir, and a kinswoman of my
master's.

135   PRINCE HENRY   Even such kin as the parish heifers are to the town
bull.— Shall we steal upon them, Ned, at supper?   *To Poins*

POINS   I am your shadow, my lord: I'll follow you.

---

109 I . . . thee Falstaff imitates **Roman** brevity by emulating the structure of Caesar's *veni, vidi,
vici* ("I came, I saw, I conquered") : "I present my kind regards, praise your virtues and say
goodbye"   **111 idle times** leisure   **mayst** can   **112 by . . . no** a mild oath   **113 familiars**
close friends   **115 steep** soak   **sack** Spanish white wine   **116 twenty** i.e. a lot   **117 use**
treat, behave toward   **120 play . . . time** pass the time foolishly   **125 frank** sty, pigpen
128 Ephesians . . . church good old companions of the usual disreputable ways   **132 pagan**
heathen/prostitute   **133 proper** respectable   **135 town bull** commonly owned bull that was
used to impregnate all the **heifers**

PRINCE HENRY   Sirrah, you boy, and Bardolph, no word to your
master that I am yet in town. There's for your   *Gives money*
140   silence.

BARDOLPH   I have no tongue, sir.

PAGE   And for mine, sir, I will govern it.

PRINCE HENRY   Fare ye well. Go.

[*Exeunt Bardolph and Page*]

This Doll Tearsheet should be some road.

145   POINS   I warrant you, as common as the way between St
Albans and London.

PRINCE HENRY   How might we see Falstaff bestow himself tonight
in his true colours, and not ourselves be seen?

POINS   Put on two leathern jerkins and aprons, and wait
150   upon him at his table like drawers.

PRINCE HENRY   From a God to a bull? A heavy declension! It
was Jove's case. From a prince to a prentice, a low
transformation: that shall be mine, for in everything the
purpose must weigh with the folly. Follow me, Ned.   *Exeunt*

Act 2 Scene 3   *running scene 6*

Enter Northumberland and his Lady, and Harry Percy's Lady

NORTHUMBERLAND   I prithee, loving wife and gentle daughter,
Give an even way unto my rough affairs.
Put not you on the visage of the times
And be like them to Percy troublesome.

5   LADY NORTHUMBERLAND   I have given over, I will speak no more.
Do what you will: your wisdom be your guide.

NORTHUMBERLAND   Alas, sweet wife, my honour is at pawn,
And, but my going, nothing can redeem it.

---

144 road i.e. whore (used by all men; **road** was slang for "vagina")   **145 way . . . London** i.e.
Watling Street, the main road from London to the Midlands   **St Albans** Hertfordshire town
twenty-five miles north of London   **147 bestow** behave   **150 drawers** bartenders, waiters
151 God . . . bull refers to the supreme god Jove's transformation into a bull, in which form he
raped Europa   **heavy declension** serious decline   **152 case** plays on the sense of "vagina"
prentice apprentice (bartender)   **154 weigh with** equal, counterbalance   **2.3 *Location:
Warkworth Castle, Northumberland***   **2 even way** smooth passage   **rough** difficult
3 visage face, i.e. attitude   **8 but** except for

LADY PERCY   O, yet, for heaven's sake, go not to these wars!
10   The time was, father, when you broke your word,
When you were more endeared to it than now,
When your own Percy, when my heart-dear Harry,
Threw many a northward look to see his father
Bring up his powers. But he did long in vain.
15   Who then persuaded you to stay at home?
There were two honours lost, yours and your son's.
For yours, may heavenly glory brighten it.
For his, it stuck upon him as the sun
In the grey vault of heaven, and by his light
20   Did all the chivalry of England move
To do brave acts. He was indeed the glass
Wherein the noble youth did dress themselves:
He had no legs that practised not his gait:
And speaking thick, which nature made his blemish,
25   Became the accents of the valiant,
For those that could speak low and tardily
Would turn their own perfection to abuse,
To seem like him: so that in speech, in gait,
In diet, in affections of delight,
30   In military rules, humours of blood,
He was the mark and glass, copy and book,
That fashioned others. And him—O, wondrous him!
O, miracle of men!—him did you leave,
Second to none, unseconded by you,
35   To look upon the hideous god of war
In disadvantage, to abide a field
Where nothing but the sound of Hotspur's name
Did seem defensible. So you left him.
Never, O, never, do his ghost the wrong

---

10 time . . . word Lady Percy refers to Northumberland's failure to join his son at Shrewsbury
(see *1 Henry IV*)   **19 grey** pale blue   **21 glass** mirror   **22 dress themselves** fashion
themselves, using him as a model   **23 He . . . gait** there was no one who did not imitate his
manner of walking   **24 thick** rapidly and loudly   **27 turn . . . abuse** spoil their naturally
pleasant manner of speaking   **29 affections of delight** enjoyment of pleasures   **30 humours
of blood** moods   **31 mark** reference point   **34 unseconded** unsupported   **36 abide a field**
face a battle   **38 defensible** to offer any defense   **39 ghost** soul, spirit

40

To hold your honour more precise and nice
With others than with him. Let them alone.
The marshal and the archbishop are strong.
Had my sweet Harry had but half their numbers,
Today might I, hanging on Hotspur's neck,

45

Have talked of Monmouth's grave.

NORTHUMBERLAND Beshrew your heart,
Fair daughter, you do draw my spirits from me
With new lamenting ancient oversights.
But I must go and meet with danger there,

50

Or it will seek me in another place
And find me worse provided.

LADY NORTHUMBERLAND O, fly to Scotland,
Till that the nobles and the armèd commons
Have of their puissance made a little taste.

55

LADY PERCY If they get ground and vantage of the king,
Then join you with them, like a rib of steel,
To make strength stronger. But, for all our loves,
First let them try themselves. So did your son.
He was so suffered; so came I a widow,

60

And never shall have length of life enough
To rain upon remembrance with mine eyes,
That it may grow and sprout as high as heaven,
For recordation to my noble husband.

NORTHUMBERLAND Come, come, go in with me. 'Tis with my mind

65

As with the tide swelled up unto his height,
That makes a still-stand, running neither way.
Fain would I go to meet the archbishop,
But many thousand reasons hold me back.
I will resolve for Scotland: there am I,

70

Till time and vantage crave my company.   *Exeunt*

---

40 precise and nice scrupulous and particular   **42 marshal . . . archbishop** i.e. Mowbray
and the Archbishop of York   **45 Monmouth's** i.e. the Prince of Wales'   **46 Beshrew**
curse   **47 spirits** vital powers   **48 new** newly, again   **ancient oversights** past mistakes
51 provided prepared, equipped   **54 puissance** power, strength   **55 ground . . . of**
superiority and advantage over   **59 so suffered** allowed to do so   **came** I I became
61 remembrance perhaps the plant of remembrance, rosemary   **63 recordation to**
commemoration of   **66 still-stand** pause, standstill   **69 for** to make for

Act 2 Scene 4

Enter two Drawers

FIRST DRAWER   What hast thou brought there? Apple-johns? Thou know'st Sir John cannot endure an apple-john.

SECOND DRAWER   Thou say'st true. The prince once set a dish of apple-johns before him, and told him there were five more Sir
5   Johns, and, putting off his hat, said 'I will now take my leave of these six dry, round, old, withered knights.' It angered him to the heart, but he hath forgot that.

FIRST DRAWER   Why then, cover and set them down, and see if thou canst find out Sneak's noise; Mistress Tearsheet would
10   fain have some music.

SECOND DRAWER   Sirrah, here will be the prince and Master Poins anon, and they will put on two of our jerkins and aprons, and Sir John must not know of it. Bardolph hath brought word.

15   FIRST DRAWER   Then here will be old Utis: it will be an excellent stratagem.

SECOND DRAWER   I'll see if I can find out Sneak.   *Exit*
Enter Hostess [Quickly] and Doll [Tearsheet]

HOSTESS QUICKLY   Sweetheart, methinks now you are in an excellent good temperality: your pulsidge beats as
20   extraordinarily as heart would desire; and your colour, I warrant you, is as red as any rose. But, you have drunk too much canaries, and that's a marvellous searching wine, and it perfumes the blood ere we can say 'What's this?' How do you now?

25   DOLL TEARSHEET   Better than I was. Hem!

2.4   *Location: Quickly's tavern in Eastcheap, London   Drawers* bartenders, waiters
1 Apple-johns type of apple said to be in best eating condition when shriveled   **8 cover** lay
the table   **9 noise** band of musicians   **10 fain** gladly   **12 anon** soon   **jerkins** close-fitting
jackets often made of leather   **15 old Utis** fine larks, high jinks (from the now obsolete word
utas, meaning "festivity")   **19 temperality** Quickly means "temper" (plays on "temporality,"
i.e. time)   **pulsidge** malapropism for "pulse"   **20 extraordinarily** malapropism for
"ordinarily"   **22 canaries** wine from the Canary Islands   **searching** penetrating, powerful
23 perfumes probably a malapropism for "perfuses," i.e. suffuses, permeates   **25 Hem!**
probably a hiccup

HOSTESS QUICKLY Why, that was well said. A good heart's worth
    gold. Look, here comes Sir John.

Enter Falstaff

FALSTAFF   'When Arthur first in court'—   *Sings*
    Empty the jordan.—   *To First Drawer*
30   'And was a worthy king'.
    How now, Mistress Doll?   *Sings*

                                                   [Exit First Drawer]

HOSTESS QUICKLY Sick of a calm, yea, good sooth.

FALSTAFF   So is all her sect. If they be once in a calm, they are
    sick.

35 DOLL TEARSHEET You muddy rascal, is that all the comfort you
    give me?

FALSTAFF   You make fat rascals, Mistress Doll.

DOLL TEARSHEET I make them? Gluttony and diseases make
    them, I make them not.

40 FALSTAFF   If the cook make the gluttony, you help to make the
    diseases, Doll. We catch of you, Doll, we catch of you. Grant
    that, my poor virtue, grant that.

DOLL TEARSHEET Ay, marry, our chains and our jewels.

FALSTAFF   'Your broaches, pearls and ouches.' For to serve
45   bravely is to come halting off, you know. To come off the
    breach with his pike bent bravely, and to surgery bravely; to
    venture upon the charged chambers bravely—

HOSTESS QUICKLY Why, this is the old fashion: you two never
    meet but you fall to some discord. You are both, in good
50   troth, as rheumatic as two dry toasts. You cannot one bear

---

28 'When . . . court' a line from the popular ballad "Sir Launcelot du Lake"   29 jordan
chamberpot   32 calm i.e. "qualm," a fit of faintness   good sooth truly   33 sect
sex/type/profession   If . . . sick for a woman or a prostitute to be quiet means she is unwell
37 rascals rogues/lean young deer   38 make possibly with sexual connotations: "have sex
with"   40 cook plays on the sense of "pimp" and puns on "cock"   41 catch of get diseases
(specifically, venereal disease) from (Doll responds to the sense of "steal from")   44 'Your . . .
ouches' presumably a line from a ballad, but broaches, pearls and ouches are also terms for
skin lesions (associated with venereal disease)   ouch gem/boil   serve in military and sexual
sense   45 bravely courageously/showily   halting limping (from injury sustained in war/as a
result of syphilitic bone erosion; "come off" could mean "dismount sexually")   46 breach gap
in fortifications/vagina   pike staff with an iron spike/penis   surgery treatment (for
injury/venereal disease)   47 charged chambers loaded barrels of small cannon/infectious
vagina   50 rheumatic Quickly probably intends "choleric," i.e. temperamentally hot and dry

with another's confirmities. What the good year! One must
bear, and that must be you: you are the weaker   *To Doll*
vessel, as they say, the emptier vessel.

DOLL TEARSHEET Can a weak empty vessel bear such a huge full
55   hogshead? There's a whole merchant's venture of Bordeaux
stuff in him. You have not seen a hulk better stuffed in the
hold. Come, I'll be friends with thee, Jack. Thou art going to
the wars, and whether I shall ever see thee again or no, there
is nobody cares.

Enter [First] Drawer

60 FIRST DRAWER Sir, Ancient Pistol is below, and would speak
with you.

DOLL TEARSHEET Hang him, swaggering rascal! Let him not
come hither: it is the foul-mouthed'st rogue in England.

HOSTESS QUICKLY If he swagger, let him not come here. I must
65   live amongst my neighbours. I'll no swaggerers. I am in good
name and fame with the very best. Shut the door, there
comes no swaggerers here. I have not lived all this while, to
have swaggering now. Shut the door, I pray you.

FALSTAFF Dost thou hear, hostess?

70 HOSTESS QUICKLY Pray you, pacify yourself, Sir John. There
comes no swaggerers here.

FALSTAFF Dost thou hear? It is mine ancient.

HOSTESS QUICKLY Tilly-fally, Sir John, never tell me: your ancient
swaggerer comes not in my doors. I was before Master Tisick,
75   the deputy, the other day, and as he said to me—it was no
longer ago than Wednesday last—'Neighbour Quickly', says

51 confirmities malapropism for "infirmities" misleadingly suggesting "resemblances"
What . . . year! common exclamation of impatience (like "What the devil!")   52 bear be
tolerant/bear the weight of a man during sex/bear children   54 vessel now takes on vaginal
connotations   55 hogshead large wine barrel, i.e. Falstaff   venture i.e. cargo (risked in a sea
voyage)   Bordeaux stuff wine from Bordeaux in France   56 hulk big, unwieldy person/large
ship   60 Ancient ensign, i.e. soldier responsible for carrying military banners   Pistol
pronounced "pizzle," generating a pun on the sense of "penis"   62 swaggering blustering,
insolent, quarrelsome   65 I'll I'll have   66 fame reputation   73 Tilly-fally nonsense
74 Tisick i.e. "phthisic" or tuberculosis, a wasting disease of the lungs   75 deputy one acting
in place of a magistrate, before whom Quickly has been summoned for keeping a disorderly
tavern

he—Master Dumbe, our minister, was by then—'Neighbour
Quickly,' says he, 'receive those that are civil; for', sayeth he,
'you are in an ill name.' Now he said so, I can tell whereupon.

80 'For', says he, 'you are an honest woman, and well thought
on; therefore take heed what guests you receive. Receive',
says he, 'no swaggering companions.' There comes none
here. You would bless you to hear what he said. No, I'll no
swaggerers.

85 FALSTAFF   He's no swaggerer, hostess: a tame cheater he.
You may stroke him as gently as a puppy greyhound. He will
not swagger with a Barbary hen, if her feathers turn back in
any show of resistance.— Call him up, drawer.

[*Exit First Drawer*]

HOSTESS QUICKLY 'Cheater', call you him? I will bar no honest
90 man my house, nor no cheater, but I do not love swaggering.
I am the worse when one says 'swagger'. Feel, masters, how
I shake. Look you, I warrant you.

DOLL TEARSHEET   So you do, hostess.

HOSTESS QUICKLY   Do I? Yea, in very truth do I, if it were an aspen
95 leaf: I cannot abide swaggerers.

Enter Pistol, and Bardolph and his Boy

PISTOL   Save you, Sir John!

FALSTAFF   Welcome, Ancient Pistol. Here, Pistol, I charge you
with a cup of sack. Do you discharge upon mine hostess.

PISTOL   I will discharge upon her, Sir John, with two bullets.

100 FALSTAFF   She is Pistol-proof, sir. You shall hardly offend her.

HOSTESS QUICKLY   Come, I'll drink no proofs nor no bullets: I will
drink no more than will do me good, for no man's pleasure, I.

77 **Dumbe** parsons who did not preach or who did so with insufficient vigor were known as
"dumb dogs"   **by** nearby   78 **receive** i.e. as customers   79 **are . . . name** have a bad
reputation   **Now . . . whereupon** and now I understand why   82 **companions** fellows
83 **bless you** be surprised/consider yourself fortunate   85 **tame** harmless   **cheater** crafty
cardplayer (with connotations of "deceiver")   87 **Barbary hen** guinea fowl/prostitute
91 **am the worse** feel ill   94 **if it** as if I were   97 **charge** load (like a gun)/toast
98 **discharge** fire/toast/ejaculate   99 **two bullets** plays on the idea of "testicles"   100 **Pistol-
proof** bulletproof/resistant to your charms, or penis/past childbearing age   **hardly** plays on
notion of erectile hardness   101 **Come** possible play on sense of "orgasm"   102 **drink** plays
on the sense of "have sex"

PISTOL   Then to you, Mistress Dorothy. I will charge you.

DOLL TEARSHEET   Charge me? I scorn you, scurvy companion.
105   What? You poor, base, rascally, cheating, lack-linen mate!
          Away, you mouldy rogue, away! I am meat for your master.

PISTOL   I know you, Mistress Dorothy.

DOLL TEARSHEET   Away, you cutpurse rascal, you filthy bung,
          away! By this wine, I'll thrust my knife in your mouldy chaps,
110   if you play the saucy cuttle with me. Away, you bottle-ale
          rascal, you basket-hilt stale juggler, you! Since when, I pray
          you, sir? What, with two points on your shoulder? Much!

PISTOL   I will murder your ruff for this.

HOSTESS QUICKLY   No, Good Captain Pistol. Not here, sweet
115   captain.

DOLL TEARSHEET   Captain? Thou abominable damned cheater,
          art thou not ashamed to be called captain? If captains were
          of my mind, they would truncheon you out for taking their
          names upon you before you have earned them. You a
120   captain? You slave, for what? For tearing a poor whore's ruff
          in a bawdy-house? He a captain? Hang him, rogue! He lives
          upon mouldy stewed prunes and dried cakes. A captain?
          These villains will make the word 'captain' odious: therefore
          captains had need look to it.

125   BARDOLPH   Pray thee go down, good ancient.   *To Pistol*

---

103 Dorothy Doll is the shortened form of the name   **104 Charge** Doll interprets this in a
sexual sense, perhaps "charge at with a (phallic) weapon" or "burden (with pregnancy)"
scurvy worthless, contemptible   **105 lack-linen mate** poorly dressed fellow   **106 meat . . .
master** i.e. too good for you (**meat** puns on "mate" and on the sense of "whore")   **107 know**
perhaps with sexual overtones (i.e. "am familiar with you sexually")   **108 cutpurse** thieving,
pickpocket   **bung** pickpocket   **109 chaps** cheeks   **110 saucy cuttle** insolent thief (a **cuttle**
was the knife used by thieves to cut the strings securing purses to people's belts)   **bottle-ale**
perhaps meaning cheap or frothy   **111 basket-hilt** i.e. swashbuckling, inadequate (literally,
sword hilt provided with a defense for the swordsman's hand, consisting of narrow plates of
steel curved into the shape of a basket)   **juggler** trickster   **Since when** i.e. how long have
you claimed to be a soldier/so manly   **112 points** laces for attaching armor   **Much!** sarcastic
exclamation (i.e. "Much manly prowess you have!"/"Two points certainly is a lot!")
113 murder i.e. rip off, tear (i.e. sexually assault; **ruff** was slang for "vagina")   **ruff** prostitutes
were known for wearing large ruffs   **114 Captain** Quickly promotes Pistol (who is an ensign),
either inadvertently or in order to flatter him   **118 truncheon** beat   **out** i.e. of their ranks,
from military service   **121 bawdy-house** brothel   **122 stewed prunes** a dish commonly
available in brothels (hence also "whores")   **dried** stale   **124 look to it** beware, look out
125 down downstairs

FALSTAFF	Hark thee hither, Mistress Doll.	
PISTOL	Not I. I tell thee what, Corporal Bardolph, I could tear her. I'll be revenged on her.	
PAGE	Pray thee go down.	*To Pistol*

130 PISTOL   I'll see her damned first

To Pluto's damnèd lake,

To the infernal deep,

With Erebus and tortures vile also.

Hold hook and line, say I.

135   Down, down, dogs! Down, Fates!

Have we not Hiren here?

HOSTESS QUICKLY   Good Captain Peesel, be quiet. It is very late. I beseek you now, aggravate your choler.

PISTOL   These be good humours indeed. Shall pack-horses

140   And hollow pampered jades of Asia,

Which cannot go but thirty miles a day,

Compare with Caesar and with cannibals,

And Trojan Greeks?

Nay, rather damn them with King Cerberus,

145   And let the welkin roar. Shall we fall foul for toys?

HOSTESS QUICKLY   By my troth, captain, these are very bitter words.

---

130 I'll . . . first this and several of Pistol's subsequent speeches are set in prose in Folio, but consist of fragments and parodies of verse plays, so they should be spoken as verse, though the rhythms and line breaks are highly irregular   **131 Pluto's damnèd lake** Pluto was the Roman god of the underworld, which had several rivers; the Romans thought that the Italian lake Avernus was the entrance to the underworld   **133 Erebus** son of Chaos and Night, used to personify the underworld   **134 Hold . . . line** i.e. don't let go (angling terminology)   **135 Fates** classical goddesses of destiny   **136 Hiren** perhaps Pistol has affectedly named his sword; Hiren (Irene) may refer to a character in George Peele's lost play *The Turkish Mahomet and Hiren the Fair Greek*; puns on "iron," again suggesting Pistol's sword   **137 Peesel** variant pronunciation of "Pistol," further emphasizing play on "pizzle" (penis)   **138 beseek** i.e. beseech   **aggravate** in fact Quickly means the opposite, perhaps "abrogate" (put an end to) **choler** anger, one of the four bodily **humours**   **139 humours** moods (literally, bodily fluids governing the temperament)   **Shall . . . day** closely modeled on lines in Christopher Marlowe's *Tamburlaine Part II*, 4.3.1–2; much of Pistol's speech parodies theatrical rhetoric **140 jades** worn-out horses/whores   **142 cannibals** Pistol may mean "Hannibal" (i.e. famous Carthaginian general who fought the Romans in the third century BC)   **143 Trojan Greeks** Greeks besieging Troy in the Trojan war, or Pistol confuses the two groups (may play on sense of "jolly, roistering fellows")   **144 King Cerberus** the three-headed dog that guarded the entrance to the underworld; not a king   **145 welkin** sky, heavens   **fall . . . toys** quarrel/be destroyed over trifles

BARDOLPH   Be gone, good ancient: this will grow to a brawl anon.

150 PISTOL   Die men like dogs! Give crowns like pins!
Have we not Hiren here?

HOSTESS QUICKLY   On my word, captain, there's none such here. What the goodyear, do you think I would deny her? I pray be quiet.

155 PISTOL   Then feed, and be fat, my fair Calipolis.
Come, give me some sack.
Si fortune me tormente, sperato me contento.
Fear we broadsides? No, let the fiend give fire.
Give me some sack. And, sweetheart, lie thou there.   *Lays down his sword*
Come we to full points here? And are etceteras
160   nothing?

FALSTAFF   Pistol, I would be quiet.

PISTOL   Sweet knight, I kiss thy neaf. What, we have seen the seven stars!

DOLL TEARSHEET   Thrust him downstairs. I cannot endure such a
165   fustian rascal.

PISTOL   'Thrust him down stairs'? Know we not Galloway nags?

FALSTAFF   Quoit him down, Bardolph, like a shove-groat shilling. Nay, if he do nothing but speak nothing, he shall be
170   nothing here.

BARDOLPH   Come, get you downstairs.

PISTOL   What? Shall we have incision? Shall we   *Snatches up*
imbrue?   *his sword*

---

150 **Die men** let men die   **Give . . . pins** give crowns away as though they were worth no more than pins   153 **deny her** deny that she is here (Quickly thinks that Pistol is referring to an actual woman, probably a prostitute)   155 **feed . . . Calipolis** parodies a line in George Peele's *The Battle of Alcazar*   157 *Si . . . contento* "If fortune torments me, hope contents me" (rather garbled Italian)   158 **broadsides** simultaneous discharge of artillery from one side of a ship   **give fire** shoot   160 **full points** an end (literally, full stops, periods); plays on the sense of "erect penises"   **etceteras nothing** both euphemisms for the vagina   162 **neaf** hand   163 **seven stars** constellation of the Pleiades; Pistol suggests they've enjoyed themselves at night   165 **fustian** cheap/bombastic   166 **Galloway nags** small Scottish horses/prostitutes   168 **Quoit** throw   **shove-groat shilling** shilling coin used in shove-groat, a board game that involved moving a coin toward a compartment   172 **incision** i.e. bloodshed   **imbrue** stain (with blood)

Then death rock me asleep, abridge my doleful days.

175   Why then, let grievous, ghastly, gaping wounds

Untwined the Sisters Three! Come, Atropos, I say!

HOSTESS QUICKLY   Here's good stuff toward.

FALSTAFF   Give me my rapier, boy.

DOLL TEARSHEET   I prithee, Jack, I prithee do not draw.

180   FALSTAFF   Get you downstairs.   *Draws and attacks Pistol*

[*Exit Pistol, driven out by Bardolph*]

HOSTESS QUICKLY   Here's a goodly tumult! I'll forswear keeping house, before I'll be in these tirrits and frights. So, murder, I warrant now. Alas, alas, put up your naked weapons, put up your naked weapons.

185   DOLL TEARSHEET   I prithee, Jack, be quiet. The rascal is gone. Ah, you whoreson little valiant villain, you!

HOSTESS QUICKLY   Are you not hurt i'th'groin? Methought he made a shrewd thrust at your belly.

[*Enter Bardolph*]

FALSTAFF   Have you turned him out of doors?   *To Bardolph*

190   BARDOLPH   Yes, sir. The rascal's drunk. You have hurt him, sir, in the shoulder.

FALSTAFF   A rascal to brave me!

DOLL TEARSHEET   Ah, you sweet little rogue, you! Alas, poor ape, how thou sweat'st! Come, let me wipe thy face. Come on, you

195   whoreson chops. Ah, rogue, I love thee. Thou art as valorous as Hector of Troy, worth five of Agamemnon, and ten times better than the Nine Worthies. Ah, villain!

---

174 death . . . asleep quotation from a song attributed to Anne Boleyn, written as she awaited execution   **abridge** shorten   **176 Untwined** unravel, spin out (like the thread of a person's life, spun by the Fates)   **Sisters Three** Fates of classical mythology   **Atropos** one of the Fates, who cut the thread of life after her sisters, Clotho and Lachesis, spun and unwound it   **177 toward** coming up, imminent   **178 rapier** lightweight sword   **181 forswear** reject, give up   **keeping house** inn-keeping   **182 tirrits** fits of fear, upsets   **183 put . . . weapons** sheathe, or hold back your swords (plays on the sense of "get an erection with your bare penises")   **188 shrewd** vicious, dangerous   **192 brave** challenge, defy   **195 chops** fat cheeks   **196 Hector of Troy** leader of the Trojan army, known for his valiant and honorable nature   **Agamemnon** leader of the Greek army when it opposed the Trojans   **197 Nine Worthies** historical figures embodying the ideals of chivalry: three Jews (Joshua, David, and Judas Maccabaeus), three pagans (Hector of Troy, Alexander the Great, and Julius Caesar), and three Christians (Arthur, Charlemagne, and Godfrey of Bouillon)

FALSTAFF   A rascally slave, I will toss the rogue in a blanket.

DOLL TEARSHEET   Do, if thou dar'st for thy heart. If thou dost, I'll
200   canvass thee between a pair of sheets.

Enter Musicians

PAGE   The music is come, sir.

FALSTAFF   Let them play.—Play, sirs.—Sit on my knee, Doll. A
rascal bragging slave! The rogue fled from me like
quicksilver.

205   **DOLL TEARSHEET**   And thou followed'st him like a church. Thou
whoreson little tidy Bartholomew boar-pig, when wilt thou
leave fighting on days and foining on nights, and begin to
patch up thine old body for heaven?

Enter the Prince and Poins, disguised

FALSTAFF   Peace, good Doll. Do not speak like a death's-head,
210   do not bid me remember mine end.

DOLL TEARSHEET   Sirrah, what humour is the prince of?

FALSTAFF   A good shallow young fellow: he would have made a
good pantler, he would have chipped bread well.

DOLL TEARSHEET   They say Poins hath a good wit.

215   **FALSTAFF**   He a good wit? Hang him, baboon! His wit is as thick
as Tewkesbury mustard. There is no more conceit in him
than is in a mallet.

DOLL TEARSHEET   Why doth the prince love him so, then?

FALSTAFF   Because their legs are both of a bigness, and he
220   plays at quoits well, and eats conger and fennel, and

---

198 toss . . . blanket proverbial punishment for cowards   **200 canvass . . . sheets** i.e. have
sex with you   **canvass** toss   **204 quicksilver** mercury, i.e. rapidly   **205 like a church**
unclear; perhaps "slowly, in a stately manner/not at all"   **206 tidy** fat, healthy
Bartholomew boar-pig pig roasts were traditional at London's St. Bartholomew's fair (24
August)   **207 foining** thrusting (with a sword; sexual connotations)   **209 death's-head** skull
used as a memento mori, a reminder of the inevitability of death   **211 humour** disposition
213 pantler servant in charge of the pantry   **chipped bread** cut away the hard crusts
216 Tewkesbury mustard creamy mustard blended with horseradish, produced in the West
Country town of Tewkesbury in Gloucestershire   **conceit** wit, understanding, imagination
219 legs . . . bigness i.e. they're the same type (vain, fashion-conscious); men were judged by
the shapeliness of their legs   **of a** the same   **220 quoits** game in which a metal ring was
thrown at a peg fixed in the ground   **conger and fennel** conger eel seasoned with fennel,
difficult to digest

drinks off candles' ends for flap-dragons, and rides the wild-mare with the boys, and jumps upon joint-stools, and swears with a good grace, and wears his boot very smooth, like unto the sign of the leg, and breeds no bate with telling of discreet
225   stories, and such other gambol faculties he hath, that show a weak mind and an able body, for the which the prince admits him; for the prince himself is such another. The weight of an hair will turn the scales between their avoirdupois.

PRINCE HENRY   Would not this nave of a wheel have   *Aside to Poins*
230   his ears cut off?

POINS   Let us beat him before his whore.

PRINCE HENRY   Look, if the withered elder hath not his poll clawed like a parrot.

POINS   Is it not strange that desire should so many years
235   outlive performance?

FALSTAFF   Kiss me, Doll.   *She kisses him*

PRINCE HENRY   Saturn and Venus this year in   *Aside to Poins*
conjunction! What says the almanac to that?

POINS   And look whether the fiery Trigon, his man, be not
240   lisping to his master's old tables, his notebook, his counsel-keeper.

FALSTAFF   Thou dost give me flatt'ring busses.   *To Doll*

---

221 **drinks . . . flap-dragons** plays a drinking game in which one must drink liquor with burning objects (in this case candles' ends) floating in it   **flap-dragons** raisins that had to be plucked from burning brandy and swallowed   **rides the wild-mare** plays a game similar to leapfrog in which players land on rather than jump over others (**mare** plays on the sense of "whore")   222 **jumps upon joint-stools** i.e. indulges in high spirits   **joint-stools** low stools made by a joiner   223 **smooth** close-fitting (to show off his legs)   224 **sign of the leg** sign over a bootmaker's shop   **breeds no bate** causes no dissent, rouses no disagreement   **discreet** cautious, prudent (i.e. dull)   225 **gambol** playful   226 **admits** receives, socializes with   227 **such another** the same type   228 **avoirdupois** weight   229 **nave of a wheel** wheel hub (puns on "knave" and on Falstaff's rotundity)   230 **ears cut off** the punishment for slandering royalty   232 **elder** elder tree/old man   **poll . . . parrot** Doll is ruffling his hair   **poll** head (plays on popular name for a **parrot**)   237 **Saturn and Venus** planets thought to govern old age and love respectively   238 **in conjunction** together in the heavens (plays on the sense of "in sexual union")   **almanac** astrological calendar   239 **fiery Trigon** i.e. red-faced Bardolph; signs of the zodiac were divided into four groups of three (**trigons**), the fiery set consisting of Aries, Leo, and Sagittarius   240 **lisping** whispering/talking in a loving voice   **tables . . . counsel-keeper** i.e. Mistress Quickly   **tables** notebook (for recording secret assignations)   242 **busses** kisses

DOLL TEARSHEET   Nay truly, I kiss thee with a most constant heart.

245   **FALSTAFF**   I am old, I am old.

DOLL TEARSHEET   I love thee better than I love e'er a scurvy young boy of them all.

FALSTAFF   What stuff wilt thou have a kirtle of? I shall receive money on Thursday. Thou shalt have a cap tomorrow. A
250   merry song, come. It grows late. We will to bed. Thou wilt forget me when I am gone.

DOLL TEARSHEET   Thou wilt set me a-weeping, if thou say'st so. Prove that ever I dress myself handsome till thy return. Well, hearken the end.

255   **FALSTAFF**   Some sack, Francis.

PRINCE HENRY and POINS   Anon, anon, sir.   *Stepping forward*

FALSTAFF   Ha? A bastard son of the king's?— And art not thou Poins his brother?

PRINCE HENRY   Why, thou globe of sinful continents, what a life
260   dost thou lead!

FALSTAFF   A better than thou: I am a gentleman, thou art a drawer.

PRINCE HENRY   Very true, sir, and I come to draw you out by the ears.

265   **HOSTESS QUICKLY**   O, the lord preserve thy good grace! Welcome to London. Now, heaven bless that sweet face of thine! What, are you come from Wales?

FALSTAFF   Thou whoreson mad compound of majesty, by this light flesh and corrupt blood, thou art welcome.

270   **DOLL TEARSHEET**   How? You fat fool, I scorn you.

POINS   My lord, he will drive you out of your revenge and turn all to a merriment, if you take not the heat.

---

248 stuff material   **kirtle** gown   **253 handsome** smartly, respectably   **254 hearken the end** judge by the outcome (whether I'm faithful or not), wait and see   **256 Anon** coming, right away   **258 Poins his** Poins'   **259 continents** parts of the world/contents   **268 compound** composition, piece   **269 light** loose, immoral (refers to Doll)   **272 take . . . heat** do not act now

PRINCE HENRY You whoreson candle-mine, you, how vilely did
you speak of me even now before this honest, virtuous, civil
275 gentlewoman!

HOSTESS QUICKLY Blessing on your good heart, and so she is, by
my troth.

FALSTAFF Didst thou hear me?   *To Prince Henry*

PRINCE HENRY Yes, and you knew me, as you did when you ran
280 away by Gad's Hill: you knew I was at your back, and spoke
it on purpose to try my patience.

FALSTAFF No, no, no, not so. I did not think thou wast within
hearing.

PRINCE HENRY I shall drive you then to confess the wilful abuse,
285 and then I know how to handle you.

FALSTAFF No abuse, Hal, on mine honour, no abuse.

PRINCE HENRY Not to dispraise me, and call me pantler and
bread-chopper and I know not what?

FALSTAFF No abuse, Hal.

290 POINS No abuse?

FALSTAFF No abuse, Ned, in the world, honest Ned, none. I
dispraised him before the wicked, that the wicked might not
fall in love with him—in which doing, I have done the part of
a careful friend and a true subject, and thy father is to give
295 me thanks for it. No abuse, Hal.— None, Ned, none.— No,
boys, none.

PRINCE HENRY See now whether pure fear and entire cowardice
doth not make thee wrong this virtuous gentlewoman to
close with us? Is she of the wicked? Is thine hostess here of
300 the wicked? Or is the boy of the wicked? Or honest Bardolph,
whose zeal burns in his nose, of the wicked?

POINS Answer, thou dead elm, answer.

---

273 candle-mine source of animal fat for making candles   **274 honest** chaste   **279 knew**
recognized   **284 wilful abuse** deliberate slander   **299 close** unite, agree   **wicked** mocking
the language of Puritan zealots   **301 burns . . . nose** another reference to Bardolph's
alcoholically red face   **302 dead elm** rotten old tree; the elm tree was traditionally used to
support vines, and to make coffins

FALSTAFF   The fiend hath pricked down Bardolph irrecoverable, and his face is Lucifer's privy-kitchen, where he doth
305   nothing but roast malt-worms. For the boy, there is a good angel about him, but the devil outbids him too.

PRINCE HENRY   For the women?

FALSTAFF   For one of them, she is in hell already, and burns poor souls. For the other, I owe her money, and whether she
310   be damned for that, I know not.

HOSTESS QUICKLY   No, I warrant you.

FALSTAFF   No, I think thou art not. I think thou art quit for that. Marry, there is another indictment upon thee, for suffering flesh to be eaten in thy house, contrary to the law,
315   for the which I think thou wilt howl.

HOSTESS QUICKLY   All victuallers do so. What is a joint of mutton or two in a whole Lent?

PRINCE HENRY   You, gentlewoman—   *To Doll*

DOLL TEARSHEET   What says your grace?

320   FALSTAFF   His grace says that which his flesh   *Knocking within*
rebels against.

HOSTESS QUICKLY   Who knocks so loud at door? Look to the door there, Francis.

Enter Peto

PRINCE HENRY   Peto, how now? What news?

325   PETO   The king your father is at Westminster,
And there are twenty weak and wearied posts
Come from the north, and as I came along,
I met and overtook a dozen captains,

---

303 **pricked** marked   304 **Lucifer's privy-kitchen** i.e. hell   305 **malt-worms** drunkards
306 **outbids** i.e is more influential than   308 **hell . . . burns** i.e. has syphilis, with which she
infects others   309 **owe . . . that** Puritans considered moneylending sinful   312 **quit**
acquitted, forgiven/paid back   314 **suffering** permitting   **flesh . . . eaten** i.e. meat to be eaten
during Lent (when it was forbidden)/prostitution to take place   315 **howl** be punished/be
damned   316 **victuallers** innkeepers   **mutton** sheep/prostitute   319 **grace** title for a
prince/honor, virtue   320 **says . . . against** i.e. the polite title **gentlewoman** is one that the
prince (or his sexual impulse) knows instinctively to be misapplied to a loose woman like Doll
325 **Westminster** location of the royal court in London   326 **posts** messengers

Bare-headed, sweating, knocking at the taverns,

330   And asking every one for Sir John Falstaff.

PRINCE HENRY   By heaven, Poins, I feel me much to blame,

So idly to profane the precious time,

When tempést of commotion, like the south

Borne with black vapour, doth begin to melt

335   And drop upon our bare unarmèd heads.—

Give me my sword and cloak.— Falstaff, goodnight.

Exeunt [Prince Henry, Poins and Peto]

FALSTAFF   Now comes in the sweetest morsel of the night, and we must hence and leave it unpicked. More knocking at the door? How now? What's the matter?   *Knocking within*

Bardolph goes to the door

340   BARDOLPH   You must away to court, sir, presently.

A dozen captains stay at door for you.

FALSTAFF   Pay the musicians, sirrah.— Farewell,   *To the Page* hostess.— Farewell, Doll. You see, my good wenches, how men of merit are sought after. The undeserver may sleep,

345   when the man of action is called on. Farewell good wenches. If I be not sent away post, I will see you again ere I go.

DOLL TEARSHEET   I cannot speak. If my heart be not ready to burst—well, sweet Jack, have a care of thyself.

FALSTAFF   Farewell, farewell.

Exeunt [Falstaff, Bardolph and Page]

350   HOSTESS QUICKLY   Well, fare thee well. I have known thee these twenty-nine years, come peascod-time, but an honester and truer-hearted man—well, fare thee well.

BARDOLPH   Mistress Tearsheet!   *Within*

HOSTESS QUICKLY   What's the matter?

355   BARDOLPH   Bid Mistress Tearsheet come to my master.   *Within*

HOSTESS QUICKLY   O, run, Doll, run. Run, good Doll!   *Exeunt*

---

329 **Bare-headed** a sign of haste; it was customary to cover the head   332 **profane** i.e. misuse   333 **commotion** insurrection   **south** south wind, thought to carry disease and storms   334 **Borne . . . vapour** carried along with dark clouds   337 **morsel** part/sexual tidbit 338 **unpicked** untasted   340 **presently** at once   341 **stay** wait   346 **post** posthaste, immediately   350 **known** perhaps with sexual connotations   351 **peascod-time** the time when peas ripen in the pod (plays on sense of "testicle time")

Act 3 Scene 1

Enter the King, with a Page

KING HENRY IV   Go call the Earls of Surrey and of   *Gives letters*
    Warwick.
    But ere they come, bid them o'er-read these letters,
    And well consider of them. Make good speed.   *Exit [Page]*
    How many thousand of my poorest subjects
5   Are at this hour asleep? O sleep, O gentle sleep,
    Nature's soft nurse, how have I frighted thee,
    That thou no more wilt weigh my eyelids down
    And steep my senses in forgetfulness?
    Why rather, sleep, liest thou in smoky cribs,
10   Upon uneasy pallets stretching thee
    And hushed with buzzing night-flies to thy slumber,
    Than in the perfumed chambers of the great,
    Under the canopies of costly state,
    And lulled with sounds of sweetest melody?
15   O thou dull god, why liest thou with the vile
    In loathsome beds, and leav'st the kingly couch
    A watch-case or a common 'larum-bell?
    Wilt thou upon the high and giddy mast
    Seal up the ship-boy's eyes, and rock his brains
20   In cradle of the rude imperious surge
    And in the visitation of the winds,
    Who take the ruffian billows by the top,
    Curling their monstrous heads and hanging them
    With deaf'ning clamours in the slipp'ry clouds,
25   That, with the hurly, death itself awakes?
    Canst thou, O partial sleep, give thy repose
    To the wet sea-boy in an hour so rude,

3.1 *Location: the royal court*   **9 cribs** hovels   **10 pallets** straw mattresses   **13 state** splendor   **15 vile** mean, wretched, lowborn   **17 watch-case** ticking watch in a case/sentry box   **common 'larum-bell** public alarm bell, rung by a night watchman in an emergency   **20 rude imperious surge** rough, overwhelming swell of the sea   **21 visitation** violent, destructive force   **22 ruffian billows** rough waves   **24 slipp'ry** rapidly passing/unable to be grasped   **25 That** so that   **hurly** tumult, uproar   **26 partial** unfair, biased/sympathetic   **27 rude** rough, dangerous

And in the calmest and most stillest night,
With all appliances and means to boot,
30   Deny it to a king? Then happy low, lie down!
Uneasy lies the head that wears a crown.

Enter Warwick and Surrey

WARWICK   Many good morrows to your majesty!

KING HENRY IV   Is it good morrow, lords?

WARWICK   'Tis one o'clock, and past.

35   KING HENRY IV   Why then, good morrow to you all, my lords.
Have you read o'er the letters that I sent you?

WARWICK   We have, my liege.

KING HENRY IV   Then you perceive the body of our kingdom
How foul it is, what rank diseases grow
40   And with what danger, near the heart of it?

WARWICK   It is but as a body yet distempered,
Which to his former strength may be restored
With good advice and little medicine:
My lord Northumberland will soon be cooled.

45   KING HENRY IV   O, heaven! That one might read the book of fate,
And see the revolution of the times
Make mountains level, and the continent,
Weary of solid firmness, melt itself
Into the sea. And other times, to see
50   The beachy girdle of the ocean
Too wide for Neptune's hips; how chance's mocks
. And changes fill the cup of alteration
With divers liquors! 'Tis not ten years gone
Since Richard and Northumberland, great friends,
55   Did feast together, and in two years after
Were they at wars. It is but eight years since
This Percy was the man nearest my soul,

---

29 to boot besides   **30 happy low** fortunate humble men   **32 morrows** mornings   **39 foul**
diseased, polluted   **rank** festering, gross, abundant   **41 distempered** out of sorts   **43 little** a
little   **44 cooled** calm down, regain equilibrium   **46 revolution** change, movement
47 continent dry land   **50 beachy . . . ocean** i.e. seashore, imaged as a belt   **51 Neptune**
Roman god of the sea   **chance's mocks** mockeries of fortune   **53 divers** various/
unfavorable   **54 Richard** Richard II   **57 This Percy** i.e. Northumberland

Who like a brother toiled in my affairs
And laid his love and life under my foot,
60   Yea, for my sake, even to the eyes of Richard
Gave him defiance. But which of you was by—
You, cousin Neville, as I may remember—   *To Warwick*
When Richard, with his eye brimful of tears,
Then checked and rated by Northumberland,
65   Did speak these words, now proved a prophecy?
'Northumberland, thou ladder by the which
My cousin Bullingbrook ascends my throne' —
Though then, heaven knows, I had no such intent,
But that necessity so bowed the state
70   That I and greatness were compelled to kiss—
'The time shall come', thus did he follow it,
'The time will come that foul sin, gathering head,
Shall break into corruption.' So went on,
Foretelling this same time's condition
75   And the division of our amity.
WARWICK   There is a history in all men's lives,
Figuring the nature of the times deceased,
The which observed, a man may prophesy,
With a near aim, of the main chance of things
80   As yet not come to life, which in their seeds
And weak beginnings lie intreasurèd.
Such things become the hatch and brood of time;
And by the necessary form of this,
King Richard might create a perfect guess
85   That great Northumberland, then false to him,
Would of that seed grow to a greater falseness,

---

59 under my foot at my service   **60 eyes** i.e. face   **62 Neville** in fact, Warwick's name is
Richard de Beauchamp, although the Earl of Warwick in *3 Henry VI* is Richard Neville
64 rated berated   **66 'Northumberland . . . throne'** for these and the other lines the king
recalls, see *Richard II*, Act 5 Scene 1   **72 head** to a head (of a boil, with play on the sense of
"insurrection/army")   **73 corruption** pus (plays on the sense of "sin, destruction")   **74 same**
current   **77 Figuring** reproducing, depicting   **deceased** past, gone by   **79 near aim**
accurate guess   **main chance** likely outcome   **81 intreasurèd** safely stored   **82 hatch and
brood** outcome and offspring   **83 necessary form** inevitable pattern   **85 false** disloyal

Which should not find a ground to root upon,
Unless on you.

KING HENRY IV   Are these things then necessities?

90 Then let us meet them like necessities;
And that same word even now cries out on us.
They say the bishop and Northumberland
Are fifty thousand strong.

WARWICK   It cannot be, my lord.

95 Rumour doth double, like the voice and echo,
The numbers of the feared. Please it your grace
To go to bed. Upon my life, my lord,
The powers that you already have sent forth
Shall bring this prize in very easily.

100 To comfort you the more, I have received
A certain instance that Glendower is dead.
Your majesty hath been this fortnight ill,
And these unseasoned hours perforce must add
Unto your sickness.

105 KING HENRY IV   I will take your counsel.
And were these inward wars once out of hand,
We would, dear lords, unto the Holy Land.   *Exeunt*

Act 3 Scene 2   *running scene 9*

Enter Shallow and Silence, with Mouldy, Shadow, Wart, Feeble, Bull-
calf [and Servants]

SHALLOW   Come on, come on, come on. Give me your hand,
sir; give me your hand, sir. An early stirrer, by the rood! And
how doth my good cousin Silence?

---

91 cries out on denounces/calls for attention from   101 A certain instance secure evidence
Glendower leader of the Welsh rebels   103 unseasoned late, unseasonable   perforce of
necessity   106 inward civil   out of hand over and done with   107 would wish to go
3.2   *Location: Gloucestershire, west England (the home of Shallow—though Falstaff*
is supposed to be going from London to York and this would not be on his way)
Shallow and Silence both Justices of the Peace (magistrates); Silence (from Lincolnshire?)
appears to be visiting his kinsman   *Mouldy . . . Bullcalf* army recruits (Folio groups their
entrance at the beginning of the scene, but they could come on individually when their names
are called from the roll)   2 rood (Christ's) cross

SILENCE   Good morrow, good cousin Shallow.

5   SHALLOW   And how doth my cousin, your bedfellow? And your fairest daughter and mine, my goddaughter Ellen?

SILENCE   Alas, a black ouzel, cousin Shallow!

SHALLOW   By yea and nay, sir. I dare say my cousin William is become a good scholar: he is at Oxford still, is he not?

10   SILENCE   Indeed, sir, to my cost.

SHALLOW   He must then to the Inns of Court shortly. I was once of Clement's Inn, where I think they will talk of mad Shallow yet.

SILENCE   You were called 'lusty Shallow' then, cousin.

15   SHALLOW   I was called anything, and I would have done anything indeed too, and roundly too. There was I, and little John Doit of Staffordshire, and black George Bare, and Francis Pickbone, and Will Squele, a Cotswold man. You had not four such swinge-bucklers in all the Inns of Court again.

20   And I may say to you, we knew where the bona-robas were and had the best of them all at commandment. Then was Jack Falstaff, now Sir John, a boy, and page to Thomas Mowbray, Duke of Norfolk.

SILENCE   This Sir John, cousin, that comes hither anon about

25   soldiers?

SHALLOW   The same Sir John, the very same. I saw him break Scoggin's head at the court-gate, when he was a crack not thus high. And the very same day did I fight with one Sampson Stockfish, a fruiterer, behind Gray's Inn. O, the

---

5 bedfellow i.e. wife   **7 black** of dark hair and/or complexion (considered less attractive than fair hair and skin)   **ouzel** blackbird   **8 By . . . nay** a mild oath   **9 Oxford** Oxford University, sixty miles northwest of London   **11 Inns of Court** in London where young men trained for the legal profession   **12 Clement's Inn** one of the Inns of Chancery, a step below the Inns of Court   **14 lusty** lively/lustful   **16 roundly** to the full   **17 Doit** an appropriate name for a **little** man; a doit is a small coin of little value   **18 Pickbone** a name suggestive of greed   **Squele** suggests an excitable man, or one with a shrill, high-pitched voice   **Cotswold** the Cotswolds are a range of hills in Gloucestershire   **19 swinge-bucklers** swashbucklers, swaggerers **20 bona-robas** attractive whores   **27 Scoggin's** John Scoggin was court jester to Edward IV **court-gate** palace gates   **crack** lively lad (picks up on the language of breaking) **29 Sampson Stockfish** ironic combination of names: **Sampson** is a biblical hero and stockfish is dried cod (used to suggest physical weakness and an impotent penis)   **Gray's Inn** one of the Inns of Court

30   mad days that I have spent! And to see how many of mine
      old acquaintance are dead!

SILENCE   We shall all follow, cousin.

SHALLOW   Certain, 'tis certain, very sure, very sure: death is
      certain to all, all shall die. How a good yoke of bullocks at
35   Stamford Fair?

SILENCE   Truly, cousin, I was not there.

SHALLOW   Death is certain. Is old Double of your town living
      yet?

SILENCE   Dead, sir.

40 SHALLOW   Dead? See, see, he drew a good bow, and dead? He
      shot a fine shoot. John of Gaunt loved him well, and betted
      much money on his head. Dead? He would have clapped in
      the clout at twelvescore, and carried you a forehand shaft at
      fourteen and fourteen and a half, that it would have done a
45   man's heart good to see. How a score of ewes now?

SILENCE   Thereafter as they be: a score of good ewes may be
      worth ten pounds.

SHALLOW   And is old Double dead?

Enter Bardolph and his Boy [Falstaff's Page]

SILENCE   Here come two of Sir John Falstaff's men, as I think.

50 SHALLOW   Good morrow, honest gentlemen.

BARDOLPH   I beseech you, which is Justice Shallow?

SHALLOW   I am Robert Shallow, sir, a poor esquire of this
      county, and one of the king's justices of the peace. What is
      your good pleasure with me?

55 BARDOLPH   My captain, sir, commends him to you—my captain,
      Sir John Falstaff, a tall gentleman, and a most gallant leader.

---

34 How what price is   **yoke of bullocks** pair of young bulls   **35 Stamford** town in
Lincolnshire famous for horse and cattle fairs; some editors suspect that this scene is in fact
located near Stamford, a more logical stopping place for Falstaff as he travels from London to
York, but Shakespeare was often careless of geographical realism   **40 drew . . . bow** was a
good archer   **41 John of Gaunt** Henry IV's father; he dies in *Richard II*   **43 clapped . . . clout**
hit the target   **clout** square of cloth marking the center   **43 twelvescore** i.e. 240 yards
(twelve times twenty)   **forehand shaft** arrow shot directly, without the usual curved
trajectory employed when shooting at distance   **44 fourteen . . . half** i.e. 280–90 yards
45 score twenty   **ewes** female sheep   **46 Thereafter . . . be** depending on their quality
51 beseech seek to know   **52 esquire** one ranking just below a knight   **53 justices of the
peace** local magistrates   **56 tall** brave

SHALLOW He greets me well, sir. I knew him a good backsword man. How doth the good knight? May I ask how my lady his wife doth?

60 BARDOLPH Sir, pardon. A soldier is better accommodated than with a wife.

SHALLOW It is well said, sir; and it is well said indeed too. Better accommodated! It is good, yea, indeed, is it. Good phrases are surely, and everywhere, very commendable.
65 Accommodated! It comes of *accommodo*. Very good, a good phrase.

BARDOLPH Pardon, sir, I have heard the word. Phrase call you it? By this day, I know not the phrase, but I will maintain the word with my sword to be a soldier-like word, and a word of
70 exceeding good command. 'Accommodated', that is when a man is, as they say, accommodated, or when a man is being whereby he thought to be accommodated, which is an excellent thing.

Enter Falstaff

SHALLOW It is very just. Look, here comes good Sir John. Give
75 me your good hand, give me your worship's good hand. Trust me, you look well and bear your years very well. Welcome, good Sir John.

FALSTAFF I am glad to see you well, good Master Robert Shallow.— Master Surecard, as I think?

80 SHALLOW No, Sir John, it is my cousin Silence, in commission with me.

FALSTAFF Good Master Silence, it well befits you should be of the peace.

SILENCE Your good worship is welcome.

85 FALSTAFF Fie, this is hot weather, gentlemen. Have you provided me here half a dozen of sufficient men?

SHALLOW Marry, have we, sir. Will you sit?

---

57 **backsword** fencing weapon with a protective basketwork hilt   60 **accommodated** equipped (a fashionable word unfamiliar to the provincial Shallow)   65 *accommodo* Shallow considers the word's Latin origin   66 **phrase** the term could refer to a single word   74 **just** true   79 **Surecard** the name means "one certain of success"   80 **in commission** authorized to act as a magistrate   83 **of the peace** a magistrate/silent   86 **sufficient** competent

FALSTAFF   Let me see them, I beseech you.   *They sit*

SHALLOW   Where's the roll? Where's the roll? Where's the roll?
90   Let me see, let me see, let me see. So, so, so, so. Yea, marry,
sir.— Ralph Mouldy! Let them appear as I call, let them do so,
let them do so. Let me see, where is Mouldy?

MOULDY   Here, if it please you.

SHALLOW   What think you, Sir John? A good-limbed fellow:
95   young, strong, and of good friends.

FALSTAFF   Is thy name Mouldy?

MOULDY   Yea, if it please you.

FALSTAFF   'Tis the more time thou wert used.

SHALLOW   Ha, ha, ha! Most excellent! Things that are mouldy
100   lack use: very singular good. Well said, Sir John, very well
said.

FALSTAFF   Prick him.

MOULDY   I was pricked well enough before, if you could have
let me alone. My old dame will be undone now for one to
105   do her husbandry and her drudgery; you need not to have
pricked me. There are other men fitter to go out than I.

FALSTAFF   Go to. Peace, Mouldy, you shall go. Mouldy, it is time
you were spent.

MOULDY   Spent?

110 SHALLOW   Peace, fellow, peace; stand aside. Know you where
you are?— For the other, Sir John, let me see.— Simon
Shadow?

FALSTAFF   Ay, marry, let me have him to sit under: he's like to
be a cold soldier.

115 SHALLOW   Where's Shadow?

SHADOW   Here, sir.

FALSTAFF   Shadow, whose son art thou?

SHADOW   My mother's son, sir.

---

95 friends family   **102 Prick** mark down on the list   **103 pricked** vexed/sour, moldy (plays
on the sense of "equipped with a penis")   **104 dame** wife (possibly mother, but the sexual
punning makes a wife seem more likely)   **undone** at a loss   **105 do her husbandry**
undertake agricultural or household work/perform the sexual role of a husband   **drudgery**
domestic/sexual labor   **108 spent** used up, consumed (plays on the sense of "sexually
exhausted after orgasm")   **111 other** others, rest   **114 cold** cool (like shade)/cowardly
117 son puns on "sun"

FALSTAFF	Thy mother's son! Like enough, and thy father's

120   shadow. So the son of the female is the shadow of the male.
       It is often so, indeed, but not of the father's substance!

SHALLOW   Do you like him, Sir John?

FALSTAFF   Shadow will serve for summer. Prick him,— for we
       have a number of shadows to fill up the muster book.   *Aside*

125 SHALLOW   Thomas Wart?

FALSTAFF   Where's he?

WART   Here, sir.

FALSTAFF   Is thy name Wart?

WART   Yea, sir.

130 FALSTAFF   Thou art a very ragged wart.

SHALLOW   Shall I prick him down, Sir John?

FALSTAFF   It were superfluous, for his apparel is built upon his
       back, and the whole frame stands upon pins. Prick him no
       more.

135 SHALLOW   Ha, ha, ha! You can do it, sir, you can do it. I
       commend you well.— Francis Feeble?

FEEBLE   Here, sir.

FALSTAFF   What trade art thou, Feeble?

FEEBLE   A woman's tailor, sir.

140 SHALLOW   Shall I prick him, sir?

FALSTAFF   You may: but if he had been a man's tailor, he
       would have pricked you. Wilt thou make as many holes in an
       enemy's battle as thou hast done in a woman's petticoat?

FEEBLE   I will do my good will, sir. You can have no more.

145 FALSTAFF   Well said, good woman's tailor! Well said,
       courageous Feeble! Thou wilt be as valiant as the wrathful

---

120 **shadow** reflection, image   121 **not . . . substance** i.e. potentially the son of another man
123 **serve** do, suffice/perform military service   124 **shadows** names of dead or imaginary
men, a ruse to enable the captain of the regiment to claim their pay   **muster** military
recruitment   130 **ragged** rough/tattered (may pun on "ragwort," a plant thought to be an
aphrodisiac)   132 **apparel . . . pins** suggesting his clothes are held together by pins, or that
his physical frame is poorly put together (**pins** plays on the sense of "legs")   139 **tailor** the
profession had a reputation for effeminacy as well as for lechery ("tail" plays on the sense of
"sexual organs," thus leading to renewed sexual play on **prick** in the following lines)
142 **pricked** clothed/stabbed with a pin/penetrated sexually   143 **battle** army   144 **good will**
best (**will** plays on the sense of "penis")

dove or most magnanimous mouse. Prick the woman's tailor well, Master Shallow, deep, Master Shallow.

FEEBLE   I would Wart might have gone, sir.

150 FALSTAFF   I would thou wert a man's tailor, that thou mightst mend him and make him fit to go. I cannot put him to a private soldier that is the leader of so many thousands. Let that suffice, most forcible Feeble.

FEEBLE   It shall suffice.

155 FALSTAFF   I am bound to thee, reverend Feeble.— Who is the next?

SHALLOW   Peter Bullcalf of the green?

FALSTAFF   Yea, marry, let us see Bullcalf.

BULLCALF   Here, sir.

160 FALSTAFF   Trust me, a likely fellow! Come, prick me Bullcalf till he roar again.

BULLCALF   O, good my lord captain—

FALSTAFF   What, dost thou roar before th'art pricked?

BULLCALF   O, sir! I am a diseased man.

165 FALSTAFF   What disease hast thou?

BULLCALF   A whoreson cold, sir, a cough, sir, which I caught with ringing in the king's affairs upon his coronation day, sir.

FALSTAFF   Come, thou shalt go to the wars in a gown. We will have away thy cold, and I will take such order that thy

170 friends shall ring for thee.— Is here all?

SHALLOW   There is two more called than your number. You must have but four here, sir, and so I pray you go in with me to dinner.

FALSTAFF   Come, I will go drink with you, but I cannot tarry

175 dinner. I am glad to see you, in good troth, Master Shallow.

---

147 **magnanimous** brave   148 **well . . . deep** i.e. firmly (with continued sexual play)   151 **go** plays on the sense of "have sex"   **put him to** enlist him as   152 **thousands** i.e. vermin/lice   157 **green** i.e. village green   160 **likely** promising   161 **again** in response   167 **ringing . . . affairs** church bell ringing on behalf of the king   **coronation day** i.e. anniversary of the coronation   168 **gown** dressing gown/nightgown   169 **take such order** issue instructions, arrange   170 **ring for thee** ring the bells instead of you/for your funeral   171 **two . . . four** Shallow counts six but we see only five   174 **tarry** stay for

SHALLOW   O, Sir John, do you remember since we lay all night in the Windmill in St George's Field?

FALSTAFF   No more of that, good Master Shallow, no more of that.

180   SHALLOW   Ha, it was a merry night. And is Jane Nightwork alive?

FALSTAFF   She lives, Master Shallow.

SHALLOW   She never could away with me.

FALSTAFF   Never, never. She would always say she could not abide Master Shallow.

185   SHALLOW   I could anger her to the heart. She was then a bona-roba. Doth she hold her own well?

FALSTAFF   Old, old, Master Shallow.

SHALLOW   Nay, she must be old. She cannot choose but be old, certain she's old, and had Robin Nightwork by old Nightwork before I came to Clement's Inn.

190

SILENCE   That's fifty-five years ago.

SHALLOW   Ha, cousin Silence, that thou hadst seen that that this knight and I have seen! Ha, Sir John, said I well?

195   FALSTAFF   We have heard the chimes at midnight, Master Shallow.

SHALLOW   That we have, that we have, in faith, Sir John, we have. Our watch-word was 'Hem boys!' Come, let's to dinner; come, let's to dinner. O, the days that we have seen! Come, come.

200   [*Exeunt Falstaff and the Justices*]

BULLCALF   Good Master Corporate Bardolph, stand my friend, and here is four Harry ten shillings in French   *Gives money* crowns for you. In very truth, sir, I had as lief be   *to Bardolph* hanged, sir, as go. And yet, for mine own part, sir, I do not

205   care; but rather, because I am unwilling, and for mine own

---

177 **Windmill** probably the name of a brothel, perhaps a tavern   **St George's Field** area between Southwark and Lambeth, south of the River Thames; known for prostitution
180 **Nightwork** her surname suggests her occupation as a prostitute   183 **away with** endure, get on with   186 **bona-roba** whore   198 **watch-word** code word, password/drinking cry
201 **Corporate** malapropism for "Corporal"   **stand** act as   202 **Harry ten shillings** shillings from the reign of Henry VII, subsequently worth only half their original value   203 **lief** willingly

part, have a desire to stay with my friends. Else, sir, I did not care, for mine own part, so much.

BARDOLPH   Go to. Stand aside.

MOULDY   And, good master corporal captain, for my old
210   dame's sake, stand my friend: she hath nobody to do anything about her when I am gone, and she is old, and cannot help herself. You shall have forty, sir.   *Gives money*

BARDOLPH   Go to. Stand aside.

FEEBLE   I care not. A man can die but once: we owe a death.
215   I will never bear a base mind. If it be my destiny, so: if it be not, so. No man is too good to serve his prince, and let it go which way it will, he that dies this year is quit for the next.

BARDOLPH   Well said. Thou art a good fellow.

FEEBLE   Nay, I will bear no base mind.

[*Enter Falstaff and the Justices*]

220 FALSTAFF   Come, sir, which men shall I have?

SHALLOW   Four of which you please.

BARDOLPH   Sir, a word with you: I have three pound to free Mouldy and Bullcalf.

FALSTAFF   Go to, well.

225 SHALLOW   Come, Sir John, which four will you have?

FALSTAFF   Do you choose for me.

SHALLOW   Marry, then, Mouldy, Bullcalf, Feeble and Shadow.

FALSTAFF   Mouldy and Bullcalf: for you, Mouldy, stay at home till you are past service.— And for your part, Bullcalf, grow
230   till you come unto it. I will none of you.

SHALLOW   Sir John, Sir John, do not yourself wrong. They are your likeliest men, and I would have you served with the best.

FALSTAFF   Will you tell me, Master Shallow, how to choose a man? Care I for the limb, the thews, the stature, bulk, and big
235   assemblance of a man? Give me the spirit, Master Shallow. Where's Wart? You see what a ragged appearance it is. He shall charge you and discharge you with the motion of a

206 friends family   **208 Go to** i.e. very well, off you go   **212 forty** i.e. shillings   **215 so** so be it   **217 quit** free   **229 service** military/domestic/sexual service   **230 come unto it** reach manhood   **232 likeliest** ablest   **234 thews** physique, strength   **235 assemblance** appearance, frame, composition   **237 charge . . . you** load and fire

pewterer's hammer, come off and on swifter than he that
gibbets on the brewer's bucket. And this same half-faced
240   fellow, Shadow, give me this man: he presents no mark to the
enemy. The foeman may with as great aim level at the edge of
a penknife. And for a retreat, how swiftly will this Feeble, the
woman's tailor, run off! O, give me the spare men, and spare
me the great ones. Put me a caliver into Wart's hand,
245   Bardolph.

BARDOLPH   Hold, Wart, traverse. Thus, thus, thus.   *Gives Wart a*

FALSTAFF   Come, manage me your caliver. So, very   *caliver*
well, go to, very good, exceeding good. O, give me always a
little, lean, old, chopped, bald shot. Well said, Wart. Thou art
250   a good scab. Hold, there is a tester for thee.   *Gives money*

SHALLOW   He is not his craft's master. He doth not do it right. I
remember at Mile-End Green, when I lay at Clement's Inn—
I was then Sir Dagonet in Arthur's show—there was a little
quiver fellow, and he would manage you his piece thus.
255   And he would about and about, and come you in and come
you in. 'Ra, ta, ta', would he say. 'Bounce', would he say, and
away again would he go, and again would he come. I shall
never see such a fellow.

FALSTAFF   These fellows will do well, Master Shallow. Farewell,
260   Master Silence. I will not use many words with you. Fare you
well, gentlemen both. I thank you. I must a dozen mile
tonight. Bardolph, give the soldiers coats.

---

238 pewterer's hammer pewter was hammered out with rapid actions   **come off and on**
advance and retreat/lower and raise (the gun)/stay still and act   **239 gibbets . . . bucket**
slightly unclear meaning; perhaps hangs on, carries, balances the beam (**bucket**) from which
the brewer's buckets are suspended   **half-faced** thin   **240 mark** target   **241 aim** chance of
hitting the target   **level** aim   **243 spare men** thin/surplus to requirement   **244 caliver** light
musket   **246 traverse** march/take aim   **247 manage me** handle skillfully   **249 chopped**
chapped, i.e. dried up   **shot** marksman (possible play on sense of "animal left over after the
best of the herd have been selected")   **said** done   **250 scab** rascal (plays on his name)
tester sixpence   **252 Mile-End Green** East London drill ground for citizen soldiers; now
Stepney Green   **253 Sir . . . show** refers to a display of archery on Mile-End Green in which
participants took the names of King Arthur's knights of the Round Table; Shallow played
Arthur's fool   **254 quiver** nimble (plays on sense of "case for arrows")   **manage . . . he
come** i.e. was quick and skillful at firing, then retreating to the rear rank of musketeers in
order to reload before advancing to fire once more; "**Ra, ta, ta**" is the noise of reloading and
"**Bounce**" that of the shot   **261 must** i.e. must go

SHALLOW   Sir John, heaven bless you and prosper your affairs, and send us peace! As you return, visit my house. Let our old
265   acquaintance be renewed. Peradventure I will with you to the court.

FALSTAFF   I would you would, Master Shallow.

SHALLOW   Go to. I have spoke at a word. Fare you well.   *Exit*

FALSTAFF   Fare you well, gentle gentlemen.— On, Bardolph.
270   Lead the men away.

[*Exeunt Bardolph, Mouldy, Shadow, Wart, Feeble and Bullcalf*]
As I return, I will fetch off these justices. I do see the bottom of Justice Shallow. How subject we old men are to this vice of lying! This same starved justice hath done nothing but prate to me of the wildness of his youth, and the feats he hath
275   done about Turnbull Street, and every third word a lie, duer paid to the hearer than the Turk's tribute. I do remember him at Clement's Inn like a man made after supper of a cheese-paring. When he was naked, he was, for all the world, like a forked radish, with a head fantastically carved upon it
280   with a knife. He was so forlorn, that his dimensions to any thick sight were invincible. He was the very genius of famine. He came ever in the rearward of the fashion. And now is this Vice's dagger become a squire, and talks as familiarly of John of Gaunt as if he had been sworn brother
285   to him, and I'll be sworn he never saw him but once in the Tilt-yard, and then he burst his head for crowding among the marshal's men. I saw it, and told John of Gaunt he beat his own name, for you might have trussed him and all his

---

265 **Peradventure** perhaps   267 **would** wish   268 **have . . . word** meant what I said
269 **gentle** noble   271 **fetch off** trick, get the better of   273 **prate** chatter   275 **Turnbull Street** in Clerkenwell, London; known haunt of thieves and prostitutes   **duer** more punctually   276 **Turk's tribute** regular tribute money due the sultan; failure to pay was punishable by death   277 **man . . . cheese-paring** figure of a man carved idly out of the rind of cheese   280 **forlorn** pitiful, meager   281 **thick** dull, weak   **invincible** impossible to make out; some editors emend to "invisible"   **genius** spirit   282 **rearward** rear   283 **Vice's dagger** thin, insubstantial wooden dagger used by the Vice character in morality plays   **squire** of a rank just below that of knight   284 **John of Gaunt** father of King Henry IV   **sworn brother** avowed companion in arms, intimate friend   286 **Tilt-yard** area for jousting tournaments near Whitehall, London   **burst . . . men** got his head beaten trying to get past the guards   288 **his own name** i.e. a **gaunt**, very thin person   **him** i.e. Shallow

apparel into an eel-skin, the case of a treble hautboy was a
290   mansion for him, a court. And now hath he land and beefs.
Well, I will be acquainted with him, if I return, and it shall go
hard but I will make him a philosopher's two stones to me. If
the young dace be a bait for the old pike, I see no reason in
the law of nature but I may snap at him. Let time shape, and
295   there an end.

Exit

Act 4 Scene 1   *running scene 10*

Enter the Archbishop, Mowbray, Hastings

ARCHBISHOP OF YORK   What is this forest called?
HASTINGS   'Tis Gaultree Forest, an't shall please your grace.
ARCHBISHOP OF YORK   Here stand, my lords, and send discoverers
    forth
To know the numbers of our enemies.
5   HASTINGS   We have sent forth already.
ARCHBISHOP OF YORK   'Tis well done.
My friends and brethren in these great affairs,
I must acquaint you that I have received
New-dated letters from Northumberland.
10   Their cold intent, tenor and substance, thus:
Here doth he wish his person, with such powers
As might hold sortance with his quality,
The which he could not levy, whereupon
He is retired, to ripe his growing fortunes,
15   To Scotland; and concludes in hearty prayers

---

289 **eel-skin** i.e. because he is so thin   **treble hautboy** oboe   290 **beefs** cattle
291 **acquainted** familiar   **go . . . will** be hard luck if I do not   292 **philosopher's two stones**
the philosopher's stone supposedly turned base metal into gold; Falstaff intends to make
money out of Shallow (**two stones** plays on the sense of "testicles")   293 **dace** small
freshwater fish   **pike** large, voracious freshwater fish (also, appropriately enough, known as a
jack)   294 **shape** shape matters   **4.1 *Location: Gaultree Forest, north of York***
2 **Gaultree Forest** ancient royal forest to the north of York   **an't** if it   3 **discoverers** scouts
9 **New-dated** of recent date   11 **powers** forces   12 **hold sortance with** correspond, agree
quality rank   13 **levy** raise, muster   14 **retired** withdrawn   **ripe** ripen, develop

That your attempts may overlive the hazard
And fearful meeting of their opposite.

MOWBRAY   Thus do the hopes we have in him touch ground
And dash themselves to pieces.

Enter a Messenger

20   HASTINGS   Now, what news?

MESSENGER   West of this forest, scarcely off a mile,
In goodly form comes on the enemy.
And by the ground they hide, I judge their number
Upon or near the rate of thirty thousand.

25   MOWBRAY   The just proportion that we gave them out.
Let us sway on and face them in the field.

Enter Westmorland

ARCHBISHOP OF YORK   What well-appointed leader fronts us here?

MOWBRAY   I think it is my lord of Westmorland.

WESTMORLAND   Health and fair greeting from our general,
30   The prince, Lord John and Duke of Lancaster.

ARCHBISHOP OF YORK   Say on, my lord of Westmorland, in peace:
What doth concern your coming?

WESTMORLAND   Then, my lord,
Unto your grace do I in chief address
35   The substance of my speech. If that rebellion
Came like itself, in base and abject routs,
Led on by bloody youth, guarded with rage,
And countenanced by boys and beggary,
I say, if damned commotion so appeared,
40   In his true, native and most proper shape,
You, reverend father, and these noble lords
Had not been here to dress the ugly form
Of base and bloody insurrection

---

16 overlive survive   **17 opposite** adversary   **18 touch ground** run aground   **22 form** formation   **24 rate** estimate, number   **25 just . . . out** exact number we estimated   **26 sway on** move forward   **27 well-appointed** well-equipped   **fronts** faces, confronts   **30 prince . . . Lancaster** Prince John, although born at Lancaster, was actually Duke of Bedford   **32 doth . . . coming** does your arrival mean   **35 If that** if   **36 like itself** in its true colors   **routs** mobs, gangs   **37 bloody** bloodthirsty   **guarded** adorned, trimmed/protected, flanked by   **38 countenanced** approved, supported   **39 commotion** insurrection, rebellion   **40 most proper** own true   **41 reverend** respected   **42 Had not** would not have been   **dress** dress up, adorn

With your fair honours. You, lord archbishop,
45   Whose see is by a civil peace maintained,
Whose beard the silver hand of peace hath touched,
Whose learning and good letters peace hath tutored,
Whose white investments figure innocence,
The dove and very blessèd spirit of peace,
50   Wherefore do you so ill translate yourself
Out of the speech of peace that bears such grace,
Into the harsh and boisterous tongue of war,
Turning your books to graves, your ink to blood,
Your pens to lances and your tongue divine
55   To a loud trumpet and a point of war?

ARCHBISHOP OF YORK   Wherefore do I this? So the question stands.
Briefly to this end: we are all diseased,
And with our surfeiting and wanton hours
Have brought ourselves into a burning fever,
60   And we must bleed for it, of which disease
Our late King Richard, being infected, died.
But, my most noble lord of Westmorland,
I take not on me here as a physician,
Nor do I as an enemy to peace
65   Troop in the throngs of military men,
But rather show awhile like fearful war,
To diet rank minds sick of happiness
And purge th'obstructions which begin to stop
Our very veins of life. Hear me more plainly.
70   I have in equal balance justly weighed
What wrongs our arms may do, what wrongs we suffer,
And find our griefs heavier than our offences.
We see which way the stream of time doth run,
And are enforced from our most quiet there

---

44 honours noble selves   **45 see** diocese   **47 letters** scholarship   **48 investments** ecclesiastical robes   **figure** symbolize   **55 point** musical signal (perhaps plays on the sense of "sword")   **58 wanton** uncontrolled/idle/self-indulgent/lascivious   **60 bleed** let blood as a medical cure/shed blood in battle   **63 take . . . me** do not take on the role of   **66 show** appear   **67 rank** coarse, gross/corrupt   **70 justly** exactly/fairly   **72 griefs** sufferings, grievances   **74 most quiet there** former peacefulness in the stream of time

75   By the rough torrent of occasion,
      And have the summary of all our griefs,
      When time shall serve, to show in articles;
      Which long ere this we offered to the king,
      And might by no suit gain our audience.
80   When we are wronged and would unfold our griefs,
      We are denied access unto his person
      Even by those men that most have done us wrong.
      The dangers of the days but newly gone,
      Whose memory is written on the earth
85   With yet appearing blood, and the examples
      Of every minute's instance, present now,
      Hath put us in these ill-beseeming arms,
      Not to break peace or any branch of it,
      But to establish here a peace indeed,
90   Concurring both in name and quality.

WESTMORLAND   Whenever yet was your appeal denied?
      Wherein have you been gallèd by the king?
      What peer hath been suborned to grate on you,
      That you should seal this lawless bloody book
95   Of forged rebellion with a seal divine?

ARCHBISHOP OF YORK   My brother general, the commonwealth,
      I make my quarrel in particular.

WESTMORLAND   There is no need of any such redress,
      Or if there were, it not belongs to you.

100   MOWBRAY   Why not to him in part, and to us all
      That feel the bruises of the days before,
      And suffer the condition of these times
      To lay a heavy and unequal hand
      Upon our honours?

---

75 occasion circumstances   77 articles account of charges, list of grievances   79 suit
supplication/legal petition   gain our audience be granted a hearing   80 unfold disclose,
explain   83 but newly gone only recently passed   84 memory . . . earth i.e. the land bears
scars of battle   85 yet appearing still visible   86 Of . . . instance of which every minute
gives us evidence/which each moment urges upon us   87 ill-beseeming unbecoming
92 gallèd vexed, wounded   93 suborned bribed   grate on harass   94 seal approve, ratify
by affixing a wax seal   96 commonwealth state, general good   103 unequal unjust

105 WESTMORLAND O, my good lord Mowbray,
           Construe the times to their necessities,
           And you shall say indeed, it is the time,
           And not the king, that doth you injuries.
           Yet for your part, it not appears to me
110   Either from the king or in the present time
           That you should have an inch of any ground
           To build a grief on. Were you not restored
           To all the Duke of Norfolk's signories,
           Your noble and right well rememb'red father's?
115 MOWBRAY   What thing, in honour, had my father lost,
           That need to be revived and breathèd in me?
           The king that loved him, as the state stood then,
           Was force perforce compelled to banish him,
           And then that Henry Bullingbrook and he,
120   Being mounted and both rousèd in their seats,
           Their neighing coursers daring of the spur,
           Their armèd staves in charge, their beavers down,
           Their eyes of fire sparkling through sights of steel
           And the loud trumpet blowing them together,
125   Then, then, when there was nothing could have stayed
           My father from the breast of Bullingbrook,
           O, when the king did throw his warder down—
           His own life hung upon the staff he threw—
           Then threw he down himself and all their lives
130   That by indictment and by dint of sword
           Have since miscarried under Bullingbrook.

---

106 Construe make sense of/judge   **to their necessities** according to what is urgent and
immediate   **109 not appears** doesn't appear   **113 signories** estates   **116 breathed**
reanimated   **117 the state** circumstances   **118 force perforce** with violent compulsion
banish him Richard II banished both Mowbray's father and **Henry Bullingbrook** (Henry IV),
rather than allow them to meet in combat, in events dramatized in *Richard II*   **120 rousèd**
raised/angry, roused   **121 coursers** horses   **daring . . . spur** i.e. eager to charge   **122 armèd**
. . . charge lances held in position   **beavers** visors or face guards of their helmets
123 sights of steel slits in their visors   **124 blowing them together** giving them the signal to
charge   **125 stayed** kept, prevented   **127 warder** staff held by one presiding over combat
129 all their lives the lives of all those   **130 indictment** legal accusation   **dint of sword** force
of arms   **131 miscarried** come to grief

WESTMORLAND You speak, Lord Mowbray, now you know not
          what.
          The Earl of Hereford was reputed then
          In England the most valiant gentleman.
135   Who knows on whom fortune would then have smiled?
          But if your father had been victor there,
          He ne'er had borne it out of Coventry,
          For all the country in a general voice
          Cried hate upon him, and all their prayers and love
140   Were set on Hereford, whom they doted on
          And blessed and graced and did more than the king—
          But this is mere digression from my purpose.
          Here come I from our princely general
          To know your griefs; to tell you from his grace
145   That he will give you audience, and wherein
          It shall appear that your demands are just,
          You shall enjoy them, everything set off,
          That might so much as think you enemies.
MOWBRAY   But he hath forced us to compel this offer,
150   And it proceeds from policy, not love.
WESTMORLAND Mowbray, you overween to take it so.
          This offer comes from mercy, not from fear.
          For, lo, within a ken our army lies,
          Upon mine honour, all too confident
155   To give admittance to a thought of fear.
          Our battle is more full of names than yours,
          Our men more perfect in the use of arms,
          Our armour all as strong, our cause the best;
          Then reason will our hearts should be as good.
160   Say you not then our offer is compelled.
MOWBRAY   Well, by my will, we shall admit no parley.

---

133 **Earl of Hereford** i.e. Bullingbrook   137 **He . . . Coventry** he would not have got away in
safety from Coventry (Midlands town, the location of the combat)   141 **did** did so, did bless
and grace (him)   145 **wherein** on those matters in which   147 **enjoy them** have those
requests granted   **set off** put aside   148 **think you** make you seem   149 **compel** oblige him
to make   150 **policy** strategy, cunning   151 **overween** go too far   153 **ken** range of sight
156 **battle** army   **names** noblemen, famed soldiers   157 **perfect** skilled   159 **reason will** it
stands to reason   161 **parley** negotiation with the enemy

WESTMORLAND   That argues but the shame of your offence:
A rotten case abides no handling.

HASTINGS   Hath the Prince John a full commission,
165 In very ample virtue of his father,
To hear and absolutely to determine
Of what conditions we shall stand upon?

WESTMORLAND   That is intended in the general's name.
I muse you make so slight a question.

170 ARCHBISHOP OF YORK   Then take, my lord of Westmorland, this
schedule,   *Gives paper*
For this contains our general grievances:
Each several article herein redressed,
All members of our cause, both here and hence,
That are insinewed to this action,
175 Acquitted by a true substantial form
And present execution of our wills
To us and to our purposes confined,
We come within our awful banks again
And knit our powers to the arm of peace.

180 WESTMORLAND   This will I show the general. Please you, lords,
In sight of both our battles we may meet,
At either end in peace, which heaven so frame,
Or to the place of difference call the swords
Which must decide it.

185 ARCHBISHOP OF YORK   My lord, we will do so.   [*Exit Westmorland*]

MOWBRAY   There is a thing within my bosom tells me
That no conditions of our peace can stand.

HASTINGS   Fear you not that. If we can make our peace
Upon such large terms and so absolute

163 rotten . . . handling something putrid won't stand close examination (**rotten case** plays on sense of "syphilitic vagina")   165 **very ample virtue** full authority   166 **determine Of** decide on   168 **intended** implied   **name** title   169 **muse** marvel   170 **schedule** list   172 **Each several article** provided that each separate charge   173 **hence** elsewhere   174 **insinewed to** an integral part of, bound to   175 **Acquitted** provided that we are cleared   **true substantial form** binding legal proceedings   176 **present . . . confined** immediate carrying out of the demands relating to us and our intentions   178 **awful banks** respectful (awe-full) boundaries   179 **knit** bind, unite   180 **Please you** if you're content   181 **battles** armies   182 **At either end** on both sides   **frame** arrange   189 **absolute** unconditional

190   As our conditions shall consist upon,
           Our peace shall stand as firm as rocky mountains.
       MOWBRAY   Ay, but our valuation shall be such
           That every slight and false-derivèd cause,
           Yea, every idle, nice and wanton reason
195   Shall to the king taste of this action,
           That, were our royal faiths martyrs in love,
           We shall be winnowed with so rough a wind
           That even our corn shall seem as light as chaff
           And good from bad find no partition.
200   ARCHBISHOP OF YORK   No, no, my lord. Note this: the king is weary
           Of dainty and such picking grievances,
           For he hath found to end one doubt by death
           Revives two greater in the heirs of life,
           And therefore will he wipe his tables clean
205   And keep no tell-tale to his memory
           That may repeat and history his loss
           To new remembrance. For full well he knows
           He cannot so precisely weed this land
           As his misdoubts present occasion:
210   His foes are so enrooted with his friends
           That, plucking to unfix an enemy,
           He doth unfasten so and shake a friend,
           So that this land, like an offensive wife
           That hath enraged him on to offer strokes,
215   As he is striking, holds his infant up
           And hangs resolved correction in the arm
           That was upreared to execution.

---

190 consist upon insist upon/consist of   **192 valuation** estimation in the eyes of the king
193 false-derivèd wrongly attributed   **194 nice and wanton** petty and frivolous   **196 were . . .
love** even if we were willing to die for love of the king   **197 winnowed** separated, as is the
corn from the worthless husks (**chaff**) by the action of the **wind   198 That . . . partition** the
king will be unable to distinguish the good from the bad in us   **201 dainty** petty   **picking**
trifling   **202 doubt** fear   **203 heirs of life** survivors   **204 tables** records   **206 history**
record, recount   **208 precisely** completely   **209 misdoubts present occasion** i.e. to the
extent that he would like   **misdoubts** suspicions, fears   **210 enrooted** entangled by the roots
214 enraged him on provoked him   **216 hangs resolved correction** forestalls the determined
punishment   **217 execution** carry out the action

HASTINGS   Besides, the king hath wasted all his rods
          On late offenders, that he now doth lack
220   The very instruments of chastisement,
          So that his power, like to a fangless lion,
          May offer, but not hold.
ARCHBISHOP OF YORK   'Tis very true,
          And therefore be assured, my good lord marshal,
225   If we do now make our atonement well,
          Our peace will, like a broken limb united,
          Grow stronger for the breaking.
MOWBRAY   Be it so.
          Here is returned my lord of Westmorland.

Enter Westmorland

230 WESTMORLAND   The prince is here at hand. Pleaseth your lordship
          To meet his grace just distance 'tween our armies.
MOWBRAY   Your grace of York, in heaven's name then forward.
ARCHBISHOP OF YORK   Before, and greet his grace.— My lord, we
          come.

Enter Prince John [and Attendants]

PRINCE JOHN   You are well encountered here, my cousin
          Mowbray.—
235   Good day to you, gentle lord archbishop.—
          And so to you, Lord Hastings, and to all.—
          My lord of York, it better showed with you
          When that your flock, assembled by the bell,
          Encircled you to hear with reverence
240   Your exposition on the holy text
          Than now to see you here an iron man,
          Cheering a rout of rebels with your drum,
          Turning the word to sword and life to death.
          That man that sits within a monarch's heart,
245   And ripens in the sunshine of his favour,

---

218 **wasted** used up   **rods** whipping rods   219 **late** recent/dead   222 **offer** threaten
225 **atonement** reconciliation   231 **just** at an equal   233 **Before** lead on   234 **cousin** form
of address between nobles, not necessarily denoting kinship   235 **gentle** noble   237 **better . . .
you** suited you better   241 **iron** armored/unyielding   243 **word** i.e. holy word of Scripture

Would he abuse the countenance of the king,
Alack, what mischiefs might he set abroach
In shadow of such greatness! With you, lord bishop,
It is even so. Who hath not heard it spoken
250   How deep you were within the books of heaven?
To us, the speaker in his parliament;
To us, th'imagined voice of heaven itself,
The very opener and intelligencer
Between the grace, the sanctities of heaven
255   And our dull workings. O, who shall believe
But you misuse the reverence of your place,
Employ the countenance and grace of heaven,
As a false favourite doth his prince's name,
In deeds dishonourable? You have taken up,
260   Under the counterfeited zeal of heaven,
The subjects of heaven's substitute, my father,
And both against the peace of heaven and him
Have here upswarmèd them.

ARCHBISHOP OF YORK   Good my lord of Lancaster,
265   I am not here against your father's peace,
But, as I told my lord of Westmorland,
The time misordered doth, in common sense,
Crowd us and crush us to this monstrous form,
To hold our safety up. I sent your grace
270   The parcels and particulars of our grief,
The which hath been with scorn shoved from the court,
Whereon this Hydra son of war is born,

246 Would he were he to   countenance favor, patronage   247 set abroach unleash
250 deep . . . heaven learned in Scripture/firmly in God's grace   251 speaker intermediary
between monarch and parliament; here, between God and the people   253 opener and
intelligencer one who explains and informs   254 sanctities holiness, sacred nature
255 workings efforts/perceptions   256 But you that you don't   place position
257 countenance favor   258 false dishonest, disloyal   259 taken up raised   260 zeal puns
on "seal," i.e. authority   261 heaven's substitute the monarch was regarded as God's deputy
on earth   263 upswarmèd made them rise up like an angry swarm   267 misordered
confused   in common sense as all acknowledge   268 monstrous unnatural   269 hold . . .
up maintain our security   270 parcels details   271 shoved i.e. dismissed   272 Hydra in
Greek mythology, a monster that grew two heads for every one that was cut off

Whose dangerous eyes may well be charmed asleep
With grant of our most just and right desires,
275   And true obedience, of this madness cured,
Stoop tamely to the foot of majesty.

MOWBRAY   If not, we ready are to try our fortunes
To the last man.

HASTINGS   And though we here fall down,
280   We have supplies to second our attempt:
If they miscarry, theirs shall second them,
And so success of mischief shall be born
And heir from heir shall hold this quarrel up
Whiles England shall have generation.

285   PRINCE JOHN   You are too shallow, Hastings, much too shallow,
To sound the bottom of the after-times.

WESTMORLAND   Pleaseth your grace to answer them directly
How far forth you do like their articles.

PRINCE JOHN   I like them all, and do allow them well,
290   And swear here, by the honour of my blood,
My father's purposes have been mistook,
And some about him have too lavishly
Wrested his meaning and authority.—
My lord, these griefs shall be with speed   *To Archbishop*
   redressed,
295   Upon my life, they shall. If this may please you,
Discharge your powers unto their several counties,
As we will ours, and here between the armies,
Let's drink together friendly and embrace,
That all their eyes may bear those tokens home
300   Of our restorèd love and amity.

ARCHBISHOP OF YORK   I take your princely word for these redresses.

---

273 **dangerous eyes** refers to another monster, Argus, whose hundred eyes kept permanent watch until **charmed** to sleep by Mercury   280 **supplies** reinforcements   **second** support, renew   282 **success** succession   284 **Whiles . . . generation** for as long as people continue to be born   286 **sound the bottom** gauge the depth, i.e. foretell   288 **How far forth** to what extent   **like** approve of, agree to   289 **allow them well** approve of them   291 **mistook** misunderstood   292 **lavishly** freely   296 **powers** forces   **several** various, separate   299 **tokens** signs

PRINCE JOHN I give it you, and will maintain my word,
And thereupon I drink unto your grace.   *Toasts Archbishop*
HASTINGS   Go, captain, and deliver to the army
305   This news of peace: let them have pay, and part.
I know it will well please them. Hie thee, captain.

Exit [Officer]

ARCHBISHOP OF YORK To you, my noble lord of   *Toasts Westmorland*
Westmorland.
WESTMORLAND I pledge your grace, and if you   *Toasts Archbishop*
knew what pains
I have bestowed to breed this present peace,
310   You would drink freely. But my love to ye
Shall show itself more openly hereafter.
ARCHBISHOP OF YORK I do not doubt you.
WESTMORLAND I am glad of it.—
Health to my lord and gentle cousin, Mowbray.   *Toasts Mowbray*
315   **MOWBRAY** You wish me health in very happy season,
For I am, on the sudden, something ill.
ARCHBISHOP OF YORK Against ill chances men are ever merry,
But heaviness foreruns the good event.
WESTMORLAND Therefore be merry, coz, since sudden sorrow
320   Serves to say thus: 'Some good thing comes tomorrow.'
ARCHBISHOP OF YORK Believe me, I am passing light in spirit.
MOWBRAY So much the worse, if your own rule be true.
PRINCE JOHN The word of peace is rendered. Hark, how they
shout!
MOWBRAY This had been cheerful after victory.
325   **ARCHBISHOP OF YORK** A peace is of the nature of a conquest,
For then both parties nobly are subdued,
And neither party loser.
PRINCE JOHN Go, my lord,   *To Westmorland*
And let our army be dischargèd too.—   *Exit [Westmorland]*

---

305 part depart   306 Hie hurry   308 pledge toast   315 happy season opportune moment
316 something somewhat   317 Against in anticipation of   318 heaviness . . . event sadness
comes over men before a positive outcome   319 coz abbreviation of "cousin"   321 passing
surpassingly, extremely   323 rendered given   324 had been cheerful would have been
uplifting

330   And, good my lord, so please you, let our trains   *To Archbishop*
      March by us, that we may peruse the men
      We should have coped withal.
      ARCHBISHOP OF YORK   Go, good Lord Hastings,
      And ere they be dismissed, let them march by.

                                                     Exit [Hastings]

335   PRINCE JOHN   I trust, lords, we shall lie tonight together.
      Enter Westmorland
      Now, cousin, wherefore stands our army still?
      WESTMORLAND   The leaders, having charge from you to stand,
      Will not go off until they hear you speak.
      PRINCE JOHN   They know their duties.
      Enter Hastings
340   HASTINGS   Our army is dispersed.
      Like youthful steers unyoked, they took their course
      East, west, north, south, or, like a school broke up,
      Each hurries toward his home and sporting-place.
      WESTMORLAND   Good tidings, my lord Hastings, for the which
345   I do arrest thee, traitor, of high treason.—
      And you, lord archbishop, and you, Lord Mowbray,
      Of capital treason I attach you both.
      MOWBRAY   Is this proceeding just and honourable?
      WESTMORLAND   Is your assembly so?
350   ARCHBISHOP OF YORK   Will you thus break your faith?
      PRINCE JOHN   I pawned thee none:
      I promised you redress of these same grievances
      Whereof you did complain; which, by mine honour,
      I will perform with a most Christian care.
355   But for you, rebels, look to taste the due
      Meet for rebellion and such acts as yours.
      Most shallowly did you these arms commence,
      Fondly brought here and foolishly sent hence.

---

330 **trains** retinues, followers   331 **peruse** look over   332 **coped withal** had to fight with
335 **lie** lodge   341 **steers unyoked** calves freed from the yoke   343 **sporting-place** place of
entertainment, leisure   347 **Of** for, on the grounds of   **attach** arrest   351 **pawned** pledged
356 **Meet** appropriate   357 **shallowly** foolishly, thoughtlessly   358 **Fondly** stupidly

Strike up our drums, pursue the scattered stray.

360 Heaven, and not we, have safely fought today.

Some guard these traitors to the block of death,

Treason's true bed and yielder up of breath.   *Exeunt*

Enter Falstaff and Coleville [separately]

FALSTAFF What's your name, sir? Of what condition are you,
and of what place, I pray?

365 COLEVILLE I am a knight, sir, and my name is Coleville of the
Dale.

FALSTAFF Well, then, Coleville is your name, a knight is your
degree, and your place, the Dale. Coleville shall still be your
name, a traitor your degree, and the dungeon your place, a

370 place deep enough so shall you be still Coleville of the Dale.

COLEVILLE Are not you Sir John Falstaff?

FALSTAFF As good a man as he, sir, whoe'er I am. Do ye yield,
sir, or shall I sweat for you? If I do sweat, they are the drops of
thy lovers, and they weep for thy death: therefore rouse up

375 fear and trembling, and do observance to my mercy.

COLEVILLE I think you are Sir John Falstaff, and in that thought
yield me.

FALSTAFF I have a whole school of tongues in this belly of
mine, and not a tongue of them all speaks any other word

380 but my name. An I had but a belly of any indifferency, I were
simply the most active fellow in Europe. My womb, my
womb, my womb, undoes me. Here comes our general.

Enter Prince John and Westmorland [with Blunt and others]

PRINCE JOHN The heat is past. Follow no further now.

Call in the powers, good cousin Westmorland.

                                                    [*Exit Westmorland*]

385 Now, Falstaff, where have you been all this while?

When everything is ended, then you come.

---

359 stray stragglers   **363 condition** rank   **370 Dale** the sense now widens from "valley" to
include "pit"   **373 drops** tears   **374 lovers** friends   **375 do observance** show respect
378 I . . . name i.e. I am known by name everywhere on account of my vast stomach   **school**
crowd   **380 An** if   **indifferency** ordinary size   **381 womb** belly

These tardy tricks of yours will, on my life,
One time or other break some gallows' back.

FALSTAFF   I would be sorry, my lord, but it should be thus: I
390   never knew yet but rebuke and check was the reward of
valour. Do you think me a swallow, an arrow, or a bullet?
Have I, in my poor and old motion, the expedition of
thought? I have speeded hither with the very extremest inch
of possibility. I have foundered nine score and odd posts, and
395   here, travel-tainted as I am, have in my pure and immaculate
valour, taken Sir John Coleville of the Dale, a most furious
knight and valorous enemy. But what of that? He saw me,
and yielded, that I may justly say, with the hook-nosed fellow
of Rome, 'I came, saw, and overcame.'

400   PRINCE JOHN   It was more of his courtesy than your deserving.

FALSTAFF   I know not. Here he is, and here I yield him. And I
beseech your grace, let it be booked with the rest of this day's
deeds; or, I swear, I will have it in a particular ballad, with
mine own picture on the top of it, Coleville kissing my foot:
405   to the which course, if I be enforced, if you do not all show
like gilt two-pences to me, and I in the clear sky of fame
o'ershine you as much as the full moon doth the cinders of
the element—which show like pins' heads to her—believe
not the word of the noble: therefore let me have right, and let
410   desert mount.

PRINCE JOHN   Thine's too heavy to mount.

FALSTAFF   Let it shine, then.

PRINCE JOHN   Thine's too thick to shine.

FALSTAFF   Let it do something, my good lord, that may do me
415   good, and call it what you will.

---

387 **tardy tricks** delaying dodges   388 **break . . . back** i.e. get you hanged (and your weight
will cause the gallows to break)   389 **but . . . be** if it were not   392 **expedition** speed
393 **with . . . possibility** as fast as possible   394 **foundered** lamed   **nine . . . posts** over 180
horses   396 **furious** violent, wrathful   398 **hook-nosed . . . Rome** i.e. Julius Caesar
402 **booked** recorded   403 **particular ballad** special ballad written about me   404 **picture**
ballads were commonly illustrated with woodcuts   406 **gilt two-pences** false coins, twopenny
pieces gilded and passed off as gold half-crowns   **to** compared to   407 **cinders . . . element**
i.e. stars   410 **desert mount** merit be recognized   411 **heavy** fat, weighty/heinous, dreadful
413 **thick** fat/dim

PRINCE JOHN Is thy name Coleville?

COLEVILLE It is, my lord.

PRINCE JOHN A famous rebel art thou, Coleville.

FALSTAFF And a famous true subject took him.

420 **COLEVILLE** I am, my lord, but as my betters are
That led me hither. Had they been ruled by me,
You should have won them dearer than you have.

FALSTAFF I know not how they sold themselves, but thou, like
a kind fellow, gav'st thyself away; and I thank thee for thee.

Enter Westmorland

425 **PRINCE JOHN** Have you left pursuit?

WESTMORLAND Retreat is made and execution stayed.

PRINCE JOHN Send Coleville with his confederates
To York, to present execution.—
Blunt, lead him hence, and see you guard him sure.

Exeunt [Blunt and others] with Coleville

430 And now dispatch we toward the court, my lords.
I hear the king my father is sore sick.
Our news shall go before us to his majesty,
Which, cousin, you shall bear to comfort him,   *To Westmorland*
And we with sober speed will follow you.

435 **FALSTAFF** My lord, I beseech you give me leave to go through
Gloucestershire, and, when you come to court, stand my
good lord, pray, in your good report.

PRINCE JOHN Fare you well, Falstaff. I, in my condition
Shall better speak of you than you deserve.

Exeunt [all but Falstaff]

440 **FALSTAFF** I would you had but the wit: 'twere better than your
dukedom. Good faith, this same young sober-blooded boy
doth not love me; nor a man cannot make him laugh. But
that's no marvel: he drinks no wine. There's never any of
these demure boys come to any proof, for thin drink doth so

---

421 **been . . . me** taken my advice   422 **won them dearer** they would have cost more, i.e. you
would have had to fight for them   423 **sold** presented/betrayed/bartered away   425 **left** left
off, given up   426 **execution stayed** bloodshed halted   428 **present** immediate   429 **sure**
carefully, securely   431 **sore** seriously   434 **sober** moderate, dignified   438 **in my condition**
according to my disposition/as military commander   440 **would** wish   444 **come . . . proof**
turn out well

445   over-cool their blood, and making many fish-meals, that
they fall into a kind of male green-sickness, and then when
they marry, they get wenches. They are generally fools and
cowards; which some of us should be too, but for
inflammation. A good sherry-sack hath a two-fold operation
450   in it: it ascends me into the brain, dries me there all the
foolish and dull and curdy vapours which environ it, makes
it apprehensive, quick, forgetive, full of nimble, fiery and
delectable shapes, which, delivered o'er to the voice, the
tongue, which is the birth, becomes excellent wit. The
455   second property of your excellent sherry is the warming of
the blood, which, before cold and settled, left the liver white
and pale, which is the badge of pusillanimity and cowardice.
But the sherry warms it and makes it course from the
inwards to the parts extremes: it illuminateth the face,
460   which as a beacon gives warning to all the rest of this little
kingdom, man, to arm. And then the vital commoners and
inland petty spirits muster me all to their captain, the heart,
who, great and puffed up with his retinue, doth any deed of
courage, and this valour comes of sherry. So that skill in the
465   weapon is nothing without sack, for that sets it a-work, and
learning a mere hoard of gold kept by a devil, till sack
commences it and sets it in act and use. Hereof comes it that
Prince Harry is valiant, for the cold blood he did naturally
inherit of his father, he hath, like lean, sterile and bare land,
470   manured, husbanded and tilled with excellent endeavour of
drinking good and good store of fertile sherry, that he is

445 making many fish-meals they eat such a lot of fish (as opposed to red meat)   446 green-
sickness anemia causing a greenish complexion; it often afflicted teenage girls   447 get
wenches father only daughters   449 inflammation roused emotions resulting from
drink/swelling weight   sherry-sack sweet Spanish white wine   450 ascends me ascends
(me is used colloquially for emphasis)   451 curdy thick, curdled   vapours noxious
exhalations supposedly produced in the body and rising to the brain   environ surround
452 apprehensive intelligent, perceptive   forgetive apt at forging, inventive   456 liver
considered the seat of the passions   457 pusillanimity lack of courage, timidity   459 parts
extremes extremities   461 vital . . . spirits the "vital spirits" were thought to be the essence
of life   462 muster me assemble   465 a-work to work   466 a mere is a mere
467 commences initiates, unleashes (puns on "Commencement," the formal term for the
degree award ceremony at Cambridge University)   470 husbanded cultivated

become very hot and valiant. If I had a thousand sons, the first principle I would teach them should be to forswear thin potations and to addict themselves to sack.

Enter Bardolph

475   How now Bardolph?

BARDOLPH   The army is dischargèd all and gone.

FALSTAFF   Let them go. I'll through Gloucestershire, and there will I visit Master Robert Shallow, Esquire. I have him already tempering between my finger and my thumb, and

480   shortly will I seal with him. Come away.   *Exeunt*

Act 4 Scene 2   *running scene 11*

Enter King, Warwick, Clarence, Gloucester

KING HENRY IV   Now, lords, if heaven doth give successful end
    To this debate that bleedeth at our doors,
    We will our youth lead on to higher fields
    And draw no swords but what are sanctified.
5   Our navy is addressed, our power collected,
    Our substitutes in absence well invested,
    And everything lies level to our wish;
    Only we want a little personal strength,
    And pause us, till these rebels, now afoot,
10   Come underneath the yoke of government.

WARWICK   Both which we doubt not but your majesty
    Shall soon enjoy.

KING HENRY IV   Humphrey, my son of Gloucester,
    Where is the prince your brother?

15   GLOUCESTER   I think he's gone to hunt, my lord, at Windsor.

KING HENRY IV   And how accompanied?

GLOUCESTER   I do not know, my lord.

---

474 **potations** liquors   479 **tempering** becoming pliant, softening like wax   480 **seal with him** come to an agreement/shape him to my purposes   **4.2**   *Location: the Jerusalem Chamber in Westminster Abbey, though here transferred to the royal court*   2 **debate** strife, conflict   3 **higher fields** i.e. to Jerusalem, on a crusade   4 **sanctified** consecrated, holy   5 **addressed** ready   6 **substitutes . . . invested** deputies installed in office   7 **level** equal   8 **want** lack   9 **pause us** rest, wait

KING HENRY IV   Is not his brother, Thomas of Clarence, with him?

GLOUCESTER   No, my good lord, he is in presence here.

20   CLARENCE   What would my lord and father?   *Comes forward*

KING HENRY IV   Nothing but well to thee, Thomas of Clarence.
How chance thou art not with the prince thy brother?
He loves thee, and thou dost neglect him, Thomas.
Thou hast a better place in his affection
25   Than all thy brothers. Cherish it, my boy,
And noble offices thou mayst effect
Of mediation, after I am dead,
Between his greatness and thy other brethren:
Therefore omit him not, blunt not his love,
30   Nor lose the good advantage of his grace
By seeming cold or careless of his will,
For he is gracious, if he be observed.
He hath a tear for pity and a hand
Open as day for melting charity:
35   Yet notwithstanding, being incensed, he's flint,
As humorous as winter, and as sudden
As flaws congealèd in the spring of day.
His temper, therefore, must be well observed:
Chide him for faults, and do it reverently,
40   When you perceive his blood inclined to mirth,
But being moody, give him line and scope,
Till that his passions, like a whale on ground,
Confound themselves with working. Learn this, Thomas,
And thou shalt prove a shelter to thy friends,
45   A hoop of gold to bind thy brothers in,
That the united vessel of their blood,
Mingled with venom of suggestion—
As, force perforce, the age will pour it in—

---

19 in presence present/in the royal presence   **22 chance** does it happen   **26 offices** services
28 brethren brothers   **29 omit** neglect   **32 observed** treated with respect   **34 melting**
tender   **35 flint** i.e. hard, unyielding   **36 humorous** moody, volatile   **37 flaws congealèd** icy
gusts of wind   **spring** dawn/gentle warmth   **38 temper** disposition/mood   **39 reverently**
respectfully   **41 line** range, scope   **42 on ground** beached   **43 Confound** defeat, overthrow
working exertion   **47 suggestion** suspicion/incitement to evil   **48 force perforce** of
necessity

Shall never leak, though it do work as strong
50   As aconitum or rash gunpowder.
CLARENCE   I shall observe him with all care and love.
KING HENRY IV   Why art thou not at Windsor with him, Thomas?
CLARENCE   He is not there today. He dines in London.
KING HENRY IV   And how accompanied? Canst thou tell that?
55   CLARENCE   With Poins, and other his continual followers.
KING HENRY IV   Most subject is the fattest soil to weeds,
And he, the noble image of my youth,
Is overspread with them: therefore my grief
Stretches itself beyond the hour of death.
60   The blood weeps from my heart when I do shape
In forms imaginary th'unguided days
And rotten times that you shall look upon
When I am sleeping with my ancestors.
For when his headstrong riot hath no curb,
65   When rage and hot blood are his counsellors,
When means and lavish manners meet together,
O, with what wings shall his affections fly
Towards fronting peril and opposed decay!
WARWICK   My gracious lord, you look beyond him quite:
70   The prince but studies his companions
Like a strange tongue, wherein, to gain the language,
'Tis needful that the most immodest word
Be looked upon and learned, which once attained,
Your highness knows, comes to no further use
75   But to be known and hated. So, like gross terms,
The prince will, in the perfectness of time,
Cast off his followers, and their memory
Shall as a pattern or a measure live,
By which his grace must mete the lives of others,
80   Turning past evils to advantages.

---

50 aconitum aconite or wolfsbane, a poisonous plant   rash hasty, violent   55 other his
continual his other constant   56 fattest richest, most fertile   60 blood . . . heart every sigh
was thought to drain a drop of blood from the heart   64 curb restraint (literally, chain passed
under a horse's jaw)   66 lavish wild, unrestrained   68 fronting advancing/confronting
opposed hostile   69 look . . . quite go too far in judging him   76 perfectness fullness
78 measure guide   79 mete measure

KING HENRY IV   'Tis seldom when the bee doth leave her comb
            In the dead carrion.

Enter Westmorland

            Who's here? Westmorland?

WESTMORLAND   Health to my sovereign, and new happiness
85   Added to that that I am to deliver!
            Prince John, your son, doth kiss your grace's hand.
            Mowbray, the Bishop Scroop, Hastings and all
            Are brought to the correction of your law.
            There is not now a rebel's sword unsheathed,
90   But peace puts forth her olive everywhere.
            The manner how this action hath been borne
            Here at more leisure may ~~your highness~~ read,   *Gives a paper*
            With every course in his particular.

KING HENRY IV   O Westmorland, thou art a summer bird,
95   Which ever in the haunch of winter sings
            The lifting up of day.

Enter Harcourt

            Look, here's more news.

HARCOURT   From enemies heaven keep your majesty,
            And when they stand against you, may they fall
100   As those that I am come to tell you of.
            The Earl Northumberland and the lord Bardolph,
            With a great power of English and of Scots
            Are by the sheriff of Yorkshire overthrown:
            The manner and true order of the fight
105   This packet, please it you, contains at large.   *Gives papers*

KING HENRY IV   And wherefore should these good news make me
            sick?
            Will fortune never come with both hands full,
            But write her fair words still in foulest letters?
            She either gives a stomach and no food—

---

81 'Tis . . . carrion i.e. people rarely give up their pleasures despite the corrupt surroundings; drawn from the biblical story of Samson, who found a bees' nest in the carcass of a lion (Judges 14:8)   87 Bishop Scroop i.e. the Archbishop of York, Richard Scroop   91 borne carried out
93 course . . . particular turn of events set out in detail   95 haunch hindquarter, back end
96 lifting up rising, breaking   105 packet i.e. of letters, dispatch   109 stomach appetite

110 Such are the poor, in health—or else a feast
And takes away the stomach—such are the rich,
That have abundance and enjoy it not.
I should rejoice now at this happy news,
And now my sight fails, and my brain is giddy.
115 O, me! Come near me, now I am much ill.

GLOUCESTER   Comfort, your majesty!

CLARENCE   O my royal father!

WESTMORLAND   My sovereign lord, cheer up yourself, look up.

WARWICK   Be patient, princes. You do know these fits
120 Are with his highness very ordinary.
Stand from him. Give him air. He'll straight be well.

CLARENCE   No, no, he cannot long hold out: these pangs,
Th'incessant care and labour of his mind,
Hath wrought the mure that should confine it in
125 So thin that life looks through and will break out.

GLOUCESTER   The people fear me, for they do observe
Unfathered heirs and loathly births of nature:
The seasons change their manners, as the year
Had found some months asleep and leaped them over.

130 CLARENCE   The river hath thrice flowed, no ebb between,
And the old folk, time's doting chronicles,
Say it did so a little time before
That our great-grandsire, Edward, sicked and died.

WARWICK   Speak lower, princes, for the king recovers.

135 GLOUCESTER   This apoplexy will certain be his end.

KING HENRY IV   I pray you take me up and bear me hence
Into some other chamber. Softly, pray.
Let there be no noise made, my gentle friends,
Unless some dull and favourable hand
140 Will whisper music to my weary spirit.

---

121 straight straightaway   122 pangs attacks, spasms of pain   124 wrought the mure
made the wall   126 fear me fill me with fear   127 Unfathered heirs children supposed to be
unnatural, conceived supernaturally   loathly births deformed infants, regarded as ill omens
128 change their manners alter their usual patterns   as as if   130 flowed flooded
131 doting weak-minded/foolish/fond, attentive   133 Edward Edward III   sicked sickened
135 apoplexy illness causing paralysis   139 dull gentle   favourable kindly

WARWICK	Call for the music in the other room.	*To Servant*
KING HENRY IV	Set me the crown upon my pillow here.	*Crown is set*
CLARENCE	His eye is hollow, and he changes much.	*on the pillow*
WARWICK	Less noise, less noise!	

Enter Prince Henry

145   PRINCE HENRY   Who saw the Duke of Clarence?

CLARENCE   I am here, brother, full of heaviness.   *Weeps*

PRINCE HENRY   How now? Rain within doors, and none abroad?
      How doth the king?

GLOUCESTER   Exceeding ill.

150   PRINCE HENRY   Heard he the good news yet?
      Tell it him.

GLOUCESTER   He altered much upon the hearing it.

PRINCE HENRY   If he be sick with joy, he'll recover without physic.

WARWICK   Not so much noise, my lords.— Sweet prince, speak
      low,

155   The king your father is disposed to sleep.

CLARENCE   Let us withdraw into the other room.

WARWICK   Will't please your grace to go along with us?

PRINCE HENRY   No, I will sit and watch here by the king.

                    [*Exeunt all but Prince Henry*]

      Why doth the crown lie there upon his pillow,
160   Being so troublesome a bedfellow?
      O polished perturbation! Golden care!
      That keep'st the ports of slumber open wide
      To many a watchful night! Sleep with it now,
      Yet not so sound and half so deeply sweet
165   As he whose brow with homely biggen bound
      Snores out the watch of night. O majesty!
      When thou dost pinch thy bearer, thou dost sit
      Like a rich armour worn in heat of day,
      That scald'st with safety. By his gates of breath

---

146 **heaviness** sadness   147 **Rain** i.e. tears   **abroad** outside   153 **physic** medicine
161 **perturbation** cause of trouble   **care** source of anxiety   162 **ports** doors, gates (i.e.
eyelids)   163 **watchful** wakeful   165 **homely biggen** plain nightcap   166 **watch** portion of
the night/watchful vigil   168 **armour . . . safety** metal armor which gets hot and burns the
wearer at the same time it protects him from attack   169 **gates of breath** i.e. mouth and nose

170　There lies a downy feather which stirs not:
Did he suspire, that light and weightless down
Perforce must move. My gracious lord, my father,
This sleep is sound indeed. This is a sleep
That from this golden rigol hath divorced
175　So many English kings. Thy due from me
Is tears and heavy sorrows of the blood,
Which nature, love, and filial tenderness,
Shall, O dear father, pay thee plenteously.
My due from thee is this imperial crown,
180　Which, as immediate from thy place and blood,
Derives itself to me. Lo, here it sits,　*Puts crown on his head*
Which heaven shall guard. And put the world's whole
　　strength
Into one giant arm, it shall not force
This lineal honour from me. This from thee
185　Will I to mine leave, as 'tis left to me.　　　　*Exit*

KING HENRY IV　Warwick! Gloucester! Clarence!　　*Waking*

Enter Warwick, Gloucester, Clarence

CLARENCE　Doth the king call?

WARWICK　What would your majesty? How fares your grace?

KING HENRY IV　Why did you leave me here alone, my lords?

190　CLARENCE　We left the prince my brother here, my liege,
Who undertook to sit and watch by you.

KING HENRY IV　The Prince of Wales? Where is he? Let me see him.

WARWICK　This door is open. He is gone this way.

GLOUCESTER　He came not through the chamber where we
　　stayed.

195　KING HENRY IV　Where is the crown? Who took it from my pillow?

WARWICK　When we withdrew, my liege, we left it here.

KING HENRY IV　The prince hath ta'en it hence. Go, seek him out.
Is he so hasty that he doth suppose
My sleep my death?

---

171 suspire breathe out   **174 rigol** circle (i.e. crown)   **180 immediate** direct successor
181 Derives itself descends   **182 put . . . strength** even if all the strength in the world were
concentrated   **184 lineal** inherited   **185 mine** i.e. my heir

200   Find him, my lord of Warwick. Chide him hither.

[Exit Warwick]

This part of his conjoins with my disease
And helps to end me. See, sons, what things you are,
How quickly nature falls into revolt
When gold becomes her object!

205   For this the foolish over-careful fathers
Have broke their sleeps with thoughts, their brains with
        care,
Their bones with industry,
For this they have engrossed and pilèd up
The cankered heaps of strange-achievèd gold.

210   For this they have been thoughtful to invest
Their sons with arts and martial exercises.
When, like the bee, culling from every flower
The virtuous sweets,
Our thighs packed with wax, our mouths with honey,

215   We bring it to the hive, and, like the bees,
Are murdered for our pains. This bitter taste
Yields his engrossments to the ending father.

Enter Warwick

Now, where is he that will not stay so long
Till his friend sickness hath determined me?

220   WARWICK   My lord, I found the prince in the next room,
Washing with kindly tears his gentle cheeks,
With such a deep demeanour in great sorrow
That tyranny, which never quaffed but blood,
Would, by beholding him, have washed his knife

225   With gentle eye-drops. He is coming hither.

---

200 **Chide** drive with rebukes   201 **part** action   **conjoins** unites   203 **falls into revolt**
betrays itself, is unnatural   208 **engrossed** amassed   209 **cankered** tarnished/corrupt
strange-achievèd ill-gotten/brought from overseas   210 **thoughtful** careful   **invest** endow
(plays on financial sense)   211 **arts** scholarship   214 **thighs . . . wax** beeswax is stored in
sacs on the upper parts of bees' legs   215 **bees . . . pains** in fact it is not workers, but drones
(bees whose sole purpose is to impregnate the queen) who die after mating or are cast out of
the hive to die   216 **This . . . engrossments** these accumulations give a bitter taste
217 **ending** dying   218 **stay** wait   219 **determined** terminated   221 **kindly** filial/gentle
gentle noble/tender   223 **tyranny** cruelty   **but** anything but

KING HENRY IV   But wherefore did he take away the crown?

Enter Prince Henry [with the crown]

Lo, where he comes.— Come hither to me, Harry.—
Depart the chamber, leave us here alone.

Exeunt [Warwick, Gloucester, Clarence]

PRINCE HENRY   I never thought to hear you speak again.

230   **KING HENRY IV**   Thy wish was father, Harry, to that thought:
I stay too long by thee, I weary thee.
Dost thou so hunger for my empty chair
That thou wilt needs invest thee with mine honours
Before thy hour be ripe? O foolish youth!

235   Thou seek'st the greatness that will o'erwhelm thee.
Stay but a little, for my cloud of dignity
Is held from falling with so weak a wind
That it will quickly drop. My day is dim.
Thou hast stolen that which after some few hours

240   Were thine without offence, and at my death
Thou hast sealed up my expectation.
Thy life did manifest thou lovedst me not,
And thou wilt have me die assured of it.
Thou hid'st a thousand daggers in thy thoughts,

245   Which thou hast whetted on thy stony heart,
To stab at half an hour of my life.
What? Canst thou not forbear me half an hour?
Then get thee gone and dig my grave thyself,
And bid the merry bells ring to thy ear

250   That thou art crownèd, not that I am dead.
Let all the tears that should bedew my hearse
Be drops of balm to sanctify thy head,
Only compound me with forgotten dust.
Give that which gave thee life unto the worms.

255   Pluck down my officers, break my decrees,

---

232 chair position/throne   **236 cloud of dignity** rank or honor, insubstantial as a cloud
240 Were would have been   **241 sealed . . . expectation** confirmed my fears   **242 manifest**
demonstrate   **245 whetted** sharpened   **247 forbear** endure, permit   **252 balm** consecrated
oil used in the coronation of the monarch   **sanctify** consecrate, render holy   **253 compound**
mix

For now a time is come to mock at form.
Henry the Fifth is crowned. Up, vanity,
Down, royal state, all you sage counsellors, hence!
And to the English court assemble now,
260   From ev'ry region, apes of idleness!
Now, neighbour confines, purge you of your scum:
Have you a ruffian that will swear, drink, dance,
Revel the night, rob, murder, and commit
The oldest sins the newest kind of ways?
265   Be happy, he will trouble you no more.
England shall double gild his treble guilt.
England shall give him office, honour, might,
For the fifth Harry from curbèd licence plucks
The muzzle of restraint, and the wild dog
270   Shall flesh his tooth in every innocent.
O my poor kingdom, sick with civil blows!
When that my care could not withhold thy riots,
What wilt thou do when riot is thy care?
O, thou wilt be a wilderness again,
275   Peopled with wolves, thy old inhabitants!
PRINCE HENRY   O, pardon me, my liege! But for my tears,
The moist impediments unto my speech,
I had forestalled this dear and deep rebuke
Ere you with grief had spoke and I had heard
280   The course of it so far. There is your crown,   *Puts it back on*
And he that wears the crown immortally   *the pillow*
Long guard it yours. If I affect it more
Than as your honour and as your renown,
Let me no more from this obedience rise,   *Kneels*
285   Which my most true and inward duteous spirit
Teacheth, this prostrate and exterior bending.
Heaven witness with me, when I here came in,

---

256 **form** established order, custom   260 **apes of idleness** fools prone to all unworthy vices
261 **confines** states, countries   266 **gild** cover with gold (puns on **guilt**)   267 **office** official
position   270 **flesh his tooth** sink his tooth into the flesh   272 **care** anxiety, concerned
efforts (sense then shifts to "chief concern")   278 **had** would have   **dear** heartfelt
282 **affect** desire   284 **obedience** i.e. kneeling posture

And found no course of breath within your majesty,
How cold it struck my heart. If I do feign,
290 O, let me in my present wildness die
And never live to show th'incredulous world
The noble change that I have purposèd.
Coming to look on you, thinking you dead,
And dead almost, my liege, to think you were,
295 I spake unto the crown as having sense,
And thus upbraided it: 'The care on thee depending
Hath fed upon the body of my father:
Therefore, thou best of gold art worst of gold.
Other, less fine in carat, is more precious,
300 Preserving life in med'cine potable,
But thou, most fine, most honoured, most renowned,
Hast eat the bearer up.'—Thus, my royal liege,
Accusing it, I put it on my head,
To try with it, as with an enemy
305 That had before my face murdered my father,
The quarrel of a true inheritor.
But if it did infect my blood with joy,
Or swell my thoughts to any strain of pride,
If any rebel or vain spirit of mine
310 Did with the least affection of a welcome
Give entertainment to the might of it,
Let heaven forever keep it from my head
And make me as the poorest vassal is
That doth with awe and terror kneel to it!
315 **KING HENRY IV** O my son,
Heaven put it in thy mind to take it hence,
That thou mightst join the more thy father's love,
Pleading so wisely in excuse of it!
Come hither, Harry, sit thou by my bed   *Prince Henry rises*

---

288 **course** current   292 **have purposèd** intend   295 **as having sense** as though it were
alive   296 **on thee depending** attached to you   299 **fine in carat** pure   300 **med'cine
potable** i.e. *aurum potabile*, a liquid medicine supposed to contain gold   301 **fine** refined, pure
304 **try** dispute, engage in   310 **affection** tendency to   311 **Give entertainment to** receive, be
hospitable to   **might** power   313 **vassal** subject   317 **join the more** be further united to

320　And hear, I think, the very latest counsel
　　　That ever I shall breathe. Heaven knows, my son,
　　　By what by-paths and indirect crooked ways
　　　I met this crown, and I myself know well
　　　How troublesome it sat upon my head.
325　To thee it shall descend with better quiet,
　　　Better opinion, better confirmation,
　　　For all the soil of the achievement goes
　　　With me into the earth. It seemed in me
　　　But as an honour snatched with boist'rous hand,
330　And I had many living to upbraid
　　　My gain of it by their assistances,
　　　Which daily grew to quarrel and to bloodshed,
　　　Wounding supposèd peace. All these bold fears
　　　Thou see'st with peril I have answerèd,
335　For all my reign hath been but as a scene
　　　Acting that argument. And now my death
　　　Changes the mood, for what in me was purchased,
　　　Falls upon thee in a more fairer sort.
　　　So thou the garland wear'st successively.
340　Yet, though thou stand'st more sure than I could do,
　　　Thou art not firm enough, since griefs are green,
　　　And all thy friends, which thou must make thy friends,
　　　Have but their stings and teeth newly taken out,
　　　By whose fell working I was first advanced
345　And by whose power I well might lodge a fear
　　　To be again displaced, which to avoid,
　　　I cut them off and had a purpose now
　　　To lead out many to the Holy Land,
　　　Lest rest and lying still might make them look

320 **latest** last, final　322 **by-paths** obscure, indirect paths　323 **met** came by　327 **soil**
grounds, foundation/stain, dishonor　329 **boist'rous** unruly, violent　330 **many** i.e. of the
men who claimed to have assisted him　333 **fears** sources of fear　336 **argument** plot,
theme/subject of contention　337 **purchased** bought, acquired not inherited　338 **fairer sort**
just manner/favorable lot　339 **garland** i.e. crown　**successively** by right of succession
341 **griefs are green** grievances remain fresh, unhealed　342 **make** work to maintain as
344 **fell working** fierce efforts　345 **lodge** harbor

350   Too near unto my state. Therefore, my Harry,
      Be it thy course to busy giddy minds
      With foreign quarrels, that action, hence borne out,
      May waste the memory of the former days.
      More would I, but my lungs are wasted so
355   That strength of speech is utterly denied me.
      How I came by the crown, O heaven forgive,
      And grant it may with thee in true peace live!

PRINCE HENRY   My gracious liege,
      You won it, wore it, kept it, gave it me.
360   Then plain and right must my possession be;
      Which I with more than with a common pain
      Gainst all the world will rightfully maintain.

Enter Lord John of Lancaster [Prince John] and Warwick [behind]

KING HENRY IV   Look, look, here comes my John of Lancaster.

PRINCE JOHN   Health, peace, and happiness to my royal father!

365   KING HENRY IV   Thou bring'st me happiness and peace, son John,
      But health, alack, with youthful wings is flown
      From this bare withered trunk. Upon thy sight
      My worldly business makes a period.
      Where is my lord of Warwick?

370   PRINCE HENRY   My lord of Warwick!

KING HENRY IV   Doth any name particular belong
      Unto the lodging where I first did swoon?

WARWICK   'Tis called Jerusalem, my noble lord.

KING HENRY IV   Laud be to heaven! Even there my life must end.
375   It hath been prophesied to me many years,
      I should not die but in Jerusalem,
      Which vainly I supposed the Holy Land.
      But bear me to that chamber. There I'll lie.
      In that Jerusalem shall Harry die.   *Exeunt*

---

350 near closely   **state** kingship   **351 giddy** foolish, restless   **352 action** war   **hence borne out** undertaken abroad   **353 waste** dispel   **354 I** I say   **wasted** worn out   **361 common pain** ordinary effort   **367 trunk** body/tree trunk   **368 a period** an end   **372 lodging** room   **swoon** faint   **374 Laud** praise   **375 years** i.e. years ago   **376 but** except   **377 vainly** foolishly/conceitedly

Act 5 Scene 1

Enter Shallow, Silence, Falstaff, Bardolph, Page and Davy

	SHALLOW	By cock and pie, you shall not away tonight. What, Davy, I say!
	FALSTAFF	You must excuse me, Master Robert Shallow.
5	SHALLOW	I will not excuse you. You shall not be excused. Excuses shall not be admitted. There is no excuse shall serve. You shall not be excused.— Why, Davy!
	DAVY	Here, sir. *Steps forward*
	SHALLOW	Davy, Davy, Davy, let me see, Davy, let me see. William Cook, bid him come hither. Sir John, you shall not be
10		excused.
	DAVY	Marry, sir, thus: those precepts cannot be served. And again, sir, shall we sow the headland with wheat?
	SHALLOW	With red wheat, Davy. But for William Cook: are there no young pigeons?
15	DAVY	Yes, sir. Here is now the smith's note for *Gives a paper* shoeing and plough-irons.
	SHALLOW	Let it be cast and paid.— Sir John, you shall not be excused.
	DAVY	Sir, a new link to the bucket must needs be had.
20		And, sir, do you mean to stop any of William's wages, about the sack he lost the other day at Hinckley Fair?
	SHALLOW	He shall answer it. Some pigeons, Davy, a couple of short-legged hens, a joint of mutton, and any pretty little tiny kickshaws, tell William Cook. *They talk aside*
25	DAVY	Doth the man of war stay all night, sir?

**5.1   *Location: at Justice Shallow's, Gloucestershire   Davy* one of Shallow's servants
1 By . . . pie** a mild oath   **cock** form of "God"   **pie** Roman Catholic service book
11 precepts writs, summons   **12 headland** strip of unplowed land in a field; used for turning
the plow it was sown later than the rest of the field   **13 red wheat** a dark-colored late variety
15 smith's note blacksmith's bill   **16 plough-irons** any iron parts of a plow   **17 cast**
calculated (plays on the sense of "form metal into shape")   **19 link . . . bucket** rope or chain,
most likely for the pail drawing water up from a well   **21 Hinckley Fair** well-known cattle fair
held every August at Hinckley, a market town on the Warwickshire/Leicestershire border
22 answer repay   **24 kickshaws** fancy dishes   **25 man of war** soldier/large warship (i.e.
Falstaff)

SHALLOW   Yes, Davy. I will use him well. A friend i'th'court is better than a penny in purse. Use his men well, Davy, for they are arrant knaves, and will backbite.

DAVY   No worse than they are bitten, sir, for they have marvellous foul linen.

SHALLOW   Well conceited, Davy. About thy business, Davy.

DAVY   I beseech you, sir, to countenance William Visor of Woncot against Clement Perkes of the Hill.

SHALLOW   There are many complaints, Davy, against that Visor. That Visor is an arrant knave, on my knowledge.

DAVY   I grant your worship that he is a knave, sir, but yet, heaven forbid, sir, but a knave should have some countenance at his friend's request. An honest man, sir, is able to speak for himself, when a knave is not. I have served your worship truly, sir, these eight years, and if I cannot once or twice in a quarter bear out a knave against an honest man, I have but a very little credit with your worship. The knave is mine honest friend, sir: therefore, I beseech your worship let him be countenanced.

SHALLOW   Go to, I say he shall have no wrong. Look about, Davy.   [*Exit Davy*]
Where are you, Sir John? Come, off with your boots.— Give me your hand, Master Bardolph.

BARDOLPH   I am glad to see your worship.

SHALLOW   I thank thee with all my heart, kind Master Bardolph, and welcome, my tall fellow.— Come, Sir John.

FALSTAFF   I'll follow you, good Master Robert Shallow.

[*Exit Shallow*]
Bardolph, look to our horses.

[*Exeunt Bardolph and Page*]
If I were sawed into quantities, I should make four dozen of such bearded hermits' staves as Master Shallow. It is a

---

26 use treat   A . . . purse i.e. it's useful to have friends in high places   28 arrant knaves absolute rogues   backbite tell tales, slander   29 bitten . . . linen i.e. clothes full of lice   31 Well conceited very witty   32 countenance favor   41 bear out support   42 credit trust/reputation   45 Look about watch out/get busy   51 tall valiant, or perhaps ironically addressed to the Page   54 quantities little bits   55 staves i.e. long and thin

wonderful thing to see the semblable coherence of his men's spirits and his: they, by observing of him, do bear themselves like foolish justices: he, by conversing with them, is turned into a justice-like servingman. Their spirits are so married in 60 conjunction with the participation of society that they flock together in consent, like so many wild geese. If I had a suit to Master Shallow, I would humour his men with the imputation of being near their master: if to his men, I would curry with Master Shallow that no man could better 65 command his servants. It is certain that either wise bearing or ignorant carriage is caught, as men take diseases, one of another: therefore let men take heed of their company. I will devise matter enough out of this Shallow to keep Prince Harry in continual laughter the wearing out of six fashions, 70 which is four terms, or two actions, and he shall laugh with intervallums. O, it is much that a lie with a slight oath and a jest with a sad brow will do with a fellow that never had the ache in his shoulders. O, you shall see him laugh till his face be like a wet cloak ill laid up.

75 SHALLOW   Sir John!   *Within*

FALSTAFF   I come, Master Shallow, I come, Master Shallow.

Exit

Act 5 Scene 2   *running scene 13*

Enter the Earl of Warwick and the Lord Chief Justice

WARWICK   How now, my Lord Chief Justice whither away?

LORD CHIEF JUSTICE   How doth the king?

WARWICK   Exceeding well, his cares are now all ended.

LORD CHIEF JUSTICE   I hope, not dead.

---

56 **semblable coherence** close correspondence   58 **conversing** associating   59 **married in conjunction** intimately connected   61 **suit to** lawsuit for/favor to beg   63 **imputation . . . near** suggestion that I am friendly with   64 **curry** curry favor, flatter   66 **carriage** behavior, bearing   70 **terms** sessions of the law courts (four in a year)   **actions** lawsuits   71 **intervallums** intervals between **terms**   72 **sad brow** straight face   **never . . . shoulders** i.e. was young and carefree   74 **ill laid up** badly folded, i.e. creased up   **5.2** *Location: the royal court*   1 **whither away** where are you going

5   WARWICK   He's walked the way of nature,
And to our purposes he lives no more.
LORD CHIEF JUSTICE   I would his majesty had called me with him.
The service that I truly did his life
Hath left me open to all injuries.
10   WARWICK   Indeed I think the young king loves you not.
LORD CHIEF JUSTICE   I know he doth not, and do arm myself
To welcome the condition of the time,
Which cannot look more hideously upon me
Than I have drawn it in my fantasy.

Enter John of Lancaster [Prince John], Gloucester and Clarence,
[Westmorland and others]

15   WARWICK   Here come the heavy issue of dead Harry.
O, that the living Harry had the temper
Of him, the worst of these three gentlemen!
How many nobles then should hold their places
That must strike sail to spirits of vile sort!
20   LORD CHIEF JUSTICE   Alas, I fear all will be overturned.
PRINCE JOHN   Good morrow, cousin Warwick, good morrow.
GLOUCESTER *and* CLARENCE   Good morrow, cousin.
PRINCE JOHN   We meet like men that had forgot to speak.
WARWICK   We do remember, but our argument
25   Is all too heavy to admit much talk.
PRINCE JOHN   Well, peace be with him that hath made us heavy.
LORD CHIEF JUSTICE   Peace be with us, lest we be heavier!
GLOUCESTER   O, good my lord, you have lost a friend indeed,
And I dare swear you borrow not that face
30   Of seeming sorrow, it is sure your own.
PRINCE JOHN   Though no man be assured what grace to find,
You stand in coldest expectation.
I am the sorrier, would 'twere otherwise.

---

8 **service . . . injuries** presumably the Lord Chief Justice is recalling the time he had Prince
Henry arrested and is worried about repercussions now that Hal is king   **truly** faithfully
14 **fantasy** imagination   15 **heavy issue** sorrowful offspring   16 **temper** disposition
18 **hold their places** retain their positions   19 **strike sail** lower their sails, i.e. submit   **vile**
base   24 **argument** subject for discussion   29 **borrow not** do not put on   30 **sure** certainly
31 **grace** favor (from Hal)   32 **coldest expectation** the least favorable situation

CLARENCE   Well, you must now speak Sir John Falstaff fair,
35   Which swims against your stream of quality.
LORD CHIEF JUSTICE   Sweet princes, what I did, I did in honour,
    Led by th'impartial conduct of my soul,
    And never shall you see that I will beg
    A ragged and forestalled remission.
40   If troth and upright innocency fail me,
    I'll to the king my master that is dead,
    And tell him who hath sent me after him.
WARWICK   Here comes the prince.

Enter Prince Henry [now King Henry V]

LORD CHIEF JUSTICE   Good morrow, and heaven save your majesty!
45   KING HENRY V   This new and gorgeous garment majesty
    Sits not so easy on me as you think.—
    Brothers, you mix your sadness with some fear.
    This is the English, not the Turkish court,
    Not Amurah an Amurah succeeds,
50   But Harry Harry. Yet be sad, good brothers,
    For, to speak truth, it very well becomes you.
    Sorrow so royally in you appears
    That I will deeply put the fashion on
    And wear it in my heart. Why then, be sad,
55   But entertain no more of it, good brothers,
    Than a joint burden laid upon us all.
    For me, by heaven, I bid you be assured,
    I'll be your father and your brother too.
    Let me but bear your love, I'll bear your cares;
60   But weep that Harry's dead, and so will I;
    But Harry lives, that shall convert those tears
    By number into hours of happiness.
PRINCE JOHN, GLOUCESTER *and* CLARENCE   We hope no other from
    your majesty.

---

35 your . . . quality the current of your nature and position   **39 ragged** wretched
forestalled remission pardon so certain to be refused it is not worth asking   **40 troth** good
faith, honesty   **49 Amurah** a Turkish sultan who, upon gaining the throne, had all his
brothers killed; his successor did the same thing   **62 number . . . happiness** i.e. for each tear
there shall be an hour of happiness

KING HENRY V You all look strangely on me.— And   *To Lord*
   you most: *Chief Justice*

65   You are, I think, assured I love you not.

LORD CHIEF JUSTICE I am assured, if I be measured rightly,
   Your majesty hath no just cause to hate me.

KING HENRY V No?
   How might a prince of my great hopes forget
70   So great indignities you laid upon me?
   What? Rate, rebuke, and roughly send to prison
   Th'immediate heir of England? Was this easy?
   May this be washed in Lethe, and forgotten?

LORD CHIEF JUSTICE I then did use the person of your father,
75   The image of his power lay then in me,
   And in th'administration of his law,
   Whiles I was busy for the commonwealth,
   Your highness pleasèd to forget my place,
   The majesty and power of law and justice,
80   The image of the king whom I presented,
   And struck me in my very seat of judgement,
   Whereon, as an offender to your father,
   I gave bold way to my authority
   And did commit you. If the deed were ill,
85   Be you contented, wearing now the garland,
   To have a son set your decrees at nought?
   To pluck down justice from your awful bench?
   To trip the course of law and blunt the sword
   That guards the peace and safety of your person?
90   Nay, more, to spurn at your most royal image
   And mock your workings in a second body?
   Question your royal thoughts, make the case yours,
   Be now the father and propose a son,

---

64 strangely in a distant, unfamiliar manner   **65 assured** convinced   **69 hopes** expectations
71 Rate berate   **72 easy** insignificant/lenient   **73 Lethe** in Greek mythology, the river in the
underworld; immersion in its waters induced forgetfulness   **74 use the person** represent
80 presented represented   **84 commit** imprison   **85 Be you** would you be   **garland** crown
87 awful awe-inspiring, majestic   **bench** judge's seat, i.e. judicial system   **90 spurn**
strike/disdain   **91 second body** deputy, substitute   **92 make . . . yours** put yourself in that
situation   **93 propose** imagine

Hear your own dignity so much profaned,

95 See your most dreadful laws so loosely slighted,

Behold yourself so by a son disdained,

And then imagine me taking your part

And in your power soft silencing your son.

After this cold considerance, sentence me;

100 And, as you are a king, speak in your state

What I have done that misbecame my place,

My person, or my liege's sovereignty.

KING HENRY V You are right, Justice, and you weigh this well:

Therefore still bear the balance and the sword.

105 And I do wish your honours may increase

Till you do live to see a son of mine

Offend you and obey you, as I did.

So shall I live to speak my father's words:

'Happy am I, that have a man so bold,

110 That dares do justice on my proper son;

And no less happy, having such a son,

That would deliver up his greatness so

Into the hands of justice.' You did commit me,

For which, I do commit into your hand

115 Th'unstained sword that you have used to bear,

With this remembrance: that you use the same

With the like bold, just and impartial spirit

As you have done gainst me. There is my hand.   *Offers his hand*

You shall be as a father to my youth,

120 My voice shall sound as you do prompt mine ear,

And I will stoop and humble my intents

To your well-practised wise directions.

And, princes all, believe me, I beseech you:

My father is gone wild into his grave,

---

94 **profaned** abused, treated with contempt   95 **dreadful** formidable, awe-inspiring   **loosely** carelessly, casually   98 **soft** gently   99 **cold considerance** calm consideration   100 **state** role as king   101 **misbecame** was not appropriate to   103 **weigh** consider, reason   104 **still . . . sword** i.e. retain your position; **balance** (scales) and **sword** are the emblems of justice   110 **proper** own   114 **commit** sense shifts from "imprison" to "entrust"   115 **used** been accustomed   116 **remembrance** reminder   120 **sound** speak out   121 **intents** intentions   122 **well-practised** experienced

125   For in his tomb lie my affections,
And with his spirits sadly I survive,
To mock the expectation of the world,
To frustrate prophecies and to raze out
Rotten opinion, who hath writ me down
130 ·   After my seeming. The tide of blood in me
Hath proudly flowed in vanity till now.
Now doth it turn and ebb back to the sea,
Where it shall mingle with the state of floods
And flow henceforth in formal majesty.
135   Now call we our high court of parliament,
And let us choose such limbs of noble counsel,
That the great body of our state may go
In equal rank with the best governed nation,
That war, or peace, or both at once, may be
140   As things acquainted and familiar to us,—
In which you, father, shall have foremost hand.   *To Lord*
Our coronation done, we will accite,   *Chief Justice*
As I before remembered, all our state.
And, heaven consigning to my good intents,
145   No prince nor peer shall have just cause to say,
Heaven shorten Harry's happy life one day!   *Exeunt*

Act 5 Scene 3   *running scene 14*

Enter Falstaff, Shallow, Silence, Bardolph, [Davy] and Page

SHALLOW   Nay, you shall see mine orchard, where, in an arbour, we will eat a last year's pippin of my own graffing, with a dish of caraways, and so forth.— Come, cousin Silence.— And then to bed.

---

125 affections wild inclinations, self-indulgent behavior   **126 sadly** solemnly, seriously
127 mock defy   **128 raze out** erase, obliterate   **129 Rotten opinion** poor, corrupt reputation
130 After my seeming in accordance with the way I appeared to be   **131 vanity**
worthlessness, folly   **133 state of floods** majesty of the sea   **136 limbs . . . counsel** i.e.
advisers   **142 accite** summon   **143 remembered** mentioned (pronounced *remembred*)
144 consigning to approving, setting its seal to   **5.3** *Location: Shallow's garden,
Gloucestershire*   **1 orchard** garden   **2 pippin** variety of apple   **graffing** grafting,
cultivation   **3 caraways** sweets or cakes made with caraway seeds

5   **FALSTAFF**   You have here a goodly dwelling and a rich.

    SHALLOW   Barren, barren, barren: beggars all, beggars all, Sir John. Marry, good air.— Spread, Davy, spread, Davy. Well said, Davy.

    FALSTAFF   This Davy serves you for good uses. He is your
10   servingman and your husband.

    SHALLOW   A good varlet, a good varlet, a very good varlet, Sir John. I have drunk too much sack at supper. A good varlet. Now sit down, now sit down. Come, cousin.

    SILENCE   Ah, sirrah, quoth a, we shall
15   Do nothing but eat, and make good cheer,   *Sings*
       And praise heaven for the merry year.
       When flesh is cheap and females dear,
       And lusty lads roam here and there
       So merrily, and ever among so merrily.

20   **FALSTAFF**   There's a merry heart. Good Master Silence, I'll give you a health for that anon.

    SHALLOW   Give Master Bardolph some wine, Davy.

    DAVY   Sweet sir, sit. I'll be with you anon. Most sweet sir, sit. Master page, good master page, sit. Proface! What you
25   want in meat, we'll have in drink, but you bear. The heart's all.   *[Exit]*

    SHALLOW   Be merry, Master Bardolph.— And, my little soldier there, be merry.

    SILENCE   Be merry, be merry, my wife has all,   *Sings*
30   For women are shrews, both short and tall.
       'Tis merry in hall when beards wag all,
       And welcome merry Shrovetide.
       Be merry, be merry.

---

5 rich fertile/well-off   **one**   **7 Spread** lay the cloth for eating   **8 said** done   **10 husband** steward   **11 varlet** servant/rogue   **14 quoth a** said he   **17 flesh** meat/whores   **dear** beloved/expensive   **18 lusty** lively/lustful   **21 health** toast   **24 Proface!** a toast or welcoming cry: "May it do you good!" (from old French or Italian)   **25 want in meat** lack in flesh, i.e. size   **bear** put up with it   **26 all** i.e. the most important thing   **30 shrews** nags and scolds   **31 in . . . all** at dinner when men's **beards** move up and down in lively conversation   **32 Shrovetide** the three feast days before Ash Wednesday and the beginning of Lent

FALSTAFF	I did not think Master Silence had been a man of	

FALSTAFF I did not think Master Silence had been a man of
35 this mettle.

SILENCE Who, I? I have been merry twice and once ere now.

[*Enter Davy with apples*]

DAVY There is a dish of leather-coats for you. *To Bardolph?*

SHALLOW Davy!

DAVY Your worship! I'll be with you straight.— A cup of
40 wine, sir?

SILENCE A cup of wine that's brisk and fine, *Sings*
And drink unto the leman mine,
And a merry heart lives long-a.

FALSTAFF Well said, Master Silence.

45 **SILENCE** If we shall be merry, now comes in the sweet of the
night.

FALSTAFF Health and long life to you, Master Silence.

SILENCE Fill the cup, and let it come, *Sings*
I'll pledge you a mile to the bottom.

50 **SHALLOW** Honest Bardolph, welcome. If thou want'st anything,
and wilt not call, beshrew thy heart.— Welcome, my little
tiny thief.— And welcome indeed too. I'll drink to *To Page*
Master Bardolph, and to all the cavalieros about London.

DAVY I hope to see London once ere I die.

55 **BARDOLPH** If I might see you there, Davy.

SHALLOW You'll crack a quart together, ha! Will you not,
Master Bardolph?

BARDOLPH Yes, sir, in a pottle-pot.

SHALLOW I thank thee. The knave will stick by thee, I can
60 assure thee that. He will not out: he is true bred.

BARDOLPH And I'll stick by him, sir.

SHALLOW Why, there spoke a king. Lack nothing: be merry.
Look who's at door there, ho! Who knocks? *Knocking within*

35 mettle character/liveliness **36 twice and once** comic inversion of "once or twice"
37 leather-coats russet apples which have tough skins **41 brisk** dry/sparkling **42 leman**
sweetheart **48 let it come** pass it round **49 pledge** toast **a . . . bottom** the whole cup,
even if it were a mile deep **51 beshrew** a curse on **53 cavalieros** fashionable young men
56 crack a quart empty a quart pot, i.e. two pints of ale **58 pottle-pot** tankard containing
two quarts (four pints), twice what Shallow proposed **59 stick by thee** keep up with you (in
drinking) **60 out** drop out **true bred** i.e. made of the right stuff

FALSTAFF	Why, now you have done me right.	*Davy goes to the door*

65 SILENCE   Do me right,   *Sings*
           And dub me knight,
           Samingo. Is't not so?

FALSTAFF   'Tis so.

SILENCE   Is't so? Why then, say an old man can do somewhat.

70 DAVY   If it please your worship, there's one Pistol come
           from the court with news.

FALSTAFF   From the court? Let him come in.

Enter Pistol

           How now, Pistol?

PISTOL   Sir John, save you, sir!

75 FALSTAFF   What wind blew you hither, Pistol?

PISTOL   Not the ill wind which blows none to good, sweet
           knight. Thou art now one of the greatest men in the realm.

SILENCE   Indeed, I think he be, but Goodman Puff of Barson.

PISTOL   Puff? Puff in thy teeth, most recreant coward base!

80 Sir John, I am thy Pistol and thy friend,
           Helter-skelter have I rode to thee,
           And tidings do I bring and lucky joys
           And golden times and happy news of price.

FALSTAFF   I prithee now deliver them like a man of this world.

85 PISTOL   A *foutre* for the world and worldlings base!
           I speak of Africa and golden joys.

FALSTAFF   O base Assyrian knight, what is thy news?
           Let King Cophetua know the truth thereof.

SILENCE   And Robin Hood, Scarlet and John.   *Sings*

90 PISTOL   Shall dunghill curs confront the Helicons?

---

64 done me right i.e. by matching me in drinking   **65 Do . . . Samingo** popular drinking song
67 Samingo Sir Mingo (*mingo* is Latin for "I urinate")   **69 somewhat** something   **77 greatest**
most influential (Silence takes the sense of "fattest")   **78 but** except for   **Goodman** title for
those below the rank of gentleman   **Puff** name suggestive of swelling (Pistol shifts the sense
to "brag, boast")   **79 recreant** cowardly   **83 price** great value   **84 man . . . world** an
ordinary mortal, i.e. in plain language   **85 A foutre** i.e. "I don't give a fuck" (from the French)
87 Assyrian native of Assyria, ancient Middle Eastern country renowned in the Bible for
robbery and pillage, later associated with luxury   **88 King Cophetua** African king who fell in
love with a beggar girl; a popular topic for ballads   **89 Robin . . . John** fragment from the
ballad *Robin Hood and the Pinder of Wakefield*   **90 curs** dogs   **Helicons** i.e. the Muses who lived
on Mount Helicon in Greece— hence "true poets"

And shall good news be baffled?
Then, Pistol, lay thy head in Furies' lap.

SILENCE   Honest gentleman, I know not your breeding.

PISTOL   Why then, lament therefore.   ↓*Silence falls asleep*↓

95 SHALLOW   Give me pardon, sir. If, sir, you come with news from
the court, I take it there is but two ways, either to utter them,
or to conceal them. I am, sir, under the king, in some
authority.

PISTOL   Under which king, Besonian? Speak or die.

100 SHALLOW   Under King Harry.

PISTOL   Harry the Fourth or Fifth?

SHALLOW   Harry the Fourth.

PISTOL   A *foutre* for thine office!—
Sir John, thy tender lambkin now is king.
105 Harry the Fifth's the man. I speak the truth.
When Pistol lies, do this, and fig me, like
The bragging Spaniard.

FALSTAFF   What, is the old king dead?

PISTOL   As nail in door. The things I speak are just.

110 FALSTAFF   Away, Bardolph!— Saddle my horse.— Master
Robert Shallow, choose what office thou wilt in the land, 'tis
thine.— Pistol, I will double-charge thee with dignities.

BARDOLPH   O, joyful day! I would not take a knighthood for my
fortune.

115 PISTOL   What? I do bring good news.

FALSTAFF   Carry Master Silence to bed.— Master Shallow, my
lord Shallow, be what thou wilt. I am fortune's steward. Get
on thy boots. We'll ride all night. O sweet Pistol! Away,
Bardolph!   [*Exit Bardolph*]

120 Come, Pistol, utter more to me, and withal devise something
to do thyself good. Boot, boot, Master Shallow. I know the

---

91 baffled frustrated/treated with contempt   **92 lay . . . lap** appeal to the Furies, mythological
goddesses of revenge   **93 breeding** social status   **99 Besonian** beggar, knave (from Italian
besogno)   **106 do . . . me** make the indecent gesture known as the "fig of Spain," which
consisted of thrusting the thumb between the index and middle fingers   **109 just** true
110 Away let's go   **112 double-charge . . . dignities** load you, like a firearm, twice over with
honors   **113 take** exchange   **116 Carry . . . bed** presumably Silence has passed out from too
much drink   **120 withal** moreover   **121 Boot** get your boots on

young king is sick for me. Let us take any man's horses. The
laws of England are at my commandment. Happy are they
which have been my friends, and woe unto my Lord Chief
125   Justice!

PISTOL   Let vultures vile seize on his lungs also!

'Where is the life that late I led?' say they.

Why, here it is. Welcome those pleasant days.   *Exeunt*

Act 5 Scene 4   *running scene 15*

Enter Hostess Quickly, Doll Tearsheet and Beadles

HOSTESS QUICKLY   No, thou arrant knave. I would I might die,
that I might have thee hanged. Thou hast drawn my
shoulder out of joint.

FIRST BEADLE   The constables have delivered her over to me, and
5   she shall have whipping-cheer enough, I warrant her. There
hath been a man or two lately killed about her.

DOLL TEARSHEET   Nut-hook, nut-hook, you lie. Come on, I'll tell
thee what, thou damned tripe-visaged rascal. If the child I
now go with do miscarry, thou hadst better thou hadst
10   struck thy mother, thou paper-faced villain.

HOSTESS QUICKLY   O, that Sir John were come, he would make
this a bloody day to somebody, But I would the fruit of her
womb might miscarry!

FIRST BEADLE   If it do, you shall have a dozen of cushions again,

---

122 sick i.e. longing, pining for (unconscious play on sense of "sick of")   **126 vultures . . .
also** refers to the punishment inflicted on Prometheus by the Greek gods; for stealing fire from
heaven, he had his liver pecked out by vultures each day (it regrew at night)   **127 'Where . . .
led?'** line from a lost poem or ballad   **5.4   *Location: London, but unspecified—almost
certainly a street*   Beadles** parish officers with the power to punish petty offenders,
perhaps synonymous with Fang and Snare   **2 that** so that   **hanged** i.e. as her murderer
4 over up (for punishment)   **5 whipping-cheer** feast of whipping, a common punishment for
whores   **6 killed about her** murdered on her account; may play on "brought to orgasm" in
her company   **7 Nut-hook** beadle or constable; literally a long pole with a hook at the end for
gathering nuts   **8 tripe-visaged** with a face like tripe (i.e. sallow, pockmarked).   **9 go** am
pregnant   **thou . . . struck** you'd have been better off if you'd struck   **10 paper-faced** i.e.
thin, pale   **12 bloody . . . somebody** he'd fight and make somebody pay for this
121 . . . miscarry either she hopes Doll will miscarry and the Beadle be punished or she's
confused and means the opposite   **14 cushions** implying that Doll is feigning pregnancy by
stuffing a cushion under her gown

15   you have but eleven now. Come, I charge you both go with
      me, for the man is dead that you and Pistol beat among you.

DOLL TEARSHEET   I'll tell thee what, thou thin man in a censer, I
      will have you as soundly swinged for this, you blue-bottled
      rogue, you filthy famished correctioner. If you be not
20   swinged, I'll forswear half-kirtles.

FIRST BEADLE   Come, come, you she knight-errant, come.

HOSTESS QUICKLY   O, that right should thus o'ercome might!
      Well, of sufferance comes ease.

DOLL TEARSHEET   Come, you rogue, come. Bring me to a justice.

25   HOSTESS QUICKLY   Yes, come, you starved bloodhound.

DOLL TEARSHEET   Goodman death, goodman bones!

HOSTESS QUICKLY   Thou anatomy, thou!

DOLL TEARSHEET   Come, you thin thing, come you rascal.

FIRST BEADLE   Very well.   *Exeunt*

Act 5 Scene 5   *running scene 16*

Enter two Grooms

FIRST GROOM   More rushes, more rushes.

SECOND GROOM   The trumpets have sounded twice.

FIRST GROOM   It will be two of the clock ere they come from the
      coronation.   *Exeunt Grooms*

Enter Falstaff, Shallow, Pistol, Bardolph and Page

5   FALSTAFF   Stand here by me, Master Robert Shallow. I will
      make the king do you grace. I will leer upon him as he comes
      by, and do but mark the countenance that he will give me.

---

15 but only   **17 man in a censer** vessels in which incense was burned were embossed
with figures   **18 swinged** thrashed   **blue-bottled** beadles wore dark-blue uniforms
19 correctioner one who administers punishment; or more specifically, officer at the Bridewell
House of Correction for prostitutes   **20 forswear half-kirtles** give up wearing skirts; a kirtle
consisted of a bodice and a skirt   **21 she knight-errant** female knight/prostitute (who
commits her misdeeds, or errs by night)   **22 right . . . might** inversion of the proverb "might
overcomes right"   **23 sufferance . . . ease** undergoing suffering/patient forbearance
produces relief/comfort   **26 Goodman . . . bones** insults referring to the Beadle's thinness
27 anatomy skeleton   **28 thing** perhaps with phallic connotations   **rascal** rogue/
underweight young deer   **5.5** *Location: a public place in Westminster, near the Abbey*
Grooms manservants   **1 rushes** with which Elizabethan floors were commonly strewn
6 leer upon look sideways at, catch his eye   **7 countenance** look/patronage

PISTOL   Bless thy lungs, good knight.

FALSTAFF   Come here, Pistol, stand behind me.— O, if I had
10   had time to have made new liveries, I would have bestowed
      the thousand pound I borrowed of you. But it is no matter,
      this poor show doth better: this doth infer the zeal I had to
      see him.

SHALLOW   It doth so.

15   FALSTAFF   It shows my earnestness in affection—

PISTOL   It doth so.

FALSTAFF   My devotion—

PISTOL   It doth, it doth, it doth.

FALSTAFF   As it were, to ride day and night, and not to
20   deliberate, not to remember, not to have patience to shift
      me—

SHALLOW   It is most certain.

FALSTAFF   But to stand stained with travel, and sweating with
      desire to see him, thinking of nothing else, putting all affairs
25   in oblivion, as if there were nothing else to be done but to see
      him.

PISTOL   'Tis *semper idem*, for *obsque hoc nihil est*. 'Tis all in
      every part.

SHALLOW   'Tis so, indeed.

30   PISTOL   My knight, I will inflame thy noble liver,
      And make thee rage.
      Thy Doll, and Helen of thy noble thoughts,
      Is in base durance and contagious prison,
      Haled thither
35   By most mechanical and dirty hand.
      Rouse up revenge from ebon den with fell

---

10 **liveries** servants' uniforms   **bestowed** laid out, used   12 **infer** imply, demonstrate
20 **shift me** change my shirt   27 *semper idem* "ever the same" (Latin)   *obsque . . . est*
"apart from this there is nothing" (Latin; *obsque* is a mistake for *absque*)   'Tis . . . **part** Pistol's
rough translation of the Latin   30 **liver** regarded as the seat of the passions   32 **Helen** i.e.
Helen of Troy, supposedly the most beautiful woman in the world   33 **durance** imprisonment
34 **Haled** hauled, dragged   35 **mechanical** vulgar, common   36 **ebon** ebony, black   **fell**
fierce

Alecto's snake,

For Doll is in. Pistol speaks naught but troth.

FALSTAFF   I will deliver her.

40   PISTOL   There roared the sea, and trumpet-clangour sounds.

The trumpets sound. Enter King Henry V, [with his] brothers [Prince
John, Clarence, Gloucester], Lord Chief Justice [and others]

FALSTAFF   Save thy grace, King Hal, my royal Hal!

PISTOL   The heavens thee guard and keep, most royal imp of
    fame!

FALSTAFF   Save thee, my sweet boy!

KING HENRY V   My Lord Chief Justice, speak to that vain man.

45   LORD CHIEF JUSTICE   Have you your wits? Know you what 'tis you
    speak?

FALSTAFF   My king, my Jove! I speak to thee, my heart!

KING HENRY V   I know thee not, old man. Fall to thy prayers.

How ill white hairs become a fool and jester!

I have long dreamed of such a kind of man,

50   So surfeit-swelled, so old and so profane.

But being awake, I do despise my dream.

Make less thy body hence, and more thy grace,

Leave gormandizing; know the grave doth gape

For thee thrice wider than for other men.

55   Reply not to me with a fool-born jest.

Presume not that I am the thing I was,

For heaven doth know—so shall the world perceive—

That I have turned away my former self,

So will I those that kept me company.

60   When thou dost hear I am as I have been,

Approach me, and thou shalt be as thou wast,

The tutor and the feeder of my riots:

Till then, I banish thee, on pain of death,

---

37 **Alecto** one of the Furies, described by Virgil as being crowned with snakes   38 **in** in prison;
possibly plays on "pregnant" (hence Falstaff's "deliver")   42 **imp** scion or offspring of a noble
house   44 **vain** foolish, worthless   46 **Jove** supreme Roman god   **heart** dear old friend
50 **surfeit-swelled** swollen from overindulgence   52 **hence** henceforth   53 **gormandizing**
excessive eating   62 **riots** debauched behavior, revelry, disorderly deeds

As I have done the rest of my misleaders,
65   Not to come near our person by ten mile.
For competence of life I will allow you,
That lack of means enforce you not to evil.
And, as we hear you do reform yourselves,
We will, according to your strength and qualities,
70   Give you advancement.— Be it your charge, my lord,   *To Chief*
To see performed the tenor of our word.— Set on.   *Justice*

Exeunt King [and his train]

FALSTAFF   Master Shallow, I owe you a thousand pound.

SHALLOW   Aye, marry, Sir John, which I beseech you to let me
have home with me.

75 FALSTAFF   That can hardly be, Master Shallow. Do not you
grieve at this: I shall be sent for in private to him. Look you,
he must seem thus to the world. Fear not your advancement.
I will be the man yet that shall make you great.

SHALLOW   I cannot well perceive how, unless you should give
80   me your doublet and stuff me out with straw. I beseech you,
good Sir John, let me have five hundred of my thousand.

FALSTAFF   Sir, I will be as good as my word. This that you heard
was but a colour.

SHALLOW   A colour I fear that you will die in, Sir John.

85 FALSTAFF   Fear no colours. Go with me to dinner.— Come,
Lieutenant Pistol. Come, Bardolph. I shall be sent for soon at
night.

[Enter Prince John, the Lord Chief Justice and Officers]

LORD CHIEF JUSTICE   Go, carry Sir John Falstaff to the Fleet.
Take all his company along with him.

90 FALSTAFF   My lord, my lord—

LORD CHIEF JUSTICE   I cannot now speak. I will hear you soon.
Take them away.

---

65 our Hal uses the royal plural pronoun   66 competence of life a sufficient allowance
67 That . . . evil so that poverty will not make you turn to crime   70 advancement promotion,
favor   charge responsibility, orders   71 tenor substance   80 doublet close-fitting jacket
83 colour pretense (of Henry's)   84 colour puns on "collar" (hangman's noose),   die puns
on "dye"   85 colours enemy flags   86 soon at night this very evening/early in the evening
88 Fleet prison in the City of London

PISTOL *Si fortuna me tormento, spero me contento.*

Exeunt all but Lancaster [Prince John] and Chief Justice

PRINCE JOHN I like this fair proceeding of the king's.

95 He hath intent his wonted followers
Shall all be very well provided for,
But all are banished till their conversations
Appear more wise and modest to the world.

LORD CHIEF JUSTICE And so they are.

100 PRINCE JOHN The king hath called his parliament, my lord.

LORD CHIEF JUSTICE He hath.

PRINCE JOHN I will lay odds that, ere this year expire,
We bear our civil swords and native fire
As far as France. I heard a bird so sing,

105 Whose music, to my thinking, pleased the king.
Come, will you hence?

Exeunt

Epilogue

[*Enter the Epilogue*]

First my fear, then my curtsy, last my speech. My fear is your
displeasure: my curtsy, my duty: and my speech, to beg your
pardons. If you look for a good speech now, you undo me, for

110 what I have to say is of mine own making, and what indeed I
should say will, I doubt, prove mine own marring. But to the
purpose, and so to the venture. Be it known to you, as it is
very well, I was lately here in the end of a displeasing play, to
pray your patience for it and to promise you a better. I did

115 mean indeed to pay you with this, which, if like an ill venture
it come unluckily home, I break, and you, my gentle
creditors, lose. Here I promised you I would be and here I

---

93 Si . . . contento "If fortune torments me, hope contents me" (Italian; the same motto Pistol uttered in Act 2 Scene 4, with the Italian differently garbled)   **94 fair proceeding** kindly/just course of action   **95 hath intent** intends   **wonted** customary   **97 conversations** behavior   **103 civil swords** used in civil wars   **107 curtsy** bow   **your** addressed to the audience   **111 doubt** fear   **marring** ruin   **112 venture** attempt/risk   **115 ill venture** unsuccessful commercial voyage   **116 break** break my promise/am bankrupt   **117 creditors** plays on both financial sense and "people who believe my promise" commit my body to your mercies: bate me some and I will pay you some and, as most debtors do, promise you infinitely.

120 If my tongue cannot entreat you to acquit me, will you command me to use my legs? And yet that were but light payment, to dance out of your debt. But a good conscience will make any possible satisfaction, and so will I. All the gentlewomen here have forgiven me: if the gentlemen will

125 not, then the gentlemen do not agree with the gentlewomen, which was never seen before in such an assembly. One word more, I beseech you: if you be not too much cloyed with fat meat, our humble author will continue the story, with Sir John in it, and make you merry with fair Katherine of

130 France, where, for anything I know, Falstaff shall die of a sweat, unless already he be killed with your hard opinions. For Oldcastle died a martyr, and this is not the man. My tongue is weary, when my legs are too, I will bid you goodnight, and so kneel down before you; but, indeed, to

135 pray for the queen.   [*Exit*]

---

118 bate me let me off   **128 continue . . . it** i.e. in *Henry V*, although in the end Falstaff did not feature in that play   **131 sweat** a fit of sweating due to either physical exertion, the plague, or a type of cure for venereal disease   **hard** unfavorable   **132 Oldcastle . . . martyr** Sir John Oldcastle, the name originally given to Falstaff, was an early fifteenth-century Lollard leader, subsequently regarded as a martyr by the Puritans; Shakespeare had to drop the name from the play due to objections from Oldcastle's descendants

TEXTUAL NOTES

Q = First Quarto text of 1600
F = First Folio text of 1623
F2 = a correction introduced in the Second Folio text of 1632
Ed = a correction introduced by a later editor
SD = stage direction
SH = speech heading (i.e. speaker's name)

List of parts: *adapted from* THE ACTORS NAMES *at end of F text*

Induction SH RUMOUR = Ed. *Not in* F **000 hold** = Ed. F = Hole
1.1.142 hard = Q. F = head **68 Spoke** = Q. F = Speake **a venture** = Q. F = aduenture **188 brought** = F2. F = bring
1.2.6 clay, man *spelled* Clay-man *in* F **91 for** = Q. *Not in* F
2.1.1 SH HOSTESS QUICKLY = Ed. F = *Hostesse* **149, 152 SH GOWER** = Ed. F = *Mes.* **164 counties** = Q. F = Countries
2.2.14 videlicet *spelled* Viz. *in* F **100 borrower's** = Ed. F = borrowed
2.3.5 SH LADY NORTHUMBERLAND = Ed. F = *Wife. (throughout the scene)*
2.4.132 With = Q. F = where **199 *SD Musicians*** = Ed. F = *Musique* **227 avoirdupois** *spelled* Haber-de-pois *in* F
3.2.138 SH FALSTAFF = Ed. F = *Shal.*
4.1.39 appeared = Ed. F = appeare **118 force** = Ed. F = forc'd **252 th'imagined** = Ed. F = th'imagine **435 My . . . report** *set as prose in* F, *but some eds set as verse because of rhyme on* court/report **450 curdy** *spelled* cruddie *in* F
4.2.262 will = Q. F = swill **277 moist** = Q. F = most **372 swoon** = Q. F = swoon'd
5.2.37 th'impartial = Q. F = th'Imperiall **45 SH KING HENRY V** = Ed. F = *Prince.* **197 your** = Q. F = you
5.3.22 Give = Q. F = Good **88 Cophetua** = Q. F = Couitha **89 SH SILENCE** = Ed. F = *Shal.*
5.4.4 SH FIRST BEADLE = Ed. F = *Off.*
5.5.16 SH PISTOL = F. *Some eds reassign to* SHALLOW **18 SH PISTOL** = F. *Some eds reassign to* SHALLOW **107 Epilogue** *text follows* F. Q *divides into three paragraphs: (1) from* First my feare *to* promise you infinitely: and so I kneele downe before you; but indeed, to pray for the Queene. *(2) from* If my tongue cannot *to* such as assemblie. *(3) from* One word more *to* wil bid you, good night. *I.e. F moves prayer for the Queen to the end. The confusion may be caused by the conflation of two distinct epilogues, perhaps one for public and one for court performance*

QUARTO PASSAGES THAT DO NOT APPEAR IN THE FOLIO

Following 1.2.193:

but it was alway yet the trick of our English nation, if they have a good thing, to make it too common. If ye will needs say I am an old man, you should give me rest. I would to God my name were not so terrible to the enemy as it is: I were better to be eaten to death with a rust than to be scoured to nothing with perpetual motion.

Following 2.2.24:

and God knows, whether those that bawl out the ruins of thy linen shall inherit his kingdom: but the midwives say the children are not in the fault; whereupon the world increases, and kindreds are mightily strengthened.

Following 2.4.14:

Dispatch: the room where they supped is too hot; they'll come in straight.

Following 2.4.58:

DOLL TEARSHEET   Hang yourself, you muddy conger, hang yourself!

Following 2.4.135:

FALSTAFF   No more, Pistol; I would not have you discharge yourself of our company, Pistol.

After "divers liquors!" *in 3.1.53:*

O, if this were seen,
The happiest youth, viewing his progress through,
What perils past, what crosses to ensue,
Would shut the book, and sit him down and die.

OATHS FROM THE QUARTO

The following oaths were altered in the Folio text as a result of the Parliamentary Act to Restrain the Abuses of Players (spelling has been modernized in this list):

	QUARTO	FOLIO
1.1.17	Good, and God will.	Good, an heaven will!
1.1.117	I would to God I had not seen	I would to heaven I had not seen
1.2.20	a face-royal, God may finish	a face-royal. Heaven may finish
1.2.30	glutton, pray God his tongue	glutton! May his tongue
1.2.84	My good lord, God give your lordship	My good lord! Give your lordship
1.2.99	Well, God mend him.	Well, heaven mend him!
1.2.179	Well, God send the prince	Well, heaven send the prince
1.2.181	God send the companion	Heaven send the companion
1.2.188	for, by the Lord, I take	for if I take
1.2.194–5	and God bless your expedition	and heaven bless your expedition
1.3.19	Yea Mary, there's the point	Ay, marry,* there's the point

* **marry** by (the Virgin) Mary.

	QUARTO	FOLIO
2.1.6	O Lord I, good Master Snare	Ay, ay, good Master Snare
2.1.104	Pray thee peace	Prithee,* peace
2.1.122	Faith you said so before	Nay, you said so before
2.1.135	Pray thee, Sir John	Prithee, Sir John
2.1.135–6	i'faith I am loath to pawn my plate so God save me law	I loath to pawn my plate, in good earnest, la
2.2.1	Before God, I am	Trust me, I am
2.2.4	Faith it does me	It doth me,
2.2.26	Yes faith, and let it be	Yes, and let it be
2.2.31	Mary I tell thee	Why, I tell thee
2.2.52	By this light I am well spoken on	Nay, I am well spoken of.
2.2.55–6	help: by the mass here comes . . .	help. Look, look, here comes . . .
2.2.60	God save your grace	Save your grace
2.2.119	God send the wench no	May the wench have no
2.3.1	I pray thee	I prithee
2.3.9	O yet for God's sake	O, yet, for heaven's sake
2.3.17	For yours, the God of heaven brighten it	For yours, may heavenly glory . . .
2.4.1	What the devil hast thou	What hast thou

* **Prithee** I pray thee.

	QUARTO	FOLIO
2.4.3	Mass thou say'st true	Thou say'st true
2.4.15	By the mass here will be	Then here will be
2.4.18	I'faith sweetheart	Sweetheart
2.4.21	rose, in good truth law: but i'faith you have	rose. But, you have
2.4.31	yea, good faith.	yea, good sooth.
2.4.34	A pox damn you, you muddy rascal	You muddy rascal
2.4.84–5	a tame cheater i'faith, you	a tame cheater he. You
2.4.95	God save you, Sir John.	Save you, Sir John!
2.4.111	sir: God's light, with	sir? What, with
2.4.112	God let me not live, but I will murder	I will murder
2.4.121–2	a captain? God's light these villains	A captain? These villains
2.4.136–7	'tis very late i'faith, I beseek	It is very late. I beseek
2.4.152–3	her? For God's sake be quiet	her? I pray be quiet
2.4.163	For God's sake thrust him	Thrust him
2.4.178	I pray thee, Jack, I pray thee	I prithee, Jack, I prithee
2.4.204	I'faith and thou	And thou
2.4.242	By my troth I kiss thee	Nay truly, I kiss thee

	QUARTO	*FOLIO*
2.4.251	By my troth thou't set me	Thou wilt set me
2.4.264–6	by my troth welcome . . . now the Lord bless . . . thine, O Jesu, are you	Welcome . . . Now, heaven bless . . . thine! What, are you
2.4.275	God's blessing of your	Blessing on your
3.1.45	O God that one	O, heaven! That one
3.1.68	Though then God knows, I	Though then, heaven knows, I
3.1.97	upon my soul,	Upon my life,
3.2.15	By the mass I was called anything:	I was called anything,
3.2.29–30	Gray's Inn: Jesu, Jesu, the mad	Gray's Inn. O, the mad
3.2.33–4	death (as the Psalmist saith) is certain	death is certain
3.2.36	By my troth I was not there	Truly, cousin, I was not there
3.2.40	Jesu, Jesu, dead! A drew	Dead? See, see, he drew
3.2.56	tall gentleman, by heaven, and	tall gentleman, and
3.2.62	It is well said in faith sir,	It is well said, sir;
3.2.70	command, by heaven, accommodated	command. 'Accommodated'

	QUARTO	**FOLIO**
3.2.75–6	hand, by my troth: Trust me	hand. Trust me
3.2.99	excellent i'faith, things	excellent! Things
3.2.100	good, in faith well said	good. Well said
3.2.113	Yea Mary	Ay, marry
3.2.160	Fore God a likely	Trust me, a likely
3.2.162	O lord, good my lord captain	O, good my lord captain
3.2.164	O Lord sir, I am	O, sir! I am
3.2.175	you, by my troth	you, in good troth
3.2.186	By the mass I could	I could
3.2.199	dinner, Jesus the days	dinner. O, the days
3.2.214	By my troth I . . . owe God a death	I . . . we owe a death
3.2.219	Faith, I'll bear	Nay, I will bear
3.2.249	Well said i'faith Wart,	Well said, Wart.
3.2.259–60	Shallow, God keep you Master	Shallow. Farewell, Master
3.2.263–4	Sir John, the Lord bless you, God prosper your affairs, God send us peace at your return,	Sir John, heaven bless you and prosper your affairs, and send us peace!
3.2.267	Fore God would you would	I would you would
3.2.268	word, God keep you.	word. Fare you well.
3.2.272	Shallow, Lord, Lord, how	Shallow. How

	QUARTO	FOLIO
4.1.182	peace, which God so	peace, which heaven so
4.1.232	in God's name then forward	in heaven's name then forward
4.1.250	the books of God	the books of heaven
4.1.252	voice of God himself	voice of heaven itself
4.1.260	zeal of God	zeal of heaven
4.1.295	Upon my soul they	Upon my life, they
4.1.360	God, and not we	Heaven, and not we,
4.1.403	or by the Lord, I will have it	or, I swear, I will have it
4.2.1	Now lords, if God doth	Now, lords, if heaven doth
4.2.182	Which God shall guard:	Which heaven shall guard.
4.2.287	God witness	Heaven witness
4.2.312	Let God for ever	Let heaven forever
4.2.316	God put it in	Heaven put it in
4.2.321	God knows	Heaven knows
4.2.356	O God forgive	O heaven forgive
4.2.374	Laud be to God,	Laud be to heaven!
5.1.37	yet God forbid	yet, heaven forbid,
5.2.20	O God, I fear	Alas, I fear
5.2.44	and God save	and heaven save
5.2.51	For by my faith it	For, to speak truth, it
5.2.144	And God consigning	And, heaven consigning
5.2.146	God shorten	Heaven shorten

	QUARTO	FOLIO
5.3.5	Fore God you have here	You have here
5.3.12	Sir John: by the mass I have	John. I have
5.3.16	praise God for	praise heaven for
5.3.56	By the mass you'll crack	You'll crack
5.3.59	By God's liggens* I thank thee	I thank thee
5.3.74	Sir John, God save you.	Sir John, save you,
5.3.78	By'r'lady** I think a be	Indeed, I think he be
5.3.84	I pray thee now	I prithee now
5.3.123–4	blessed are they that	Happy are they which
5.4.1	I would to God that I might	I would I might
5.4.11	O the Lord that	O, that
5.4.12	but I pray God the	But I would the
5.4.22	O God that right	O, that right
5.5.8	God bless thy lungs	Bless thy lungs
5.5.41	God save thy grace	Save thy grace
5.5.43	God save thee	Save thee,
5.5.57	For God doth know	For heaven doth know
5.5.73	Yea Mary	Aye, marry

* **God's liggens** the precise meaning is unclear.
** **By'r'lady** By our lady, i.e. the Virgin Mary.

SCENE-BY-SCENE ANALYSIS

INDUCTION

The allegorical figure of Rumour opens the play, posing questions about the nature of truth and the power of language. Rumour's speech emphasizes confusion and uncertainty, not just in battle, but in the whole kingdom, divided by civil war. Rumour has given deliberately misleading information as to the outcome of the battle of Shrewsbury (at the end of *Henry IV Part I*) claiming that the king and Prince Henry were defeated and Hotspur triumphant, whereas in fact the opposite is true. The significance of past to present is clear and the inability to come to terms with the past leads to conflict in the future.

ACT 1 SCENE 1

Lines 1–146: Lord Bardolph reports to Northumberland that King Henry has been mortally wounded at Shrewsbury and that Northumberland's son, Hotspur, has killed Prince Henry. He compares their victory to "Caesar's fortunes," placing the events of the play in a wider historical context and raising the recurrent theme of time. It becomes clear, however, that he has not witnessed these events and is merely repeating what he has been told, reinforcing the arguments made by Rumour in the Induction. Travers and Morton bring different reports. Travers' information is also based on rumor, but suggests that the rebels have not done as well as Lord Bardolph believes. Despite Bardolph's attempts to reassure Northumberland, Morton reveals the truth: Hotspur is dead. Northumberland does not need to be told this, however, as he can see the truth in Morton's appearance: "the whiteness in thy cheek / Is apter than thy tongue to tell thy errand." When Bardolph refuses to believe him, Morton explains that he actually saw Prince Henry kill

Hotspur. He describes how the death of Hotspur, "whose spirit lent a fire / Even to the dullest peasant in his camp," caused the rebel soldiers to flee from the battle. Morton announces that the king's forces, led by Prince John and Westmorland, are on their way to fight Northumberland.

Lines 147–225: Playing on the theme of oppositions, Northumberland announces that "In poison there is physic": the death of his son has given him the strength to fight. "Enraged with grief," he makes a rousing declaration, calling for an end to everything ("Let order die!"), using the meta-theatrical image of a play that has gone on too long, "a ling'ring act," to describe the civil conflict. Bardolph and Morton urge him to be rational, arguing that they all knew the possible outcome, and that none of their apprehensions could have prevented Hotspur's "stiff-borne action" and death. Bardolph declares that they must go into battle again, and Morton agrees, adding that he has heard that the Archbishop of York is prepared to join the rebels. He argues that the presence of the Archbishop "Turns insurrection to religion," giving credence to their cause and fresh confidence to their troops.

ACT 1 SCENE 2

Lines 1–51: In direct contrast to the serious nature of the previous scene, Falstaff's disreputable behavior generates comedy. He delivers a long complaint about how, although he is "witty," he is also "the cause" of wit in others. He complains that his Page, a gift from Prince Henry, makes him look foolish, comparing himself to a "sow that hath o'erwhelmed all her litter but one." He continues to joke about the disparity in their sizes, referring to his Page as an "agate" and threatening to return him to the prince as an ornament. He also comments humorously on the youthful nature of the prince. He is interrupted by the arrival of the Lord Chief Justice, and tries to sneak away.

Lines 52–220: The Lord Chief Justice recognizes Falstaff from his role in a robbery (see *Henry IV Part I*), but his Servant tells him that

Falstaff did "good service" in the battle at Shrewsbury, another instance of rumor belying truth. The Lord Chief Justice sends his Servant to attract Falstaff's attention, but Falstaff tells his Page to pretend that he is deaf. This episode generates comedy but also highlights the wider theme of miscommunication. The Lord Chief Justice reminds Falstaff that, before the battle of Shrewsbury, he sent for him to answer to charges that might have resulted in the death penalty. Falstaff uses his military service as a defense, and the Lord Chief Justice concedes that this "hath a little gilded over" his part in the robbery. He warns Falstaff that he should stay out of trouble and suggests that he should act more appropriately, reinforcing the sustained images of opposing youth and age: Falstaff's "white beard" contrasts with his earlier references to the prince's youthful, beardless countenance. The Lord Chief Justice wishes the prince had a "better companion." Falstaff continues to antagonize him until he leaves. Falstaff then expresses his intention to profit from the wars, ironically echoing Northumberland's claim that "In poison there is physic" with his intention to "turn diseases to commodity."

ACT 1 SCENE 3

The Archbishop of York, Hastings, Mowbray, and Lord Bardolph discuss the preparations of the rebels and the odds on their success. Mowbray sees the need to fight, but questions whether their numbers are strong enough. Hasting reports that they have "five and twenty thousand men," and that they are in "hope" of Northumberland joining them. Lord Bardolph questions whether their army will be strong enough without Northumberland's forces, and suggests that they wait until they are certain of his support, revealing his cautious nature as he warns against "Conjecture, expectation and surmise." In contrast, Hastings is optimistic, insisting that the king must divide and therefore weaken his powers by fighting the French, the Welsh, and the rebels at the same time. York announces that they should proclaim their cause publicly, suggesting that the English people are "sick of their own choice" of king, and commenting scathingly that they are treating Henry in the same way as they treated Richard II. He concludes that "Past and to come seems best; things present worst," again emphasizing the theme of time and its effects.

ACT 2 SCENE 1

Lines 1–117: Hostess Quickly has summoned two officers, Fang and Snare, to arrest Falstaff, who she claims has "stabbed" her in his refusal to pay the money he owes. In a long-winded speech, laden with unwitting sexual innuendo, she describes how Falstaff has wronged her, and how he "cares not what mischief he doth, if his weapon be out." Falstaff arrives, accompanied by Bardolph (no relation to Lord Bardolph), whom he instructs to cut off Fang's head, and throw the "quean" (whore), Hostess Quickly, into the gutter. A noisy fight breaks out, which is interrupted by the arrival of the Lord Chief Justice. He chastises Falstaff, who should be on his way to York by now. Hostess Quickly complains about his behavior and the money he owes her. Falstaff pretends that she is mad, but the Lord Chief Justice is unmoved, showing his understanding of Falstaff's character and immunity to his fabrications and charm. He commands him to pay his debts, and Falstaff takes the Hostess aside as Gower enters.

Lines 118–172: While the Lord Chief Justice asks Gower for news, Falstaff persuades the Hostess to pawn her "plate and tapestry" to lend him yet more money, and arranges that the prostitute Doll Tearsheet will join him that evening for supper at the tavern. Falstaff is left with the Lord Chief Justice and Gower, who ignore him while they discuss the king's affairs.

ACT 2 SCENE 2

For the first time in the play, we see a member of the royal household: so far, the narrative, and therefore audience interest, has focused on the rebels and Falstaff. Even now, we only hear of the king through report, a device suggesting that, despite its eponymous title, the play is about more than Henry IV; concerning itself instead with his country and people, and the development of the character of Prince Henry. The prince is with Poins, one of his former, disreputable, companions. The prince complains that he is "weary" and torn between his old ways and his new responsibilities. He describes how his "heart bleeds" because of his father's illness, but that he is unable to show his true feelings, because, like Poins, people would think that he was being "a most princely hypocrite." Bardolph brings a nonsensical letter to Prince Henry from Falstaff. When the prince learns that Falstaff will be dining with Doll Tearsheet at the tavern that evening, he and Poins decide to disguise themselves as waiters so as to see Falstaff "in his true colours," emphasizing that Henry has yet to complete his metamorphosis from reprobate to royal prince.

ACT 2 SCENE 3

Northumberland urges his wife and widowed daughter-in-law to support him in his decision to fight the king, but Lady Percy begs him not to go to war. She reminds him that he did not go when Hotspur needed his support, effectively leaving him to die. Her grief is evident, and her description of the noble Hotspur, "the glass / Wherein the noble youth did dress themselves," serves to contrast with Prince Henry, who, while in the process of becoming a more responsible and honorable character, is still attracted to his old, irresponsible lifestyle. Northumberland is swayed by Lady Percy's arguments, showing his weakness as an ally in the rebels' cause. He agrees to go to Scotland while the first stages of the battle are under way.

ACT 2 SCENE 4

Once again, the low-status characters provide comic contrast to the events of the main plot, while reinforcing some of its key themes and concerns. This scene also serves to establish the growing estrangement between Falstaff and the prince.

Lines 1–207: Two waiters discuss the arrangements for Falstaff's meal, and go to find the disguises for Prince Henry and Poins. Hostess Quickly and Doll Tearsheet arrive, followed by Falstaff, and a humorous, bawdy exchange follows between them all. There are a number of joking references to venereal disease, a subject that is returned to throughout the scene and which, although comic, serves as a metaphor for the wider corruption of the kingdom. They are interrupted by a waiter who informs Falstaff that "Ancient Pistol" has asked to speak to him. When Pistol enters, the conversation becomes more riotous and confusing, compounded by Pistol's nonsensical speeches and threats against Doll Tearsheet, to which she replies with bawdy indignation. The emphasis on Pistol's and Bardolph's military titles reminds the audience of wider events, but Doll's mockery of Pistol, "You a captain?" contrasts with the more serious soldiery in the play. Bardolph tells Pistol to leave before it "grow[s] to a brawl" but, when he tries to throw him out, Pistol draws his sword. Despite Doll's protests, Falstaff draws as well, and Pistol is driven out. Doll Tearsheet sympathizes with Falstaff and, although her language is rough, it is also strangely tender, revealing a gentler side to Falstaff in his relationship with her. The Musicians arrive, and Falstaff invites Doll to sit on his knee. She good-naturedly asks him when he is going to "leave fighting" and "begin to patch up" his "old body for heaven," one of the increasing number of references to Falstaff's age.

Lines 208–355: Prince Henry and Poins enter, disguised. As they listen in, Doll questions Falstaff about them, reinforcing the theme of misrepresentation/rumor as he describes Henry as a "shallow young fellow" and dismisses Poins' reputed wit as being "as thick as Tewkesbury mustard." Finally, Falstaff recognizes the prince and Poins, and Henry reveals angrily that they have heard everything. As Falstaff tries to make excuses, they are interrupted by Peto, who reports that the king is at court and that there is a great deal of military activity under way: "weak and wearied" messengers are arriving from the north, and "a dozen captains" are searching for Falstaff to take command of his troops. Henry is ashamed that he has "idly" wasted "precious time" when the "tempest of commotion, like the south / Borne with black vapour, doth begin to melt." His language provides a sudden, serious note and the previous humor is forgotten in his brief, dismissive "goodnight" to Falstaff. Falstaff takes a fond farewell of Hostess Quickly and Doll Tearsheet.

ACT 3 SCENE 1

Late at night, the king is occupied with the business of war. He sends his Page with letters and embarks on a soliloquy that reveals his troubled mind, a technique that moves the audience from the previously distanced presentation of the character to a position of sudden, intimate insight. He dwells on how his "poorest subjects" are "at this hour asleep," comparing the simple lives of everyday people with the overbearing responsibilities of kingship: "Uneasy lies the head that wears a crown." Surrey and Warwick arrive, and King Henry compares his kingdom to a "body" that is infected with "rank diseases," echoing the imagery of the previous scene. He wishes he could know the future, and then considers the past, reinforcing the theme of time as he dwells on how Richard II and Northumberland had once been "great friends" and then, "two years after / Were they at wars," and how "but eight years since" Northumberland had been his own ally, only to betray him. He reminds them how Richard prophesied "this same time's condition / And the division of our amity." Warwick reasons that Richard could guess that Northumberland might betray Henry, having betrayed him. Focusing once more on the present, the king reports that "the bishop and Northumberland / Are fifty thousand strong," but Warwick responds that "Rumour doth double / Like the voice and echo," and urges Henry to go to bed before he makes himself more unwell. Henry agrees, comforting himself with the thought that once the "inward wars" of his kingdom are over, he will make his long-planned pilgrimage "unto the Holy Land."

ACT 3 SCENE 2

Justices Shallow and Silence await the arrival of Falstaff in Gloucestershire (a diversion from his march to York). This inclusion of characters from rural, "middle-class" England serves to emphasize the country-wide impact of the civil war, providing a contrast to the city and court, and the diametric of nobles and low-status characters seen so far. The presentation of Shallow and Silence is gently mocking: their names characterize their conversational styles, as Shallow talks endlessly about his past and his previous acquaintance with Falstaff, and Silence says very little. Underlying this mild humor, however, their preoccupation with the past echoes that of the king, and their constant return to the theme of death emphasizes the growing focus on mortality in the play.

They are interrupted by Bardolph and Falstaff, who inspect the men that Shallow and Silence have assembled for recruitment. Comedy is generated through the recruits' names and corresponding characters: "Mouldy," "Wart," and "Feeble," for example, and the humor that Falstaff derives from this. When Falstaff goes to dinner with Silence and Shallow, Bardolph accepts bribes from two recruits to ensure that they will not have to join up. When the others return, he tells Falstaff, who praises him and avoids selecting these men, revealing Falstaff's essentially corrupt nature. The scene ends with Falstaff's soliloquy, in which he mocks his old acquaintance, Shallow, and claims that he will make some money from him in the future, "if" he returns from the wars, a qualification that reminds us of the play's increasing concerns with mortality.

ACT 4 SCENE 1

Lines 1–185: The Archbishop of York meets with Mowbray and Hastings in Gaultree forest to prepare for battle. They have sent scouts to find out the strength of the king's armies. The Archbishop tells them that he has received a letter from Northumberland, claiming that he cannot raise satisfactory support and will not be joining them. A Messenger arrives with the news that the king's men are "scarcely off a mile" and that his armies number about thirty thousand. As Mowbray urges the others to battle, they are approached by Westmorland, acting as emissary from Prince John. Westmorland addresses the Archbishop, reminding him of his holy position and suggesting that the role of a "reverend father" is to sustain peace. He asks why the Archbishop has turned to "the harsh and boisterous tongue of war." The Archbishop returns to the recurring image of disease as he describes how the country has been brought "into a burning fever / And we must bleed for it." He argues that he has "justly weighed" the arguments for and against war, but that the king's refusal to hear the "griefs" of his subjects has left him no choice. Westmorland reiterates that it is not the Archbishop's role to involve himself, but Mowbray argues that it is the role of "all / That feel the bruises of the days before," emphasizing once again the influence of the past. Westmorland agrees to take a "schedule" of the rebels' "general grievances" to Prince John.

Lines 186–362: Mowbray worries that, even if they can succeed in a peaceful resolution, the king will make their families suffer in the future, but the Archbishop argues that the king has learned that sustaining grievances from generation to generation leads to greater troubles and that he is convinced that the king will "wipe his tables clean / And keep no tell-tale to his memory." Westmorland returns and invites them to meet with Prince John. The prince arrives and, like Westmorland, suggests that the Archbishop has no place in "Turning the word to sword and life to death." The rebels remind Prince John of the list of grievances that they sent him and ask him to "answer them directly." The prince argues that his "father's purposes have been mistook," but promises that "these griefs shall be with speed redressed." He calls for the rebels to discharge their armies, promising that the royal forces will do the same. They all toast each other, and the rebel soldiers are heard cheering the "word of peace." The prince sends Westmorland to discharge the royal army. He returns to report that the prince's men will not leave until they have heard him give the order, just as Hastings returns to announce that the rebel armies have dispersed. Westmorland arrests the rebels for "high treason" and, when they protest, the prince reminds them that he promised to redress their grievances, and that he will do this "with a most Christian care," but that they are traitors to the king and will be executed.

Lines 363–480: Falstaff meets with a rebel knight, Coleville, and persuades him to surrender, relying on his false reputation for having killed Hotspur (see *Henry IV Part I*). Prince John and his followers arrive, and the prince accuses Falstaff of keeping out of the way until everything is over. Falstaff argues that he has, with "pure and immaculate valour," taken Coleville prisoner, but the prince remains cynical. Westmorland brings the news that the rebels have retreated, and Prince John sends Coleville to be executed. Falstaff asks permission to go to Gloucester and begs the prince to give a "good report" of him to the court. Prince John agrees, reluctantly, and leaves. Alone, Falstaff muses on the prince's dislike of him, blaming his "sober-blooded" disposition on the fact that he "drinks no wine." He dwells on the faults of those who do not drink, and, through this round-about and lengthy diatribe, passes negative comment on both the prince and King Henry, who both have "cold blood" and are like "lean, sterile and bare land." He leaves for Gloucester, aiming to get money from Justice Shallow.

ACT 4 SCENE 2

Lines 1–82: Although extremely ill, King Henry talks with Warwick and two of his sons, Clarence and Gloucester, about his plans for a crusade once the rebels are "underneath the yoke of government." He asks after Prince Henry and advises Clarence that, as the brother who is closest to Henry, he must act as guide and mediator to him. He asks why Clarence is not with Henry and learns that he is dining with Poins. The king complains that his son is "overspread" with "weeds," but Warwick argues that "in the perfectness of time" Henry will "Cast off his followers."

Lines 83–228: Westmorland brings news from Prince John that the rebel leaders have been executed and that "peace puts forth her olive everywhere." Harcourt follows, announcing that Northumberland and Lord Bardolph are defeated. Despite his joy, the king grows more unwell. He calls for his crown to be set upon his pillow. Prince Henry arrives and Clarence reports that their father is "Exceeding ill." The others withdraw, leaving Henry with his sleeping father. The prince sees the crown and muses on the pressures of kingship, seeing the crown as a "Golden care" and echoing his father's words in Act 3

Scene 1, as he considers how much sounder common men must sleep without the "pinch" of "majesty." Believing King Henry to be dead, he places the crown on his own head before leaving.

The king wakes and calls for his sons and followers, demanding to know why he has been left alone. Clarence explains that Henry was there. Seeing his crown missing, the king sends Warwick to find Prince Henry, furious at his apparent haste to succeed to the throne. As Warwick searches, the king laments sons who "revolt" against their fathers. Warwick finds Henry weeping in the next room. The prince returns, holding the crown, and the king sends everyone out so that they may speak privately.

Lines 229–379: Angry and disappointed, the king accuses Prince Henry of wishing him dead. He claims that Henry did not need to steal the crown, as it will be his anyway "after some few hours," and laments that he will be leaving his "poor kingdom" in the hands of a sinful, irresponsible king. Deeply moved, Henry replaces the crown on his father's pillow and kneels beside him. He explains that he thought his father had died, and that this thought "struck" his heart "cold." He tells the king of the speech that he made to the crown, rebuking it for placing the burden of care on his father to the extent that it "Hast eat the bearer up." He describes how he put the crown on, not out of greed, but to "try" it as "an enemy," and to test his own response, looking for "pride" or an inclination to enjoy "the might of it." Instead, he feels the same "awe and terror" of any subject in the face of its power.

King Henry asks his son to sit beside him, promising that however "troublesome" the crown sat on his own head, it will "descend with better quiet" upon the prince. Echoing Northumberland's meta-theatrical imagery in Act 1 Scene 1, he describes his reign as "a scene / Acting that argument" of civil war. He describes his own ascension to the throne as "purchased," but argues that it "falls upon" Prince Henry "in a more fairer sort." He warns his son that he is inheriting a troubled kingdom "since griefs are green," and advises him to unite the country through "foreign quarrels." He dwells on "how [he] came by the crown," but the prince reassures him that he "won it, wore it, kept it," and that when he himself inherits it, he will rightfully maintain possession of it. Prince John arrives, accompanied by Warwick, and they take the king to the "Jerusalem chamber," where he wishes to die, having had it prophesied that he "should not die but in Jerusalem."

ACT 5 SCENE 1

Falstaff is greeted by Shallow, who insists that he stay the night. Briefly alone, Falstaff mocks Shallow for his resemblance to his own serving men, observing that "wise bearing or ignorant carriage is caught, as men take diseases . . . therefore let men take heed of their company," an ironic statement in the light of Prince Henry's forthcoming rejection of Falstaff.

ACT 5 SCENE 2

The Lord Chief Justice and Warwick discuss the death of King Henry IV and their own positions. Warwick agrees that the Lord Chief Justice is right to be concerned as the new king, Henry V, "loves you not." Henry's three brothers arrive and Warwick observes that Henry has the "worst" temperament of all of the old king's sons. The two men worry for the future, fearing that "all will be overturned." The princes, Warwick, and the Lord Chief Justice are discussing their sorrow at recent events, when the new king himself enters. Henry's language reflects the change in his character: he shows humility in his description of how "This new and gorgeous garment majesty" does not sit "easy" on him.

He sees that his brothers are mourning, but also that they seem afraid of him and he reassures them that he intends to look after them: "I'll be your father and your brother too." His listeners seem unconvinced, and the Lord Chief Justice openly acknowledges that he is aware that Henry does not like him. Henry asks why he should, when in the past he has seen fit to "Rate, rebuke, and roughly send to prison / Th'immediate heir of England." The Lord Chief Justice replies that, in the past, he was acting on behalf of "law and justice" in the name of Henry IV. He asks Henry what, under those circumstances, he did wrong. Surprisingly, Henry replies that the Lord Chief

Justice was right, and insists that he wishes him to continue in his current role. He gives the Lord Chief Justice his hand and assures them all that although his blood has "flowed in vanity" in the past, it will "flow henceforth in formal majesty," an image which signals a shift in focus from the all-dominating past to a more hopeful future.

ACT 5 SCENE 3

In a moment of bathos, the action focuses on the drunken Falstaff, Shallow, and Silence, the latter of whom keeps bursting into song. They are interrupted by Pistol, who claims that he has important news, but exasperates everyone by talking nonsense and arguing with Silence. Eventually, he announces that Falstaff's "tender lamb-kin," Henry, has become king. Falstaff is delighted, describing him-self as "fortune's steward" in anticipation of being a favorite of the new king, and calls for Bardolph to saddle their horses. Falstaff's lack of grief at the old king's death and his selfish response to the news show he is incapable of change.

ACT 5 SCENE 4

Hostess Quickly and Doll Tearsheet are manhandled along by two Beadles who have arrested Doll for prostitution. There is comedy in the exchange of insults, but the episode serves to represent a restora-tion of law and order under the rule of the new king.

ACT 5 SCENE 5

Preparations are under way for the coronation, and Falstaff, Shal-low, Bardolph, and Pistol await the arrival of the king. Full of self-importance, Falstaff tells them that he will "make the king do [them] grace," and promises Shallow that he will soon be able to repay the thousand pounds that he has borrowed. Henry V enters, followed by his royal train, and Falstaff calls out to him. Henry does not acknowledge him, instead directing the Lord Chief Justice to "speak to that vain man." When Falstaff persists, Henry responds "I know thee not, old man," and advises him to "Fall to thy prayers." He describes his past existence with Falstaff and the others as a "dream" from which he has woken. He makes it clear that he has "turned away [from his] former self" and, although he will make him an allowance, Henry banishes Falstaff until he reforms his character.

The king and his train leave. Falstaff retains the hope that this is merely "a colour" on the part of Henry, returning to the play's original premise of the distance between words and truth, but Shallow (and the audience) can see that this is not so. As they leave, they are stopped by Prince John and the Lord Chief Justice, who orders that Falstaff and his companions be taken to prison. Despite Falstaff's protests, they are led away, emphasizing the new regime of law and justice under Henry V. The Lord Chief Justice and Prince John discuss the future, foreseeing that the country will soon unite in war against France.

EPILOGUE

The Epilogue provides a lighthearted conclusion as the speaker expresses his hope that the audience approved of the play, and promises that "our humble author will continue the story," outlining some of the events in *Henry V*.

HENRY IV IN PERFORMANCE: THE RSC AND BEYOND

The best way to understand a Shakespeare play is to see it or ideally to participate in it. By examining a range of productions, we may gain a sense of the extraordinary variety of approaches and interpretations that are possible—a variety that gives Shakespeare his unique capacity to be reinvented and made "our contemporary" four centuries after his death.

We begin with a brief overview of the theatrical and cinematic life of the two parts of *Henry IV*, offering historical perspectives on how the two plays have been performed. We then analyze in more detail a series of productions of *Henry IV Part II* staged over the last half-century by the Royal Shakespeare Company. The sense of dialogue between productions that can only occur when a company is dedicated to the revival and investigation of the Shakespeare canon over a long period, together with the uniquely comprehensive archival resource of promptbooks, program notes, reviews, and interviews held on behalf of the RSC at the Shakespeare Birthplace Trust in Stratford-upon-Avon, allows an "RSC stage history" to become a crucible in which the chemistry of the play can be explored.

We then go to the horse's mouth. Modern theater is dominated by the figure of the director. He or she must hold together the whole play, whereas the actor must concentrate on his or her part. The director's viewpoint is therefore especially valuable. Shakespeare's plasticity is wonderfully revealed when we hear the directors of two highly successful productions answering the same questions in very different ways. And finally, we offer the actor's perspective: a view of the two parts of the play through the eyes of Prince Hal.

FOUR CENTURIES OF *HENRY IV*: AN OVERVIEW

Henry IV Part I was probably written and performed between 1596 and 1597 with *Part II* following a year later. The first performances of which records survive were at court in 1612–13 when a total of twenty plays were presented to celebrate the marriage of James I's daughter Elizabeth to Frederick, the Elector of Palatine. They are listed as *The Hotspurre* and *Sir John Falstaffe*, and were only later identified as the two parts of Shakespeare's *Henry IV*. These alternative titles suggest that both were originally seen in terms of their star parts rather than as a political study of kingship with Prince Hal at the center. As scholars and theater historians have pointed out:

> That change of emphasis required a change of format. It takes both parts of *Henry IV* followed by *Henry V* to make Prince Hal into a fully-fledged hero, or anti-hero, and it was not until the mid-twentieth century that an influential cycle of these plays . . . was staged in the English theatre.[1]

Until this point the plays were performed individually and, although *Part II* was clearly designed as a sequel to *Part I*—probably in order to capitalize on the enormous and immediate popularity of the first play—there is little evidence to suggest that they were performed in sequence. Numerous contemporary references and reprints of the Quarto editions all point to their popularity and success, however. The writer Nicholas Breton mentions seeing "the play of Ancient Pistol,"[2] and Leonard Digges' prefatory poem to the 1640 edition of Shakespeare's poems provides further evidence of their popularity:

> . . . let but Falstaff come,
> Hal, Poins, the rest, you scarce shall have a room,
> All is so pestered . . .

In his commendatory poem to the Folio edition of Beaumont and Fletcher (1647), Sir Thomas Palmer claims he could "tell how long / Falstaff from cracking nuts have kept the throng."

Falstaff was originally played either by company clown Will Kempe or comic actor Thomas Pope, while Prince Hal was almost certainly played by Richard Burbage, the leading tragedian with Shakespeare's acting company, the Lord Chamberlain's (later the King's) Men. John Lowin took over the role of Falstaff: "before the Wars Lowin used to act, with mighty applause Falstaff."[3] During the Interregnum from 1642 to 1660 the theaters were technically closed, although various means were employed to get around the prohibition on plays, such as the introduction of music and dancing into sketches from popular plays known as drolls; a collection of twenty-seven of these, *The Wits, or Sport Upon Sport*, by Francis Kirkman, was published in 1662 with three featuring episodes from Shakespeare's plays, including *The Bouncing Knight, or the Robbers Robbed*, centered on Falstaff's exploits. The frontispiece illustration places Falstaff and the Hostess in prominent positions.

Henry IV Part I continued to be popular after the Restoration and was one of the first plays performed by Thomas Killigrew's King's Company in 1660. Samuel Pepys' diary records his attendance at no fewer than four performances over the period 1660–68. The play's main attractions were still Hotspur and Falstaff. Thomas Betterton, the great Restoration actor-manager, played Hotspur in 1682, with "wild impatient starts" and "fierce and flashing fire,"[4] but in the 1700 revival he took on the role of Falstaff. Thomas Davies records how "the versatility of Betterton's genius was never more conspicuous than in his resigning the choleric Hotspur, in his declining years, and assuming the humour and gaiety of Falstaff, in which he is said to have been full as acceptable to the public as in the former."[5] In contrast to most Shakespearean revivals in the period, it underwent relatively few changes apart from textual cuts of long political speeches, the Welsh dialogue and song, and much of the mock trial in the tavern. Betterton's continued popularity as Falstaff was largely responsible for a revival of *Part II* during the eighteenth century, in which the star turns were Falstaff and Justice Shallow.

In the next generation, James Quin, who had previously played Hotspur and the king, was the most notable Falstaff. David Garrick played Hotspur on five occasions, dressed "in a laced frock and a Ramilie wig,"[6] but was plainly unsuited to the role, and the part was taken over by Spranger Barry. One of the theatrical highlights seems to have been Falstaff carrying Hotspur offstage:

No joke ever raised such loud and repeated mirth, in the galleries, as Sir John's labour in getting the body of Hotspur on his back . . . Quin had little or no difficulty in perching Garrick upon his shoulders, who looked like a dwarf on the back of a giant. But oh! how he tugged and toiled to raise Barry from the ground![7]

His successor, John Henderson, reportedly had so much difficulty with his Hotspur that a small gang of "Falstaff's ragamuffins" were used instead to bear the body offstage.[8] Other late eighteenth-century Falstaffs included at least one woman, Mrs. Webb, who "excelled in corpulent and grotesque characters" in Norwich in 1786.[9]

John Philip Kemble played Hotspur at Covent Garden in the early nineteenth century and his brother, Stephen, was one of a number of actors to play Falstaff without padding, although William Hazlitt remarked of his performance, "Every fat man cannot represent a great man."[10] The American actor James Henry Hackett played the part in England and America for forty years, and his Hotspurs included John Philip and Charles Kemble, as well as Edmund Kean and William Charles Macready. He received mixed reviews; *The Athenaeum* reported:

His is the best Falstaff that has been seen for many a day,— which, however, is not saying much for it. But it has positive merits that deserve recognition. He did not . . . reach the full conception which Shakespeare has here embodied . . . but he aimed at it, and accomplished much; his soliloquy on honour, in particular, was well delivered, and, take him for all in all, we are disposed to give him a cordial welcome.[11]

His identification with the role was such that he became known as "Falstaff Hackett."

In 1821 a spectacular production of *Henry IV Part II* with Macready as King Henry and Charles Kemble as Prince Hal included a magnificent staging of the coronation procession as a tribute to the coronation of George IV. Kemble's production of *Part I* in 1824 with himself as Hotspur was mainly noted for the historical accuracy of costumes and sets, which included "the King's Chamber in the old Palace of Westminster; the inn-yard at Rochester with the castle, by night; Hotspur's Camp; a distant view of Coventry; and Shrewsbury from the field of battle."[12] Samuel Phelps' production at Sadler's Wells in 1846 was similarly spectacular:

> All has been done with a lavish and judicious hand, without a regard to cost or aught beside, save the desire of gratifying the public. The accoutrements, armour, and trappings worn by the several armies in the fourth and fifth acts are indeed splendid, and the minutest care has been shown in the arrangement of the costumes, even to the very crests of the different parties. The battle was admirably managed—the scenery was entirely new, and elicited much applause.[13]

The 1864 revival at Drury Lane which included the Glendower scene in full for the first time was distinguished by Phelps' Falstaff: "He lays stress not on Falstaff's sensuality, but on the lively intellect that stands for soul as well as mind in his gross body," in a performance marked by "a smooth delicate touch that stamps the knight distinctly as a man well born and bred."[14] Phelps' remarkable doubling of the king and Justice Shallow in *Part II* later that year earned further praise.[15]

Herbert Beerbohm Tree's 1896 production at the Haymarket Theatre used a fuller text of the play and was well received by the critics, with the exception of George Bernard Shaw. William Archer praised the overall conception—"There has been no nearer approach in our day to the complete performance of a Shakespearian drama."[16] Of Tree's performance, *The Athenaeum* reported: "it is the fat knight himself that comes before us."[17] Shaw, however, thought that "Mr Tree only wants one thing to make him an excellent Falstaff, and that is to get born over again as unlike himself as possible."[18]

Victorian spectacle went out of fashion in the early twentieth century influenced by the ideas of William Poel and the English Stage Society, which favored performances on a thrust stage with minimal scenery and faster-paced, fluid action.

History does not update in the same way as the comedies and tragedies that have lent themselves to a variety of settings, costumes, and periods. The effect on the history plays has been to emphasize

1. Herbert Beerbohm Tree as Falstaff in his 1896 production at the Haymarket Theatre. *The Athenaeum* reported: "it is the fat knight himself that comes before us."

their historicity. Between 1901 and 1906 Frank Benson staged a cycle of Shakespeare's history plays for the first time at the Stratford-upon-Avon festival season which omitted *Henry IV Part I* but included *King John*, *Richard II*, *Henry IV Part II*, *Henry V*, *Henry VI Part II*, and *Richard III*. W. B. Yeats was impressed by the way in which "play supports play"[19] when presented in this way. *Henry IV Part I* was included in the new cycle in 1905, as was Marlowe's *Edward II*. In 1921 Barry Jackson had staged both parts of *Henry IV* on the same day (23 April) in Birmingham. The two parts of *Henry IV* were the first plays performed after the opening of the New Memorial Theatre in Stratford by the Prince of Wales in 1932— *Part I* in the afternoon and *Part II* in the evening.

In 1935 Robert Atkins and Sydney Carroll staged a production of *Henry IV Part I* with the popular vaudeville comedian George Robey as Falstaff. Despite his lack of classical training many critics were impressed by his performance; Herbert Farjeon reflected that "We learn from Mr Robey's Falstaff many things. One of them is that it is a tremendous advantage to have Shakespeare's clowns . . . played by men who are funny *before they begin* . . . Mr Sydney Carroll's brilliant casting of Falstaff should put an end to the long dreary line of legitimate actors who have made soggy hay of Shakespeare's comics."[20] However, *The New Statesman* regarded Robey's Falstaff as an "old soak rather than the fallen gentleman . . . nothing more than a super-Bardolph."[21]

John Burrell's production a decade later at the New Theatre was warmly received:

> *Feliciter audax* [pleasingly audacious] is, indeed, the phrase for Mr Burrell's production. Choosing not to adopt the uninterrupted flow of the Elizabethan method, he closes each scene with a moment of dumb-show, shadowy and significant. I shall never forget Glendower, standing at the window (the actor is Harcourt Williams, who knows how to stand)— standing and staring after Hotspur as he gallops away, with the two women weeping at his feet while we know what they guess, that they will never see Hotspur again.[22]

Harcourt Williams' performance was not the only one to be widely praised. Ralph Richardson's Falstaff was universally admired:

> a grand buffoon and rapscallion in *Part I*, proceeded in *Part II* to a still richer understanding which could catch the sombre

2. Ralph Richardson as Falstaff and Laurence Olivier as Justice Shallow in John Burrell's 1945 New Theatre production: Ralph Richardson's Falstaff was universally admired, and Laurence Olivier triumphed as Hotspur in *Part I* and Justice Shallow in *Part II*.

illumination of "Do not bid me remember mine end" and suggest, as Falstaffs rarely do, the attraction of the man for the Prince as well as the considerable brain behind the wit. This was a metamorphosis assisted by make-up but by no means entirely dependent on it: for Richardson's greatness—and I think the word is justifiable—in the part was a greatness of spirit that transcended the mere hulk of flesh.[23]

Laurence Olivier, meanwhile, played Hotspur in *Part I* and Justice Shallow in *Part II*, and triumphed in both.

But it was the 1951 presentation of the tetralogy of *Richard II*, *Henry IV Part I*, *Henry IV Part II*, and *Henry V* by Anthony Quayle, John Kidd, and Michael Redgrave at the Shakespeare Memorial Theatre that was to prove decisive in the plays' fortunes. Anthony Quayle explained the thinking behind the productions:

it seemed to us that the great epic theme of the Histories had become obscured through years of presenting the plays single, and many false interpretations had grown up, and come to be accepted, through star actors giving almost too persuasive and

3. The 1951 Shakespeare Memorial Theatre presented *Richard II*, *Henry IV Part I* and *Part II*, and *Henry V* as a tetralogy: with Harry Andrews as Henry IV and Richard Burton as Hal.

dominant performances of parts which the author intended to be by no means sympathetic.[24]

One critic suggested: "One will never again think of these plays as single entities, and when they are played as such we shall feel them to have been lopped."[25] Tanya Moiseiwitsch designed a single set of "plain unvarnished oak" that could be "embellished as the occasion demanded with props or with hangings" and "provided three acting spaces and a large variety of entrances; it allowed the action to move in an uninterrupted flow."[26] There *were* star performances though— "Mr Redgrave's poetic Richard and dazzling Hotspur, Mr Quayle's splendidly rich Falstaff and Mr Richard Burton's sultry intriguing Hal," as well as "Mr Harry Andrews's superb and masterly Boling-broke";[27] the balance was shifted decisively away from Hotspur and Falstaff toward Hal.

Douglas Seale directed both parts of *Henry IV* at the Old Vic in 1955 in productions admired for being "simple and direct and, while comparatively and mercifully static within each individual scene . . . they are driven with a brilliant sense of the narrative speed over all."[28] Again, a strong cast achieved unanimous praise, from Paul Rogers' Falstaff—"leaner and considerably dilapidated, is already some of the way downhill," to Robert Hardy's Prince—"a very strong and charming performance," while "John Neville makes a fine Hotspur and a whirlwind Pistol, and Paul Daneman an ominous Worcester followed, in a miraculous transformation, by an extremely funny Shallow, withered with senility and malice. Rachel Roberts and Gwen Cherrell draw fruitfully on Hogarth for Mistress Quickly and Doll Tearsheet."[29]

It has become the norm since then for the two plays of *Henry IV* to be performed together, often within the context of a larger cycle of Shakespeare's history plays. The resources required for such ambitious projects are only realistically available to the national subsidized companies, and productions by the RSC (discussed below) have constituted the majority of these. In 1986 Michael Bogdanov and Michael Pennington formed the English Shakespeare Company with the aim of promoting and presenting the works of Shakespeare both nationally and internationally. The inaugural production, *The Hen-*

rys, consisted of *Henry IV Part I* and *Part II* plus *Henry V*. The following year they presented *The Wars of the Roses*, comprising *Richard II*, *Henry IV Part I*, *Henry IV Part II*, *Henry V*, the three plays of *Henry VI* telescoped into two plays (*Henry VI: House of Lancaster*, *Henry VI: House of York*), and *Richard III*. The production toured successfully for two years, both within the UK and internationally. The company deliberately worked against the dominant mode of theatrical realism to present radical and exciting productions, designed to engage a modern audience:

> We would provide a space that would allow the plays to range over the centuries in imagery. We would free our, and the audiences' imaginations by allowing an eclectic mix of costumes and props, choosing a time and a place that was most appropriate for a character or a scene. Modern dress at one moment, medieval, Victorian or Elizabethan the next. We would use a kit of props . . . [which], as far as possible, would remain on stage. The means of transformation from one scene to the next would remain visible. No tricks up our sleeves (until we needed one). We would create a style that was essentially rough theatre, but would add, when we needed it, a degree of sophistication.[30]

The relatively few American productions of *Henry IV* have concentrated historically on *Part I*, focusing on the roles of Hotspur and Falstaff. Stuart Vaughan directed both parts which played in repertory at New York's Phoenix Theater in 1960: the emphasis on Eric Berry's widely praised, compelling Falstaff led to the accusation that it "might accurately be called 'The Decline and Fall of Sir John Falstaff, Fat Old Knight.'"[31] In 1993, Ron Daniels directed back-to-back stagings of *Part I* and *Part II* for the American Repertory Theater, updated to an American Civil War setting which enjoyed a mixed critical reception:

> Mr. Daniels has created a wildly anachronistic, culturally mixed salad in which different elements of Shakespeare's epic portrait are accorded theatrical analogues from wholly dis-

parate historical moments. The result, given visual life by John Conklin's time-traveling, slightly ragged scenic shorthand, is less disjunctive than one might expect.[32]

Barbara Gaines' 1999 production of both plays at Chicago's Shakespeare Repertory Theater was widely praised for its simple staging and strong performances. In 2003 Dakin Matthews conflated the texts of both plays in a production at Lincoln Center's Vivian Beaumont Theater, directed by Jack O'Brien. The resulting adaptation lasted nearly four hours with two intervals but compressed the action to create a fast-paced, fluid text. Kevin Kline's Falstaff was:

> made up to resemble a threadbare Santa Claus with a blimp of a prosthetic belly and a snowy beard, Mr. Kline looks like the most traditional Falstaff imaginable. The wonderful surprise is how he deviates from the convention of bluster and braggadocio. Mr. Kline has never had more of a chance to make a meal of the scenery. Instead, he delivers a finely measured performance that matches the actor's infinite resourcefulness with that of the character he plays.[33]

Remarkably, London's National Theatre did not stage a performance of *Henry IV* until Nicholas Hytner's production in 2005 played on a "roughly arrow-shaped stage" in the large Olivier Theatre. The production managed "to suggest the mighty sweep of the plays— their oscillation from uptight court to frowsty lowlife, from the frenetically urban to the peacefully pastoral, from the battlefield to the boozer—with depth and definition."[34] Michael Gambon was praised for the way he:

> wonderfully incorporates the contradictions of Falstaff. He looks like the kind of wily, drunken bohemian tramp that Just William would ill-advisedly let into the Brown household, where he would later be found comatose in the wine cellar. In the moveable feast of his accent, you hear the tones of a parvenu whose poshness is pretty precarious and inclined to slip

into saloon-bar bravado. This is not a sentimentalised fat knight. He's utterly out for himself, and the last thing we're treated to in *Part 1* is the sight of him shamelessly robbing two venerable corpses.[35]

Matthew McFadyen made a "shrewd witty prince," and David Bradley played the "haunted cadaverous king," while:

> The scenes in Gloucestershire are delectably comic, thanks to the great John Wood, whose Justice Shallow is a transcendent study in florid, nervously energetic self-delusion about a wild youth that he did not experience. He is delightfully partnered by Adrian Scarborough, who, as Silence, is like a little slip of death inadequately warmed up—until he gets a few glasses inside him, when he cannot be restrained from providing quavering, unwanted cabaret.[36]

The two parts of *Henry IV* with their broad cross section of scenes and characters have come to be regarded as a sort of national epic firmly established at the heart of the Shakespearean repertory. The most remarkable film version is Orson Welles' 1966 film adaptation, *Chimes at Midnight*, in which the entire tetralogy from *Richard II* to *Henry V* is telescoped into less than two hours. In 1938 Welles directed an unsuccessful play called *Five Kings* in which he had gathered all the Falstaff material from the *Henrys* and *The Merry Wives of Windsor*. This formed the basis of Welles' film, shot while he was supposedly making *Treasure Island*. As Scott McMillin suggests, "he was not interested in the historical epic formed by the histories; he was interested in Falstaff—or, perhaps more accurately, in a certain angle of vision which he thought of as Falstaffian."[37] The star-studded cast included Jeanne Moreau, Margaret Rutherford, John Gielgud (as Henry IV), with Ralph Richardson as the narrator. The film's brilliance lies in Welles' characteristically bravura film vocabulary and style. As McMillin puts it: "If Falstaff had made films, he would have made something like this one."[38]

The BBC Shakespeare version, by contrast, offers a conventional historical cycle of the second tetralogy (*Richard II*, *Henry IV Part I*,

Henry IV Part II, Henry V) made for television and directed by David Giles. Anthony Quayle, who had played Falstaff so successfully in 1951, reprised the role. The narrow focus of television does not, however, lend itself easily to the broad sweep of history:

> If cycle-thinking puts the realm and its rulers ahead of Fal-
> staff, and if the performance of Falstaff puts him well ahead of
> the realm and its rulers, trouble is brewing. Quayle's assured
> performance as Falstaff is the strongest element of the pro-
> duction, and the separate "sphere of intelligence" provided
> by his addresses to the audience happily interrupts the duti-
> ful effort to capture history in the space of the television stu-
> dio. He is in better control of the medium—and this makes
> Prince Hal's efforts to take better control of the kingdom seem
> second-rate.[39]

The English Shakespeare Company's highly politicized, eclectic *Wars of the Roses* was recorded for television in 1989.

AT THE RSC

The Disease of the Body Politic

The plays of *Henry IV* are pervaded by a sense of national disintegra-
tion—the curse on the usurper Bullingbrook for the sacrilegious act
of usurping and killing a king by divine right, Richard II. *Part I* ends
with the possibility of hope, of triumph for Henry and his seemingly
reclaimed son. From the start of *Part II*, however, we are aware of a
very different tone. The old England is dying—at court, tavern, and
on the battlefield:

> The second part of *Henry IV* presents actors with the difficulty
> of keeping up the theatrical energy through what is, in effect,
> one long "dying scene." There is a sense of the characters
> being all covered in cobwebs and disease, saying the same sorts
> of things as they said in *Part One*, but now it's all falling on deaf

ears. They are all older now, the country is going down in wrack and ruin, and the king is going with it.[40]

When thinking of *Henry IV Part II*, the words of another of Shakespeare's sacrilegious usurpers come to mind:

> There's nothing serious in mortality.
> All is but toys; renown and grace is dead,
> The wine of life is drawn, and the mere lees
> Is left this vault to brag of.   (*Macbeth*, Act 3 Scene 1)

What emerges in twentieth-century productions is an emphasis on this melancholic, elegiac aspect of the play, showing how it pervades all levels of society. The decay of the country stems from the top, the king's illness and his lack of a reliable heir to the throne in Hal, and displays itself in lawlessness:

> In *Part Two*, the whole country is afflicted by a mortal sickness. The London streets are filled with lawless mobs and unruly carnivals; . . . This is an England turbulent with decay . . . in which disease spreads through the whole body politic.[41]

> The three contrasting worlds of court, rebel camp and tavern run throughout both plays; they interlock dramatically and offer a panoramic view of the state of the country. As a national epic, the plays link high and low life, and their engagement with the condition of England provides great scope for directors and designers.[42]

It is notable that the two parts of *Henry IV* have not been radically reconceptualized by the RSC. Even in 2000, *Henry IV*'s traditional setting was sandwiched in between two thoroughly modern representations of *Richard II* and *Henry V*. The modernization of the play happens mainly in the representation of the characters. In postwar Britain, the ideal of chivalric death in battle had died out after two bloody world wars. The jingoism of the 1950s had evaporated by the 1960s and a new skeptical generation emerged, unconvinced by their politicians, and doubtful about the necessity for a monarchy at all. *Henry IV* therefore does not particularly lend itself to a modern setting, as the England represented in the play appears a long distant memory. This fact, especially in *Part II*—which contains so much dialogue evoking thoughts of days gone by, of pleasures experienced, but lost—often leads directors to add a feeling of nostalgia to productions, evoked by autumnal imagery. Mirroring the atmosphere and themes of the play, that time of the year when life in nature begins to die reflects the death of the "old order." In 1964, Peter Hall used this autumnal metaphor to great effect:

> Mr Hall has a clear preference for autumn over the other seasons of the year . . . The play itself is autumnal. The leaves are falling, and on all sides life is coming to an end. The King is dying, his conscience incurably sick and his crusade only metaphorically achieved. Falstaff is ageing, his wit not quite what it has been, and his body—like Doll Tearsheet's—is diseased . . . Where honour is in question, it is now six of one, half-a-dozen of the other. Old Double is dead, and the apples are ripening in the straw. Lancastrian England is sick with internal division, and there is no longer a chivalry to divide. It is crying out for new blood, even if more blood must be spilt to acquire it. Peace will be dearly bought, and it will not last for long. More will be required than two chantries, a hospice, and an agonized prayer before a battle to exorcise the curse of regicide.[43]

> In the second part the tone darkens into elegy, and so far as the comic scenes are concerned the result is pure gain, for without some such deliberate change in mood the later revels can appear as mere echoes of their counterparts in the first play. As it is, they sometimes develop an almost Chekhovian atmosphere; there is a sense that time is running out and that the best days are already past.[44]

As these reviews of Peter Hall's production indicate, *Henry IV Part II* has lent itself to Chekhovian interpretation. The characters walk a tightrope at all times, with farcical, absurdist comedy on the one side and abject tragedy on the other. The passage of time is a constant preoccupation, as is the desultory and unsuccessful search for life's meaning. The play has an emphasis on moments of epiphany and illumination, a demand for psychological realism, and melancholy surrender to inevitability.

The work of Bertolt Brecht also proved a source of inspiration for Hall. In examining the brutal mechanics of power that moved behind Shakespeare's history plays, Hall also laid special emphasis on the social detail, showing the effect that politics have on the ordinary people who inhabit this world:

> The allegorical figure of Rumour was turned into the realistic figure of a maimed soldier, but Henry Knowles' snarling performance and the uncannily successful echoic effects restored the symbolic quality.[45]

> What the Royal Shakespeare's producing triumvirate—Peter Hall, John Barton, Clifford Williams—have done is to turn the Histories into Brecht. Again and again, as unshaven, carefully muddied soldiery pulled their little canteen-wagons into stark, straw-strewn farmyards, I looked for Mother Courage to follow with her children. The result is impressive in many respects. It rationalises and humanises those miles of blank verse, explaining, motivating, lending historical and psychological solidity.[46]

This Brechtian element was also present in the performance of Ian Holm, who played Hal. He appeared to many reviewers to take on Brecht's idea of actors alienating themselves from rather than inhabiting their roles. In doing so he created a coldly analytic Hal, an observer taking part, rather than engaged in the action of the play. He was criticized by many reviewers for his reading of the part, but several others thought that this style of acting suited Hal's character, who does indeed appear manipulative, cold, and disengaged at times, and who remains an enigma.

Terry Hands in 1975 took on the Brechtian level of social detail and successfully evoked the epic nature of *Henry IV Part II* by his inventive symbolism:

> it brings the best out of Terry Hands, whose direction expresses a joy in the sheer diversity of experience. He is not out to disclose any grand design, but to show all kinds of unconnected things happening simultaneously; and he shows his hand immediately by casting the Rumour Prologue for a chorus of hooded figures who then disperse into separate characters. What most holds the production together is its sense of time. It is divided between past and future, looking back regretfully to the straight heroics and gaiety of *Part One*, and forward to the new age which will follow the king's death. Rightly, the Eastcheap scenes are played as an elegiac echo.[47]

> One curious trait in Hands's directorial character is that when he faces scenes which require plain, even pedantic, storytelling, he has a tendency to get bored with them and to stray into ornate symbolism . . . he presents us with some extraordinary images. The regional rebels cluster like black ravens, to pick the carcass of a king (and a kingdom) who is by no means dead. When Hal is crowned, Hands lays a glistening white carpet across the stage with the courtiers lined up one side and Falstaff's friends roughly gathered on the other. Then Hal appears, covered from nose to toenail in gleaming gold. He walks downstage, to RSC trumpets, and raises his golden visor to speak to Falstaff: and reject him.[48]

In an episodic play that covers the whole gamut of society—from court, to tavern, to rural Gloucestershire, to the battlefield—a strong directorial vision and an excellent designer are needed to hold the strands of the play together in a unified way that doesn't detract from the variety of tone. Adrian Noble's production in 1991 had a versatile staging which:

> heighten[ed] the play's wide variety of tones, from the grim Expressionist intensity with which the whole milling cast deliver Rumour's many tongued Prologue, through the many

sight-gags which erupt round Albie Woodington's crazed leather bike-boy of a Pistol in the Eastcheap scenes, to the elegiac rhythms of Shallow's misty, autumnal Gloucestershire, with its slow-motion apple pickers and beekeepers. In a dream-like, non-naturalistic touch, the corpse of Henry is borne off-stage through this last landscape, suggesting that none of the play's seemingly separate worlds has been immune to the infection of his reign.[49]

This production achieved cohesion of setting and tone by having Henry IV wander through the worlds of his realm in different states of being. Thus:

the King delivers his great speech on the sleepless cares of majesty not from within the Palace of Westminster but while wandering like his own troubled ghost, through the darkened tavern at Eastcheap, to which his insomniac thoughts appear literally to have conveyed him. He sits down frailly in the arm-chair vacated only moments before by Falstaff on his way out to a night of pleasure with Doll Tearsheet. Around him, the disarrayed furniture betokens the riots and revels from which, as monarch, he is by definition excluded. It offers a haunting image of the emotional isolation which is one of the costs of kingship.[50]

FOR LAUGHTER FRAMES THE LIPS OF DEATH[51]

This is in many ways a twilight play: its characters are stalked by death, betrayal and disappointment.

—John Peter[52]

For a play, which deals with such melancholy themes, there is a tangible poignancy evoked by its comedic aspects. Where *Part I* offered a brightness and energy in the characters outside the court and the influence of Henry IV, in *Part II* there is a diminished joy, and a darkening in the laughter of the audience. This is nowhere more evident than in the Gloucestershire scenes where Silence and Shallow provide the most plangent and uproariously funny parts of this play, and Falstaff reveals a darker, melancholic side to his character.

In 1964, these scenes were played too darkly for the critics' tastes as they adjusted to modern cynicism infiltrating productions. Hugh Griffith, who played Falstaff, was considered definitive in his day. He surprised critics when, in *Part II*, he gave us "an ageing Falstaff whose interior gaiety, if he ever had any, is stilled by the thought of the grave":[53]

> for once, [Falstaff] abandons his role as the clown and speaks with a melancholy reflectiveness heavy with the sense of mortality. This strain is picked up again in the scenes with Shallow when the two old men confront one another—Shallow talking of death but in fact envying his friend's life, and Falstaff finding in Shallow's absurdity another proof of the world's vanity.[54]

There is no doubt that Falstaff finds solace in the fact that he is, by comparison, younger and healthier than his companions. His stint

4. Benjamin Whitrow as Justice Shallow, Desmond Barrit as Falstaff, and Peter Copley as Justice Silence in Michael Attenborough's 2000 RSC production.

in Gloucestershire is not just for financial reasons but, in escaping the tavern and the decay pervading his life in London, Shallow and Silence take him mentally away from his proximity to the Grim Reaper.

Desmond Barrit, who played the role in 2000, found self-serving and cynical motives behind Falstaff's visit to the country:

> Things aren't working for him at this time and he needs to find somewhere else where he might be important, and one of those places might be among these yokels who find even his most obvious witticisms terribly funny . . . Falstaff realizes that their sense of humour is very basic, and just sends them up. He also realizes that there's money in the country, plenty to eat, and plenty to drink, that nobody's short of anything, that recruits who will buy themselves out are easy to find, and that, at last, there's some possibility of getting that thousand pounds that has eluded him for so long . . . What's more, he suddenly finds himself with people much older than himself, or, with the recruits, with bumpkins and buffoons, so that here he can feel superior to (and younger than) those around him. Looking down on them almost, as if they belonged on a much lower level than himself.[55]

Likewise, Robert Stephens in 1991 gave a Falstaff of psychological complexity, egocentric, but not without emotional depth. On the line "If I had a thousand sons . . . ," he broke down, reminding us of his parental longings, found but now lost in Hal. The critic Michael Billington noted how he

> starts out as a guileful charmer who supplies the tactile warmth and paternal affection that Hal cannot find at court. But in *Part Two* Mr Stephens becomes a much more vicious predator who reaches an apex of cruelty when he enlists the shambling, disabled Wart for his rag-and-bobtail military recruits.[56]

Sympathy for Falstaff hangs in the balance here. Conversely, John Peter found the recruits too ridiculous to find out Shakespeare's darker edge:

> The savage political comedy of Falstaff's and Bardolph's re-cruiting activities are rendered harmless and almost improba-ble by the grotesquely bedraggled appearance of the men, one of whom, in a state of near epilepsy, can barely walk. Shake-speare was writing lethally biting political drama; Noble blandly draws its teeth.[57]

The melancholy inherent in the Gloucestershire scenes was empha-sized with gentle humor:

> old men remember their lost youth, lament their dead com-panions, get drunk and sing songs, Noble scrupulously avoids an easy sentimentality. As in [Robert] Stephens's performance as Falstaff, you are made sharply aware of these characters' faults even as you warm to their flawed humanity. In these bittersweet autumnal passages, Shakespeare was writing like Chekhov 250 years before Chekhov was born, and David Bradley and Anthony Douse are superbly sad and funny as the ancient Justices.[58]

In a very different reading of the part, belonging to the more tra-ditional view of Falstaff, Brewster Mason in 1975 emphasized Fal-staff's humanity. Critic John Elsom commented that Mason:

> concentrates on the loving tolerance of the scenes at East-cheap and his gradual recognition of age and approaching death, in the scenes with Shallow and Silence. His cunning is pragmatic, not malicious, and we sense that when his ship comes home and Hal is king, he plans genuinely to repay his friends.[59]

The performance is entirely sympathetic, and amounts to a walking testimonial to his speech in praise of sack. He is magnanimous, seignorial and valiant brushing assailants aside like flies. And down in Gloucestershire with Sydney Bromley's Shallow, he is clearly relishing the immediate party more than planning to fleece his host. The fact that a collection of death's-heads like Trevor Peacock's double up Silence (doubled into an O so perfect that you could bowl him like a hoop[60]) and Tim Wylton's hideously dilapidated Bardolph still manage to make a very good party, is another index of the production's balance between fun and mortality.[61]

. . . Whose Common Theme Is Death of Fathers[62]

Hal represents the future, the possibility of hope and fortune for both Henry IV and Falstaff. For Henry, the hope is that he has taught his son enough to take the crown with firm hands and lead the country out of civil strife. For Falstaff the hope is for financial security and the social standing that will afford him comfort in his old age. However, Hal is not a certainty that either man can rely on. Against this deeply flawed, complex, and enigmatic character, the final act depicts terrible acts of betrayal. Hal's rise to the throne sees the fall and death of both men—as one father dies, the other is cast off.

In the last act of this eventful history, both fathers die, the old king in a prolonged deathbed struggle in which his destiny, England's future, and an intensely self-absorbed relationship with his son war with the fever in his bones. Death does not come until his will allows it to: satisfied that Hal has the mettle to command honorably, the old king allows himself to be borne into the Jerusalem chamber. Meanwhile,

Falstaff's "death" is quieter but no less categoric. It begins by being "caught out," by the Lord Chief Justice and Mistress Quickly combined. It continues in the countryside, traipsing up north with his band of pub belligerents and stopping off on the way to con Justice Shallow and all. It ends in London, with his rejection by Hal, the young King, in front of his friends, drinking partners and those whom he needs to impress. With this cruel snub, Falstaff's optimism and his will to live disperse, with the other rebels against the state. Only his paunch and distended liver twitch on nervously: the man is dead.[63]

The significance of Hal's taking the crown from Henry before his actual death was explained by David Troughton:

> finally for Henry comes the scene in which he has a sudden relapse and asks for his crown to be placed beside him on his pillow: "Set me the crown upon my pillow here" [4.2.142]. The line is immensely important, though it is hard to convey to a modern audience the symbolic idea of the crown on the pillow being temporarily in abeyance, waiting for the king to die before it is placed on his successor's head. To remove it is an act of sacrilege—almost as bad as stealing it from Richard II.[64]

Linking Hal's sin with the sin of Bullingbrook implies a cyclical pattern in the history of the family's reign in England, and not one that bodes well for the security of the country. In 1975 a visual motif showed the ominous nature of Hal's future, one that he appeared unaware of:

> There is a fine moment in *Part Two* when Hal, framed by the guillotine-like structure of his dying father's bed, looked down from behind the crown at the King he believed to be dead.[65]

Having seen what possession of the crown has done to his father, Michael Maloney's Hal, although aware of the necessity, had severe misgivings about carrying the burden himself. During *Part II*:

> Henry seems increasingly tormented by guilt as he views both the nobles' insurrection and Hal's apparent profligacy as retri-

bution for his usurpation of Richard II. Julian Glover appears unkempt, gaunt and ravaged. Instead of wearing the crown, he held it loosely by his side, as if he had forfeited the right to wear it. In his relationship with Hal, he changed from the embodiment of cold, distant paternal authority seen in *Part One*, to the sick and fearful father of *Part Two*.[66]

When he mistakenly supposes that Henry has expired, there is no sense, in this production, that Hal's fingers are itchy to take possession of his right with an unseemly haste. Instead, he makes a wild lunge for the crown, ramming it on his head like someone trying to get a necessary torture over with quickly. So it's all the more agonising for him when Henry, reviving and taking the dimmest view of the situation, here summons up the last vestiges of his strength to subject his son to a brutal mock coronation, pressing the golden circlet into his temples as though it were a crown of thorns. The unfairness of this is piercing and, for once, the prince's impassioned self-defence sounds in no way like a face-saving operation.[67]

Henry's emotional repression in his relationship with his son breaks down in this final scene between the two, and in many productions it can emerge as the emotional apex of the play:

the only time he ever does show affection is when he's dying— when his son has broken through to him. When all his defences are down, when he's within ten minutes of his death. Then he calls him "my son" and "my Harry" [4.2.315, 321, 350]. Only then does he use endearment.[68]

His final confrontation with Prince Hal is one of the climactic moments in all Shakespeare, not, as has often been thought, because of the reconciliation between father and son, but because of the great Oedipal recognition which precedes it. Henry has to realise here that his son both loves him and wants his crown, that filial love can be sadly and bitterly compatible with ambition and a knowledge of what it must cost.[69]

Henry dies of an unspecified illness—one assumes that the cares of both state and son have worn away at his reserves to such a degree that his physical strength has been dissipated by psychological and spiritual debility, his obsession with the crown, and his own and Hal's dubious right to kingship. In order to play the part with physical realism, David Troughton based his performance on a fatal wasting illness, common and recognizable to the audience:

I decided that my Henry was dying of cancer, and because he says, just before he is carried out to die, that "my lungs are wasted so / That strength of speech is utterly denied me" [4.2.354–5], I took lung cancer as the illness. There are a lot of half lines in Henry's speeches here, and having made this decision about the illness, it seemed to me appropriate to use the missing half lines to show the audience how ill he was. In this way you avoid acting illness on the line: you can use normal energy when you have verse to speak and then take a big heave of a breath in the missing half line, thus suggesting that you have urgent things to say, and that you can still speak perfectly well—but only briefly. Henry is an energetic man, and always has been, and that energy is still there, still a part of the character, even as he approaches death. That's why I decided that he must get out of his bed for the final berating of his son. The anger inside him for what Hal has done—for what he has done to me, throughout his life—all comes together in this final speech . . . I used to start crawling towards the exit as Hal began his speech of excuse and explanation.

. . .

Henry believes him—or is taken in by him . . . but whether it's genuine or not, Henry believes him. So the last thing I say to him is to . . . "Go and beat up the French, like we always used to, to take your subjects' minds off the problems at home; go to the Falklands and beat up the Argentinians and get re-elected; give them something to shout and cheer about" . . . And Hal takes my advice.

. . .

   For my Henry . . . in spite of all the hopes and yearnings, there was never going to be an arrival in a Jerusalem of any kind: he died as they were carrying him off the stage.[70]

Although we do not see the death of Falstaff, we know by the end that, rejected and humiliated in front of the people he wishes to impress, Falstaff has not long to live—a fact confirmed by Mistress Quickly in Act 2 Scene 3 of *Henry V*—"The rejection of Falstaff is, as it should be, a crucial moment, encapsulating much of the evening."[71]

In 1982 the stately dignity and solemn procession of the coronation was interrupted by Falstaff's embarrassing shouts:

In the final sequence, Joss Ackland sustained both his aware-ness of mortality and his vigour, revived from senility by the prospect of power. The rejection was electrifying. He main-tained an upright dignity as he was publicly rebuked, and his first "My lord" to the Lord Chief Justice had all the old defiance; with the second "my lord" he at last fell silent. There was one final telling moment. The Lord Chief Justice was obviously moved to sympathy with Falstaff, reacting with shock not only to the harsh treatment of another old man but also to the extent to which the King's zeal for justice exceeded his own: already the pupil had left the master far behind. In such moments, this *Henry IV* responded fully to the rich implica-tions about human behaviour that so distinguish these two plays.[72]

Ackland's Falstaff did not crumble until the King had gone and the order arrives to carry him to the Fleet, making it "a powerful and moving scene . . . in its presentation of the crushing of an individual by the panoply of the regal and political organisation."[73]

In the following extract, Desmond Barrit's description of the rejection scene encompasses many of the ideas central to *Part II:* of disease connecting and spreading from the monarchs of court and tavern; fatherhood to Hal; and how the political machine crushes the personal:

> The king, we soon learn, is very ill, so Hal has had to be preparing himself for kingship. Falstaff, too, is ill—very clearly so, in our production—the pox and the gout having manifested themselves on his body . . . I always work on the assumption that the audience doesn't know the play, and I certainly did that for the rejection scene . . . Whether Falstaff has any deeply hidden, sub-conscious inkling of what is going to happen to him it is hard to say, but in no way is he consciously expecting it; he's the sort of person who always goes for the optimistic option. I think he believes that now Henry IV is out of the way he can at last become Hal's father . . . Falstaff's silence is the really extraordinary thing about this meeting . . . I think that, for once in his life, Falstaff was going to beg for forgiveness . . . is going to appeal to him to remember their past, their great friendship, the good times they have had together. But he isn't given the chance to speak at all . . . He then starts trying to convince himself that he mustn't worry about it, that Hal is only behaving like this because he has to do so in public: "I shall be sent for soon at night" [5.5.86–87]. I used to say that, not to the other characters on stage, but to myself. He's trying to be firm with himself . . . But, of course, he knows that they won't be and that there will be no going back . . . the crime for which he is being imprisoned is that of loving someone too much, the crime of being a good friend—well, and a bit of a rogue as well. Hal has to move on; there is no choice. And Falstaff, I'm sure, dies of a broken heart.[74]

William Houston's Hal showed "no vestiges of fondness for his old low-life companions as his coming of age leads him to dwell on his imminent assumption of power. He has a propensity for paranoia,

5. Alan Howard, "all gold from forehead to toes" in his coronation robe, "lumbers like some gorgeous robot over to the palpitating [Brewster] Mason" as Falstaff in Terry Hands' 1975 RSC production.

and his grin is maliciously vulpine."[75] Benedict Nightingale pointed out how his "heart is clearly moving on to another plane," feeling that he will, as he assured his father, become a responsible king. However, Houston's performance gave the audience cause for concern in handing power to such a "cold fish": "That's a gain, but maybe also a loss. Was I imagining the tiny worried look Clifford Rose's ultra-honest Lord Chief Justice gave when Houston and his chilling brother, Dickon Tyrrell's Prince John walked off?"[76]

The dehumanizing effect of power was symbolically visualized in Terry Hands' 1975 production by Henry's coronation robe:

In comes [Alan] Howard, all gold from forehead to toes, and lumbers like some gorgeous robot over to the palpitating [Brewster] Mason. He wears a mask, and it seems that the mask has trapped and depersonalised him. But, after a few moments, he lifts it, and it's the same Hal underneath, saying what he must and hating himself for saying it: man as well as totem, but totem as much as man. As Mr Howard sees it, the character is constantly trying and failing to achieve human wholeness, an integrity of personality in which public and private selves are reconciled.[77]

In a haunting last image:

Hands stresses the finality of Falstaff's decline with a short tableau. The stage has been cleared of kings, courtiers and riff-raff: only the tangled, white branches of a dead tree stretch across, wall-to-wall bones. The massive figure of Brewster Mason's Falstaff stands, head bowed, beneath them. He could be dangling in the drying wind.[78]

In order for Hal to rule he must eliminate the former division of his self—between court and tavern, duty and extravagance. The necessity of casting off Falstaff is never really in question. As much as the audience enjoy the adventures of this extraordinary character, Shakespeare never lets them forget what a rogue he truly is:

As Hal distances himself from the tavern and is reconciled with his father, the signs of Falstaff's rejection are there to be read. In consequence of Falstaff's opportunist recruiting activities and the unleashing of his predatory instincts towards Shallow, the audience has in a sense been prepared for his inevitable rejection.[79]

Hal's rejection of [Falstaff] is, thus, a tragedy in miniature, and not just for the sake of Sir John's feelings. "If I had the choice between betraying my friends and betraying my country," E. M. Forster once wrote, "I hope that I would have the courage to betray my country." Hal thinks otherwise; and that is his tragedy, inevitable perhaps, even creditable, but painful, nonetheless.[80]

THE ACTOR'S VOICE AND THE DIRECTOR'S CUT: INTERVIEWS WITH MICHAEL PENNINGTON, ADRIAN NOBLE, AND MICHAEL BOYD

Michael Pennington, born in 1943, was brought up in London and read English at Cambridge University. While at university he appeared with the National Youth Theatre. He went on to join the RSC, playing small parts in *The Wars of the Roses* directed by Peter Hall (1964). He has since returned to the RSC on many occasions, playing Angelo in *Measure for Measure* (1974), Edgar in *King Lear* (1976), Berowne in *Love's Labour's Lost* (1978), Hamlet (1980), and Timon in *Timon of Athens* (2000). He has numerous radio and television parts to his credit, as well as film roles. He has written books on acting Shakespeare and Chekhov. In 1986 he and Michael Bogdanov founded the English Shakespeare Company (ESC), dedicated to taking Shakespeare to new audiences. Their inaugural production, *The Henrys*, comprising the two parts of *Henry IV* plus *Henry V*, in which he played Prince Hal/King Henry V, was enormously successful. *Richard II*, the three *Henry VI* plays, and *Richard III* were subsequently added, and their *Wars of the Roses* toured the world to great acclaim. He launched his one-man show, *Sweet William*, about Shakespeare's life and writing and his own relationship with those works, in 2006. He talks here both about playing the part of Hal and about wider aspects of the ESC staging of the two parts.

Adrian Noble, born in 1950, arrived at the RSC from the Bristol Old Vic, where he had directed several future stars in productions of classic plays. His first production on the main stage of the Royal Shakespeare Theatre in Stratford was the acclaimed 1982 *King Lear*. Two years later, his *Henry V* sowed the seed for Kenneth Branagh's film. Among his other major productions during his two decades at the RSC were *Hamlet*, again with Branagh in the title role; *The Plantagenets*, based on the *Henry VI/Richard III* tetralogy; and the two parts of *Henry IV*. Noble's 1994 *A Midsummer Night's Dream* was made into a film. He was artistic director from 1991 to 2003, since when he has been a freelance director. His production style is characterized by strong use of colors and objects (such as umbrellas), and fluid scenic structure. He talks here about his 1991 production with

Robert Stephens as Falstaff, making reference to both *Part I* and *Part II* of *Henry IV*.

Michael Boyd was born in Belfast in 1955, educated in London and Edinburgh, and completed his MA in English literature at Edinburgh University. He trained as a director at the Malaya Bronnaya Theatre in Moscow. He then went on to work at the Belgrade Theatre in Coventry, joining the Sheffield Crucible as associate director in 1982. In 1985 Boyd became founding artistic director of the Tron Theatre in Glasgow, becoming equally acclaimed for staging new writing and innovative productions of the classics. He was drama director of the *New Beginnings Festival of Soviet Arts* in Glasgow in 1999. He joined the RSC as an associate director in 1996 and has since directed numerous productions of Shakespeare's plays. He won the Laurence Olivier Award for Best Director for his version of the *Henry VI* plays in the RSC's *This England: The Histories* in 2001. He took over as artistic director of the RSC in 2003 and oversaw the extraordinarily successful Complete Works Festival in 2006–07. He followed this up with a cycle of all eight history plays, from *Richard II* through to *Richard III*, with the same company of actors. This transferred to London's Roundhouse Theatre in 2008 and won multiple awards. He talks here about both parts of *Henry IV*.

These plays can be thought of as individual works, as parts of a pair, or of a tetralogy, or even of a longer cycle of English history plays. There are cross-references across the two parts, back to *Richard II* and forward to *Henry V*. Some audience members know the back-story and the forward-story, some don't. How do you cope with all this?

MP: Each of the history plays has to stand alone—that's how Shakespeare planned them—but it's almost as if he had an idea that they might one day be seen in sequence, as they often are now, because each generally "trails" the next episode of the story at its end. So *Part II* closes by looking forward to Henry V's French campaign, and indeed the end of *Henry V* to the reign of Henry VI. With the *Henry IV*s it doesn't really matter if the audience doesn't know *Henry V* since it's in the future, except as general interest as to how Henry V became Henry V. The backstory of *Richard II* is more of a problem: you need to know about the shakiness of Henry IV's claim to the throne and his own conscience—if he has any—about having usurped. The only real answer is to make sure the actors make the audience truly listen to Hotspur's argument against Henry in *Part I* and what the king himself says, so that they miss none of it. It's a matter of emphasis in the acting, of determination to get it across.

AN: In two ways. First of all one, has to start with the very simple premise that people are buying a ticket for one show, therefore it has to stand alone. But from the point of view of the acting company and as somebody involved at the RSC with the history plays for quite some time, I'd say it's very hard not to appreciate the wider context, going back to the *Henry VI* plays. It seems to me impossible that Shakespeare did not have an architectural form in his head as he wrote them. The *Henry VI/Richard III* tetralogy was the first time since Sophocles and Euripides that someone had attempted a cycle of interrelated plays for the secular stage. It hadn't happened for two thousand years. I cannot believe that, writing it as a man in his mid- to late twenties, Shakespeare wasn't conscious of that. And of course they were enormously successful, so slightly later in his career, when his gaze cast upon the *Henry IV* plays, I think he must again have had some sort of ghost of the architecture in his mind all the time. But because the first tetralogy tackled events that chronologically took place after those of the second, you get a very strong sense of moving forward toward anarchy and chaos. If you look at all eight, you start with the formality of *Richard II* and end up with the butchery of *Richard III*. It's a divine untidiness. In the second tetralogy you can see the architecture but also a maturity of construction and a depth of characterization within each play, which makes them highly satisfactory as individual plays.

MB: We conceived our *Henry IVs* as part of an eight-play cycle of Shakespeare's history plays, and a large proportion of our audience saw them in this context. Clive Wood had not only played Bullingbrook in *Richard II* but, as Richard of York, had spent three plays trying to take the crown from Henry VI and failing. We staged the plays initially in the order of their writing so York was seen on a Sisyphean journey toward the crown, which faltered in *Henry VI Part III* and began again with renewed vigor and sophistication in *Richard II*. The *Henry IV* plays revealed the eventual fruits of his labors as bitter.

Shakespeare had five very successful histories behind him as he wrote the *Henry IVs*, and *Henry V* was a popular title long before Shakespeare wrote his version, so I think it's fair to say that both author and audience were conscious of context as they experienced the events of *Henry IV*.

These plays move between very distinctive settings: royal court, rebels' castles, Eastcheap tavern, Gloucestershire orchard, battlefield. How did you and your designer set about creating these contrasting worlds?

MP: On their own terms, eclectically. The court wore Edwardian dress, the rebels harked back variously to the eighteenth century and forward to twentieth-century warfare; the tavern was more or less 1980s, the Gloucestershire orchard perhaps a little pre–First World War, the battlefield went back to medieval chainmail and broadsword. All the time we were responding to the temperament of the characters and the atmospherics of each scene and asking the audience to accept unexpected contrasts. The plays are in a sense about the entire history of Britain.

AN: Bob Crowley designed the set and Deirdre Clancy the costumes. We started with a very beautiful wooden floor fringed with gold, that both functioned as a practical space and had a strong resonance that could operate as a metaphor. The second thing we decided was that we would spend a lot of our money (because in the end it comes down to that) on the Boar's Head in Eastcheap, because we felt it was an aspect of the play that really needed to jump into the audience's imagination. In any of Shakespeare's plays, some parts require what I would loosely call "social realism" and some don't. *King Lear* does not require much social realism. *The Merry Wives of Windsor* requires a lot, because the plots operate and are triggered by different things. There are certain aspects of *Henry IV Part I* that require that social realism, and the Boar's Head tavern is one of those.

The tavern in *Part I* was a well of life: it absolutely teemed with energy and life. The tavern in *Part II* was a much emptier place. It was a lonely and quite sad place, a place for losers, a place where folk were in danger, so everyone got out very fast when they were told there was another war starting. I used it for Henry IV's great monologue, "How many thousand of my poorest subjects / Are at this hour asleep?" [3.1.4–5]. I had King Henry wander through the tavern, in which the down-and-outs and the losers were all lying drunk and asleep.

This relates to the structure of *Part II*, which is absolutely brilliant. It all works contrapuntally. It's contrapuntal between town and country, between war councils and petty quarrels. And one of the great pieces of counterpoint is at the death of King Henry IV. Henry IV dies in the Jerusalem chamber in the Palace of Westminster and the next scene is in Gloucestershire. From the very beginning of *Part I* he has wanted to go to the Holy Land. He keeps talking about how he wants to go to Jerusalem and eventually he does go there, but he goes there in death. I had his sons and the courtiers lift his body and carry him, and as his bed was lifted aloft and he came weaving downstage then upstage, I did a transformation into the countryside in Gloucestershire. I had a huge canopy with ladders poking up through it and all you saw were the legs of the actors. They were up the ladders, throwing apples down, and the dead body of the king was carried up through the canopy, up through this orchard, the orchard of England. We did this strange picture in slow motion, so it was like he'd gone to heaven, and so we had this fabulous juxtaposition which I think completely fulfilled Shakespeare's purpose. It was a wonderful juxtaposition of the realistic—we had real beekeepers and real apple pickers in the orchard—and the imagistic, the metaphorical. The man had finally found his way to Jerusalem: it was just eighty miles up the Thames in Gloucestershire. So we found a way in *Part II* of being much freer, much bolder, in the integration of the scenery with the structure of the play.

MB: Henry's court was characterized by a simple silver bowl of water where he tried to wash his hands of the blood of Richard II.

Eastcheap was dominated by a battered old armchair that had

taken the shape of David Warner's Falstaff, and was framed by a large and tattered red velvet drape, which spoke of warmth, theatrical artifice, and backstage assignations. Staff and customers also emerged from and disappeared into a smoky purgatory beneath the stage.

Nearly all the castles from Orleans and Bordeaux in *Henry VI Part I* to Harfleur in *Henry V* were carried by our great rusty Louise Bourgeois–style tower, that rose from its hell mouth gates up past an "I'm the King of the Castle" balcony to an ambiguous spiral stair, which rose to and fell from the grid seven meters above the stage.

Gloucestershire was a bale of hay, some bunting, blossom, and a barbecue.

Our battlefields were the bodies of men fighting over the rusty body of England, which Tom Piper created. Our set suggested arms and legs and a head and viscera.

The plays dramatize the movement from feudalism (with the powerful barons of the North) to the early modern state (with an absolutist idea of monarchy). But they also speak to very Elizabethan concerns, such as the administration of the nation by means of a network of local justices (not all of whom are entirely free from corruption . . .). And at the same time, the idea of the education of a future leader is a timeless theme. So: medieval setting, Elizabethan, modern, or some eclectic mixture of them all?

MP: I'm not so sure about this education of Hal. I think he has a great struggle between his impulses and his duties; he realizes what he will have to sacrifice, and in playing the part I came to think it costs him something. Not that he lets on: in *Henry V* he hardly mentions his past and is completely ruthless about hanging Bardolph for robbing a church, the kind of thing he might once have done himself. So if this is an education, it is not a very inclusive or compassionate one, more a hard lesson in realpolitik.

AN: We chose to set it pretty accurately in its period. I think it becomes a nonsense if you take it out of its period, to be absolutely honest, because we all know too much about other periods in which

you might set it, and its own period is itself so interesting and reso-
nant. When you've got a wonderful company of actors and you do it
reasonably well, relevance jumps out at you.

MB: We found ourselves more interested in Shakespeare as a story-
teller for his own age than as medievalist scholar. After the corruption of the old world, the old faith, and the would-be absolutist
Richard, comes the cold wind of religious and political reform. Elizabeth may have seen herself characterized as Richard II, but she is
also the reforming Protestant ruler beset with a dissenting and
unruly populace that we see in *Henry IV*. The Archbishop of York,
who "Turns insurrection to religion," can't fail to have reminded
Shakespeare's audience of the Pilgrimage of Grace which threatened Elizabeth's father Henry VIII with a militarized Catholic back-
lash from the North.

   We opted for three generations: the glamorous remnants of
Richard/Elizabeth's golden age; the new black, simple, puritanical
broom of Bullingbrook/Elizabeth; and the new generation of Hal
and Poins willfully revisiting some of the decadent glamour of the
past (with a little help from the saloon glamour of Westerns).

**Prince Hal is sometimes one of the lads, sometimes coolly
detached from his companions. Does this change over the two
parts of the drama? Or, to ask the same question in another way:
his first soliloquy, "I know you all," is crucial, isn't it? Do you see
him speaking it essentially to himself or to the audience in the
theater? Does it reveal him as a Machiavellian manipulator from
the start, just playing a game in order to improve his own image,
always intending to reject his companions when the time is ripe?
Or is there much more ambivalence in the progress from "I know
you all" early in *Part I* to the rejection speech, "I know thee not,"
at the end of *Part II*?**

MP: Yes, he oscillates—he's tugged in two directions, as anybody
might be. He pulls princely rank sometimes in the tavern, and in the
court he plays the bad boy. He's quite unresolved.

   "I know you all" is a very unusual soliloquy in that it seems to be
addressed not to the audience but to his offstage friends and is over-

heard by the audience. Shakespeare hardly ever does this. A solilo-
quizer normally confides in the theater audience more intimately
than this, more trustingly. The effect here is to make Hal seem a little
remote from us.

Playing him as what you call a Machiavellian is possible but it's
not very interesting theatrically, like playing the Duke in *Measure for
Measure* simply as a manipulator.

Hal is very monosyllabic when he comes to the point—as in those
two cases [his first soliloquy in *Part I* and the rejection speech at the
end of *Part II*], and also "I do, I will" when he promises Falstaff he
will reject him. I think what keeps the play and the part alive is that
he has great difficulty in resolving his conflicting urges. He sets out
his program at the start, but he doesn't find it that easy to execute.
He leaves the tavern and goes to the court, but is disappointed by his
father, who is manipulative and self-absorbed; he goes back to Falstaff, but realizes he can't truly be part of that world either. There is
a lot of implied conflict in him.

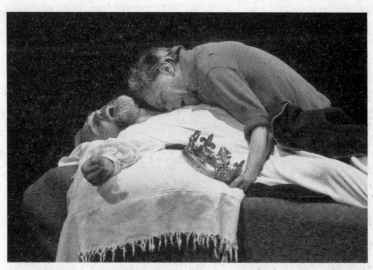

6. "O polished perturbation! Golden care!" Michael Pennington as Prince
Hal and John Castle as Henry IV in the English Shakespeare Company's
Wars of the Roses, 1986–89.

AN: He is all of those things. He's very complex because if you try and play it as somebody who's being manipulative and Machiavellian, in terms of a great scheme, it doesn't sustain itself. It's unactable and it's incredible to the audience. The only way it works is if he thoroughly embraces the Eastcheap world and is a protagonist within it. You have to work back from that and from the fact that he says "I know you all." Some people find it necessary to have the character one or the other; I think he's both. I think he's a human being and human beings are extremely complex people. Young people, especially, live several lives: they live the life they live with their parents and they live a completely different life with other people. That's part of growing up and of how you relate to your parents. Hal has, in a way, been very lucky, in the sense that he has two fathers who each represent the two aspects of his character, so again you get this counterpoint which is very creative and very abrasive; it creates intellectual energy. I think Hal embraces that world fully, and the key moment for him is when he finally answers his dad: "Do not think so. You shall not find it so" [*Henry IV Part I*, 3.2.130]. It's a monosyllabic line and you can't rush that line, because there are too many vowels in it. That's a turning point for the character; that's when he realizes he actually has to decide. It's also, interestingly enough, when he finds a voice. I think it's when he finds the voice that will attack Hotspur and will attack the French in *Henry V*. He embraces both worlds happily, and I think that's part of his personality. It's part of the education of the king, but it's more particularly part of the humanity of the king. Another way of looking at it is to think of Hal's time with Falstaff as a time of disguise; the disguise allows him the freedom to explore and develop and thereby achieve wisdom. The character is both with and outside the disguise at one and the same time.

MB: Hal's genuine longing to be a hard-drinking, womanizing Corinthian is in tension from the beginning with his dark understanding that he is heir to the throne and therefore the target of flattery and envious rumor. He starts by flirting with the political theater of the deferred appearance of the sun from behind the cloud, and ends as the leading player in a much darker piece of political theater as he renounces Falstaff, and is groomed for war with France.

The comparison and contrast between Prince Harry and Harry Hotspur is obviously crucial. Did you have particular stylistic or visual devices for establishing and exploring it?

MP: Hotspur seemed like a version of Bonnie Prince Charlie—quite a romantic, eighteenth-century rebel. Hal was completely modern except on the battlefield when he went into chain mail. So as I said above we handled these things not so much conceptually as expressionistically.

AN: It's unavoidable, isn't it? All you have to do is read the play. It's totally and utterly in your face. It's a constant reminder to the audience of what the danger of Prince Hal's behavior is, that he is messing up big-time, because it's a dominating dramatic presence. Hotspur is such a charismatic man. He's a natural leader, he has such command of language, and he has all the other things that audiences want kings to have, like a good wife, a great sense of humor, the ability to deal with his elders in a fair, just, but respectful manner. He's got all of those things; they're there like this great big elephant in the room.

MB: Our Percies were descended from Shakespeare's earlier father-and-son duo in *Henry VI*: the Talbots. By now the honorable code of chivalry of this pairing has become warped. The father caves in horribly in *Part II* and the son is bold but arrogant and reckless. Chivalry is stone dead by *Henry IV*.

Prince Hal moves in the other direction, from selfish, hedonistic criminality to a new contingent morality which will find its fullest paradoxical expression in *Henry V* (and then of course in *Hamlet*).

To answer the question: Geoffrey Streatfeild's Hal was more of a decadent dandy in *Part I* and Lex Shrapnel's Hotspur a glamorized vision of martial prowess.

It's sometimes said that in *Part I* Hal learns the military virtues of the true prince, in *Part II* the civic virtues. So Hotspur is a key

opponent in *Part I*, the Lord Chief Justice a key figure in *Part II*. Was that a productive way of looking at it for you?

MP: That didn't occur to me, and I don't think Shakespeare writes that programmatically. The developments in his characters are more subtle, less easily explained. And I'm not sure Hal learns any virtues really, only pragmatism—how to handle everybody effectively, in fact. The Lord Chief Justice is his third father figure, after Falstaff and the king—Falstaff is the one that loses out of course.

AN: Not at the time, but yes, that's quite interesting!

MB: No, but it is one template to apply to the plays. It feels more like the Lord Chief Justice's template than Shakespeare's and it makes the royalist assumption that "becoming a true prince" is Shakespeare's subject.

Having staged all the histories, I began to realize that the drive for power and the yearning for the crown is one big politically acceptable MacGuffin [plot device] that allows Shakespeare to examine the nature of humanity under pressure. Shakespeare is consistently skeptical and critical of those in power, and this famously nonjudgmental author makes an exception for any character showing signs of being overinfluenced by *Il Principe*.*

In *Part I* Hal wrestles with authority and his father, trying to find/avoid his place in life. In *Part II* Hal confronts the mortality of the very man he has defined himself against and therefore confronts his own mortality. And he kills Falstaff.

Another difference between the two parts is that, simply in terms of size of parts, *Part I* is dominated by Hal, Falstaff, Hotspur, and King Henry, whereas *Part II* has a far larger number of substantial roles. Does that suggest that they are very different kinds of plays? *Part I* a star vehicle and *Part II* an ensemble vision?

MP: They're both ensemble pieces—fabulously so. Hotspur's death and Hal's withdrawal from events in *Part I* makes room for Shallow

---

* *Il Principe* (1532) *The Prince* (Italian): Niccolò Machiavelli's examination of Renaissance realpolitik.

and Silence and the rest, and there's much more Falstaff too. I think *Part II* is just *Part I* rebalanced—not essentially different, except that there's definitely a sense of imminent change, and loss, with the king dying; the tavern scenes have less vitality and Hal generally keeps away from Falstaff, as if he was preparing himself for his future.

AN: The second half is for me the great director's challenge, because it is symphonic. Some plays work as concerti, with a series of solo turns, and some operate more symphonically. This is particularly true of the eight history plays. *Henry VI Part I*, *Part II*, and *Part III* operate symphonically. My mistake when I did *Richard III*, as the last of that tetralogy, is that until I started rehearsing it I thought it also operated symphonically, but it doesn't: it's written in a completely different manner to the *Henry VIs*. It's written as a series of concerti: one after the other, somebody stands up and plays the violin, plays the viola, plays the cello, plays the trumpet. Edward IV, Clarence, Hastings, one after the other they all stand up. It's not true to such an extent with the two parts of *Henry IV*, but it is to a degree.

I'd wanted to do *Henry IV Part I* and *Part II* for years, but for me you don't even start until you've got Falstaff, which I was very fortunate to get in Robert Stephens. That's the character that not only sets half the agenda of the plays, but is also the person who attracts all the other actors. If you don't have a genius Falstaff, then you won't get a brilliant Henry IV, and if you don't have a brilliant Henry IV, then the spine of the two plays is very shaky. Hal and Hotspur are much easier. It's for Falstaff, Henry IV, and Shallow that you really need people at the top of their game to fulfil the majesty of those two plays.

MB: Not really. *Part II* was in part conceived as a vehicle for the runaway success of Falstaff as a "turn" in *Part I*.

Does Falstaff change between the two parts?

MP: In *Part I*, Hal and he are wonderfully matched, especially in their capacity for (more or less) friendly insults. Falstaff feels Hal's absence in *Part II* very keenly—he knows in his heart the best times are past. Falstaff talks about him all the time, wistfully.

AN: He matures somehow and gets wiser in the second part. I think the reason he appears to get older in the second part is because he has the Page. That's why Shakespeare gives him a young person to walk about with, so you realize he's old. Also in *Part II* he associates much more with people of his own age, particularly with his fellow students from when he was a law student at Temple. By hanging out with Silence and Shallow, on the one hand, and with a twelve-year-old boy, on the other hand, we get a strong whiff of mortality coming off Falstaff in *Part II*, which we don't so much get in *Part I*.

MB: Falstaff has become a star in *Part II* because of his false success in Shrewsbury, and his real success in the theater in *Henry IV Part I*. Shakespeare promotes him to the courtly world and gives him exchanges with the most powerful people in the land, but then punishes him with cynicism, gout, and mortality.

He's a force of nature in *Part I*, and in *Part II* he's someone clinging on to influence, and opportunity, and life.

What did you learn in the process of rehearsing the great play-acting scene in *Part I*—the pre-enactment by Hal and Falstaff of Hal's confrontation with his father? And did it teach you things that you could use when working on the actual encounters between the prince and his father?

MP: Not so much that, but the two successive scenes are at the center of the part. The scene in the Boar's Head has terrific tension—how far will Hal go in mocking his father? How far will he let Falstaff go? The onlookers don't know how loudly they're allowed to laugh. It's a great relief to Hal to make fun of his father; then he goes to see him for real and is very disappointed. He apologizes to the king and promises to toe the line but gets little thanks for it. Hal is very frustrated by his father. It's interesting that he takes Falstaff into battle with him and even lets him take credit for the death of Hotspur—it's as if he were serving notice that he'll do his duty by his father but he's not giving up his old ways that easily.

AN: Not particularly. It's most important because it stands as a rehearsal of the denial of Falstaff; that seems its main function to me. It was fun and funny—it couldn't not be that and I made it that—and I made it very anarchic, but my main purpose related to the denial of Falstaff. I remember feeling it was profoundly wrong that Hal engaged in this playacting. The whole idea of impersonating the monarch had a slight whiff of danger about it, and I think for an Elizabethan audience it would have been almost obscene: a very dangerous thing to do and very disrespectful. The dice are loaded very heavily against Hal in *Part I* and I think that's why it is such a dramatic piece: it's because he turns the stakes around, he overturns the odds, that it is remarkable.

MB: Clive Wood had already shaped his testosterone-fueled, reforming Bullingbrook in our *Richard II*, so we already knew that Hal's encounters with his father would be bruising and straight out of Eugene O'Neill or Tennessee Williams.

There was a moving mismatch of styles in the playacting scene: David Warner's Falstaff revealing an old-fashioned delicacy that had no place in Bullingbrook's actual cold, pragmatic palace.

It's mostly a male world, but, small as they are, the female parts—Hotspur's wife, Quickly, Doll—seem very significant, don't they? What was your take on the women in these plays?

MP: I think Doll's little scene with Falstaff in *Part II* is a real love scene—both of them at their best; open, honest, and affectionate in ways they aren't elsewhere. Mistress Quickly represents one kind of female constancy in her love of Falstaff, and in a sense, Lady Percy the other, in her anger at Hotspur's withdrawing from her and her grief at his loss. They're very good parts, all three of them.

AN: They're wonderful parts and you can do fantastic things with them with the right people. I was very lucky and we did great things with those parts. What Shakespeare does is genuinely present a great portrait of a nation. Look at the language of the scene of the two carriers in Rochester: it's a couple of lorry drivers at Watford Gap services, it's a couple of guys who have done an overnight stay in a B&B somewhere. What he creates with that language—and of course it's distilled and slightly heightened—is the cadence of Elizabethan England. Shakespeare perfectly captures it: people working in an industrial situation. Now compare that with the sound of Shallow and Silence. Again, the cadence there is extraordinary. It's a remarkable soundscape, probably of Warwickshire when he was a boy, and that's part of the richness of the play. The *Henry VI* plays don't attempt that at all: you get little snippets of them with Cade and Dick the Butcher, but they are only snippets. In *Henry IV* they are in-depth portraits of a nation. You get the clergy, you get the courtiers, you get the tapsters, you get the prostitutes. Doll Tearsheet is an amazing portrait of a prostitute. Shakespeare captures the language in an extraordinary way.

MB: And Glendower's daughter possibly wins the war for Bullingbrook.

Ann Ogbomo's Kate Percy was an intelligent, beautiful, and feisty sketch for Shakespeare's later leading women, Rosalind and Beatrice.

As Mistress Quickly, Maureen Beattie brought her own instinctive understanding of comedic rhythms from Scottish variety to a much-loved character that can trace its ancestry to Noah's wife, the wife of

7. Robert Stephens as Falstaff and Joanne Pearce as Doll Tearsheet at Hostess Quickly's tavern in Eastcheap in *Part II* of Adrian Noble's 1991 RSC production.

Bath, and beyond. Together with Alexia Healy's Doll, she maintained a haven of imperfect warmth in the cold world of Bullingbrook, until at last Eastcheap was literally dismantled in *Part II*.

Shakespeare's friend and rival Ben Jonson mocked his history plays for representing battles by means of nothing more than "three rusty swords"—and modern audiences are used to the epic battles of the Hollywood screen, complete with hundreds of extras. In light of this, how do you set about staging the battles convincingly? What balance between stylization and realism?

MP: That was quite snobbish of Jonson—they couldn't afford anything else. And Shakespeare always forestalls that argument, as he does in the first chorus in *Henry V*—the means are limited but, as he knows, his imaginative suggestiveness is great.

I think the battles should be as realistic as possible, especially the Hal/Hotspur—traditional one-to-one combat, sweating it out, like Richard III and Richmond; Hamlet and Laertes, too, if you like. They're cathartic confrontations. The difficulty is greater in the general battle scenes and skirmishes; the rhetoric can be a bit thumpy and there's a lot of rushing around without much character (though when Falstaff is on the battlefield there's terrific comic counterpoint). Sometimes directors stylize Shakespeare's battle scenes—slow motion, banners, mime, and so on. I don't much care for it myself, but I appreciate why it happens. I think you have to create the fog of war as realistically as you can. Interestingly enough, in the ESC version, though we used guns often, the big one-to-one set pieces we always did in chain mail and armor and broadswords, two individuals timelessly slugging it out to the death.

AN: You've answered the question actually: you get a balance between stylization and realism. Very simple technology plus a lot of imagination can lead you to extraordinary things. You first ask the question, "What is the battle about? What is this one saying?" At the end of *Part I* it's Shrewsbury: the subject of that battle is the throne, it's a fight for the throne. There was a piece of technology in the old Royal Shakespeare Theatre that no longer exists, which I discovered when I was doing *King Lear* with Michael Gambon. There were two huge lifts running up to the stage, each one nine meters by four meters, that could hold about seventy people each. On certain occasions like Gad's Hill I used the great hole on stage where the lift shaft was. At the Battle of Shrewsbury there were people talking downstage but the hole was down, and in the trap under the stage I'd loaded the throne surrounded by the whole of King Henry's courtiers, and then, with a huge amount of music and drumming, this throne came out of the earth. Not only did this trap ascend to stage level, it went above it. So when it hit stage level it was attacked in quite a stylized way by Hotspur's men, with the entire company onstage, and it carried on up into the air until it was about eight feet off the ground, and then it started to descend. Everyone was fighting, but they were actually fighting for the throne, and then when it came down to stage level it went into realistic swordplay. It's a bit unfair of Ben Jonson to say that, but he is absolutely right. What we delivered was a quite spectacular battle based upon the technology of that theater. We were just very lucky that we had it there. I think I used that huge hole in each of the seven history plays I did.

8. The battle scenes dramatized the essential qualities of a conflict with "three rusty swords" and the audience as extras in Michael Boyd's 2007–08 RSC history cycle.

MB: Over eight plays, we worked on the battles employing many approaches, including the following:

1. Shakespeare's battles must serve the play in the same way as a song in a musical: they must move the story forward.

2. Renaissance dance was in part physical training for the men at court for battle. Our battles were to a greater or lesser extent all dances.

3. Our battles often carried a cosmological burden: i.e. they were a battle between heaven and hell fought out on earth. This combined with the spatial excitement of the Courtyard Theatre encouraged us to use four dimensions. Violence burst out from the grid, the stage, and the audience as often as from backstage.

4. Battles were staged with consciously shifting points of view, e.g. Shrewsbury was seen mostly from the rebels' perspective and picked up on the practice of decoy kings. We dramatized the courage it took to challenge an "anointed" king by opposing Hotspur with an army of kings.

5. We wanted to celebrate the chief advantage of theatrical over filmic battles: we were not the slaves of naturalism pursuing ever more plausible wounds and dismemberments. We were free to attempt to dramatize the essential qualities of a conflict. The hundreds of extras were supplied by the audience.

SHAKESPEARE'S CAREER
IN THE THEATER

BEGINNINGS

William Shakespeare was an extraordinarily intelligent man who was born and died in an ordinary market town in the English Midlands. He lived an uneventful life in an eventful age. Born in April 1564, he was the eldest son of John Shakespeare, a glove-maker who was prominent on the town council until he fell into financial difficulties. Young William was educated at the local grammar in Stratford-upon-Avon, Warwickshire, where he gained a thorough grounding in the Latin language, the art of rhetoric, and classical poetry. He married Ann Hathaway and had three children (Susanna, then the twins Hamnet and Judith) before his twenty-first birthday: an exceptionally young age for the period. We do not know how he supported his family in the mid-1580s.

Like many clever country boys, he moved to the city in order to make his way in the world. Like many creative people, he found a career in the entertainment business. Public playhouses and professional full-time acting companies reliant on the market for their income were born in Shakespeare's childhood. When he arrived in London as a man, sometime in the late 1580s, a new phenomenon was in the making: the actor who is so successful that he becomes a "star." The word did not exist in its modern sense, but the pattern is recognizable: audiences went to the theater not so much to see a particular show as to witness the comedian Richard Tarlton or the dramatic actor Edward Alleyn.

Shakespeare was an actor before he was a writer. It appears not to have been long before he realized that he was never going to grow into a great comedian like Tarlton or a great tragedian like Alleyn. Instead, he found a role within his company as the man who patched up old plays, breathing new life, new dramatic twists, into tired repertory pieces. He paid close attention to the work of the university-educated dramatists who were writing history plays and tragedies for the public stage in a style more ambitious, sweeping, and poetically grand than anything that had been seen before. But he may also have noted that what his friend and rival Ben Jonson would call "Marlowe's mighty line" sometimes faltered in the mode of comedy. Going to university, as Christopher Marlowe did, was all well and good for honing the arts of rhetorical elaboration and classical allusion, but it could lead to a loss of the common touch. To stay close to a large segment of the potential audience for public theater, it was necessary to write for clowns as well as kings and to intersperse the flights of poetry with the humor of the tavern, the privy, and the brothel: Shakespeare was the first to establish himself early in his career as an equal master of tragedy, comedy, and history. He realized that theater could be the medium to make the national past available to a wider audience than the elite who could afford to read large history books: his signature early works include not only the classical tragedy *Titus Andronicus* but also the sequence of English historical plays on the Wars of the Roses.

He also invented a new role for himself, that of in-house company dramatist. Where his peers and predecessors had to sell their plays to the theater managers on a poorly paid piecework basis, Shakespeare took a percentage of the box-office income. The Lord Chamberlain's Men constituted themselves in 1594 as a joint stock company, with the profits being distributed among the core actors who had invested as sharers. Shakespeare acted himself—he appears in the cast lists of some of Ben Jonson's plays as well as the list of actors' names at the beginning of his own collected works—but his principal duty was to write two or three plays a year for the company. By holding shares, he was effectively earning himself a royalty on his work, something no author had ever done before in England. When the Lord Chamberlain's Men collected their fee for performance at court in the Christmas season of 1594, three of them went along to the Treasurer of the Chamber: not just Richard Burbage the tragedian and Will Kempe the clown, but also Shakespeare the scriptwriter. That was something new.

The next four years were the golden period in Shakespeare's career, though overshadowed by the death of his only son Hamnet, aged eleven, in 1596. In his early thirties and in full command of both his poetic and his theatrical medium, he perfected his art of comedy, while also developing his tragic and historical writing in new ways. In 1598, Francis Meres, a Cambridge University graduate with his finger on the pulse of the London literary world, praised Shakespeare for his excellence across the genres:

> As Plautus and Seneca are accounted the best for comedy and tragedy among the Latins, so Shakespeare among the English is the most excellent in both kinds for the stage; for comedy, witness his *Gentlemen of Verona*, his *Errors*, his *Love Labours Lost*, his *Love Labours Won*, his *Midsummer Night Dream* and his *Merchant of Venice:* for tragedy his *Richard the 2*, *Richard the 3*, *Henry the 4*, *King John*, *Titus Andronicus* and his *Romeo and Juliet*.

For Meres, as for the many writers who praised the "honey-flowing vein" of *Venus and Adonis* and *Lucrece*, narrative poems written when the theaters were closed due to plague in 1593–94, Shakespeare was marked above all by his linguistic skill, by the gift of turning elegant poetic phrases.

PLAYHOUSES

Elizabethan playhouses were "thrust" or "one-room" theaters. To understand Shakespeare's original theatrical life, we have to forget about the indoor theater of later times, with its proscenium arch and curtain that would be opened at the beginning and closed at the end of each act. In the proscenium arch theater, stage and auditorium are effectively two separate rooms: the audience looks from one world into another as if through the imaginary "fourth wall" framed by the proscenium. The picture-frame stage, together with the elaborate scenic effects and backdrops beyond it, created the illusion of a self-contained world—especially once nineteenth-century developments in the control of artificial lighting meant that the auditorium could be darkened and the spectators made to focus on the lighted stage. Shakespeare, by contrast, wrote for a bare platform stage with a standing audience gathered around it in a courtyard in full day-light. The audience were always conscious of themselves and their fellow spectators, and they shared the same "room" as the actors. A sense of immediate presence and the creation of rapport with the audience were all-important. The actor could not afford to imagine he was in a closed world, with silent witnesses dutifully observing him from the darkness.

Shakespeare's theatrical career began at the Rose Theatre in Southwark. The stage was wide and shallow, trapezoid in shape, like a lozenge. This design had a great deal of potential for the theatrical equivalent of cinematic split-screen effects, whereby one group of characters would enter at the door at one end of the tiring-house wall at the back of the stage and another group through the door at the other end, thus creating two rival tableaux. Many of the battle-heavy and faction-filled plays that premiered at the Rose have scenes of just this sort.

At the rear of the Rose stage, there were three capacious exits, each over ten feet wide. Unfortunately, the very limited excavation of a fragmentary portion of the original Globe site, in 1989, revealed nothing about the stage. The first Globe was built in 1599 with sim-ilar proportions to those of another theater, the Fortune, albeit that the former was polygonal and looked circular, whereas the latter was rectangular. The building contract for the Fortune survives and allows us to infer that the stage of the Globe was probably substan-tially wider than it was deep (perhaps forty-three feet wide and twenty-seven feet deep). It may well have been tapered at the front, like that of the Rose.

The capacity of the Globe was said to have been enormous, per-haps in excess of three thousand. It has been conjectured that about eight hundred people may have stood in the yard, with two thousand or more in the three layers of covered galleries. The other "public" playhouses were also of large capacity, whereas the indoor Blackfri-ars theater that Shakespeare's company began using in 1608—the former refectory of a monastery—had overall internal dimensions of a mere forty-six by sixty feet. It would have made for a much more intimate theatrical experience and had a much smaller capacity, probably of about six hundred people. Since they paid at least sixpence a head, the Blackfriars attracted a more select or "private" audience. The atmosphere would have been closer to that of an indoor performance before the court in the Whitehall Palace or at Richmond. That Shakespeare always wrote for indoor production at court as well as outdoor performance in the public theater should make us cautious about inferring, as some scholars have, that the opportunity provided by the intimacy of the Blackfriars led to a significant change toward a "chamber" style in his last plays—which, besides, were performed at both the Globe and the Blackfriars. After the occupation of the Blackfriars a five-act structure seems to have become more important to Shakespeare. That was because of artificial lighting: there were musical interludes between the acts, while the candles were trimmed and replaced. Again, though, something similar must have been necessary for indoor court performances throughout his career.

Front of house there were the "gatherers" who collected the money from audience members: a penny to stand in the open-air yard, another penny for a place in the covered galleries, sixpence for the prominent "lord's rooms" to the side of the stage. In the indoor "private" theaters, gallants from the audience who fancied making themselves part of the spectacle sat on stools on the edge of the stage itself. Scholars debate as to how widespread this practice was in the public theaters such as the Globe. Once the audience were in place and the money counted, the gatherers were available to be extras on stage. That is one reason why battles and crowd scenes often come later rather than early in Shakespeare's plays. There was no formal prohibition upon performance by women, and there certainly were women among the gatherers, so it is not beyond the bounds of possibility that female crowd members were played by females.

The play began at two o'clock in the afternoon and the theater had to be cleared by five. After the main show, there would be a jig—which consisted not only of dancing, but also of knockabout comedy (it is the origin of the farcical "afterpiece" in the eighteenth-century theater). So the time available for a Shakespeare play was about two and a half hours, somewhere between the "two hours' traffic" mentioned in the prologue to *Romeo and Juliet* and the "three hours' spectacle" referred to in the preface to the 1647 Folio of Beaumont and Fletcher's plays.

The prologue to a play by Thomas Middleton refers to a thousand lines as "one hour's words," so the likelihood is that about two and a half thousand, or a maximum of three thousand lines, made up the performed text. This is indeed the length of most of Shakespeare's comedies, whereas many of his tragedies and histories are much longer, raising the possibility that he wrote full scripts, possibly with eventual publication in mind, in the full knowledge that the stage version would be heavily cut. The short Quarto texts published in his lifetime—they used to be called "Bad" Quartos—provide fascinating evidence as to the kind of cutting that probably took place. So, for instance, the First Quarto of *Hamlet* neatly merges two occasions when Hamlet is overheard, the "Fishmonger" and the "nunnery" scenes.

The social composition of the audience was mixed. The poet Sir John Davies wrote of "A thousand townsmen, gentlemen and whores, / Porters and servingmen" who would "together throng" at the public playhouses. Though moralists associated female play-going with adultery and the sex trade, many perfectly respectable citizens' wives were regular attendees. Some, no doubt, resembled the modern groupie: a story attested in two different sources has one citizen's wife making a post-show assignation with Richard Burbage and ending up in bed with Shakespeare—supposedly eliciting from the latter the quip that William the Conqueror was before Richard III. Defenders of theater liked to say that by witnessing the comeuppance of villains on the stage, audience members would repent of their own wrongdoings, but the reality is that most people went to the theater then, as they do now, for entertainment more than for moral edification. Besides, it would be foolish to suppose that audiences behaved in a homogeneous way: a pamphlet of the 1630s tells of how two men went to see *Pericles* and one of them laughed while the other wept. Bishop John Hall complained that people went to church for the same reasons that they went to the theater: "for company, for custom, for recreation . . . to feed his eyes or his ears . . . or perhaps for sleep."

Men-about-town and clever young lawyers went to be seen as much as to see. In the modern popular imagination, shaped not least by *Shakespeare in Love* and the opening sequence of Laurence Olivier's *Henry V* film, the penny-paying groundlings stand in the yard hurling abuse or encouragement and hazelnuts or orange peel at the actors, while the sophisticates in the covered galleries appreciate Shakespeare's soaring poetry. The reality was probably the other way around. A "groundling" was a kind of fish, so the nickname suggests the penny audience standing below the level of the stage and gazing in silent openmouthed wonder at the spectacle unfolding above them. The more difficult audience members, who kept up a running commentary of clever remarks on the performance and who occasionally got into quarrels with players, were the gallants. Like Hollywood movies in modern times, Elizabethan and Jacobean plays exercised a powerful influence on the fashion and behavior of the young. John Marston mocks the lawyers who would open their lips, perhaps to court a girl, and out would "flow / Naught but pure Juliet and Romeo."

THE ENSEMBLE AT WORK

In the absence of typewriters and photocopying machines, reading aloud would have been the means by which the company got to know a new play. The tradition of the playwright reading his complete script to the assembled company endured for generations. A copy would then have been taken to the Master of the Revels for licensing. The theater book-holder or prompter would then have copied the parts for distribution to the actors. A partbook consisted of the character's lines, with each speech preceded by the last three or four words of the speech before, the so-called cue. These would have been taken away and studied or "conned." During this period of learning the parts, an actor might have had some one-to-one instruction, perhaps from the dramatist, perhaps from a senior actor who had played the same part before, and, in the case of an apprentice, from his master. A high percentage of Desdemona's lines occur in dialogue with Othello, of Lady Macbeth's with Macbeth, Cleopatra's with Antony, and Volumnia's with Coriolanus. The roles would almost certainly have been taken by the apprentice of the lead actor, usually Burbage, who delivers the majority of the cues. Given that apprentices lodged with their masters, there would have been ample opportunity for personal instruction, which may be what made it possible for young men to play such demanding parts.

9. Hypothetical reconstruction of the interior of an Elizabethan playhouse during a performance.

After the parts were learned, there may have been no more than a single rehearsal before the first performance. With six different plays to be put on every week, there was no time for more. Actors, then, would go into a show with a very limited sense of the whole. The notion of a collective rehearsal process that is itself a process of discovery for the actors is wholly modern and would have been incomprehensible to Shakespeare and his original ensemble. Given the number of parts an actor had to hold in his memory, the forgetting of lines was probably more frequent than in the modern theater. The book-holder was on hand to prompt.

Backstage personnel included the property man, the tire-man who oversaw the costumes, call boys, attendants, and the musicians, who might play at various times from the main stage, the rooms above and within the tiring-house. Scriptwriters sometimes made a nuisance of themselves backstage. There was often tension between the acting companies and the freelance playwrights from whom they purchased scripts: it was a smart move on the part of

Shakespeare and the Lord Chamberlain's Men to bring the writing process in-house.

Scenery was limited, though sometimes set pieces were brought on (a bank of flowers, a bed, the mouth of hell). The trapdoor from below, the gallery stage above, and the curtained discovery-space at the back allowed for an array of special effects: the rising of ghosts and apparitions, the descent of gods, dialogue between a character at a window and another at ground level, the revelation of a statue or a pair of lovers playing at chess. Ingenious use could be made of props, as with the ass's head in *A Midsummer Night's Dream*. In a theater that does not clutter the stage with the material paraphernalia of everyday life, those objects that are deployed may take on powerful symbolic weight, as when Shylock bears his weighing scales in one hand and knife in the other, thus becoming a parody of the figure of Justice who traditionally bears a sword and a balance. Among the more significant items in the property cupboard of Shakespeare's company, there would have been a throne (the "chair of state"), joint stools, books, bottles, coins, purses, letters (which are brought onstage, read, or referred to on about eighty occasions in the complete works), maps, gloves, a set of stocks (in which Kent is put in *King Lear*), rings, rapiers, daggers, broadswords, staves, pistols, masks and vizards, heads and skulls, torches and tapers and lanterns which served to signal night scenes on the daylit stage, a buck's head, an ass's head, animal costumes. Live animals also put in appearances, most notably the dog Crab in *The Two Gentlemen of Verona* and possibly a young polar bear in *The Winter's Tale*.

The costumes were the most important visual dimension of the play. Playwrights were paid between £2 and £6 per script, whereas Alleyn was not averse to paying £20 for "a black velvet cloak with sleeves embroidered all with silver and gold." No matter the period of the play, actors always wore contemporary costume. The excitement for the audience came not from any impression of historical accuracy, but from the richness of the attire and perhaps the transgressive thrill of the knowledge that here were commoners like themselves strutting in the costumes of courtiers in effective defiance of the strict sumptuary laws whereby in real life people had to wear the clothes that befitted their social station.

To an even greater degree than props, costumes could carry symbolic importance. Racial characteristics could be suggested: a breastplate and helmet for a Roman soldier, a turban for a Turk, long robes for exotic characters such as Moors, a gabardine for a Jew. The figure of Time, as in *The Winter's Tale*, would be equipped with hourglass, scythe, and wings; Rumour, who speaks the prologue of *2 Henry IV*, wore a costume adorned with a thousand tongues. The wardrobe in the tiring-house of the Globe would have contained much of the same stock as that of rival manager Philip Henslowe at the Rose: green gowns for outlaws and foresters, black for melancholy men such as Jaques and people in mourning such as the Countess in *All's Well That Ends Well* (at the beginning of *Hamlet*, the prince is still in mourning black when everyone else is in festive garb for the wedding of the new king), a gown and hood for a friar (or a feigned friar like the Duke in *Measure for Measure*), blue coats and tawny to distinguish the followers of rival factions, a leather apron and ruler for a carpenter (as in the opening scene of *Julius Caesar*—and in *A Midsummer Night's Dream*, where this is the only sign that Peter Quince is a carpenter), a cockle hat with staff and a pair of sandals for a pilgrim or palmer (the disguise assumed by Helen in *All's Well*), bodices and kirtles with farthingales beneath for the boys who are to be dressed as girls. A gender switch such as that of Rosalind or Jessica seems to have taken between fifty and eighty lines of dialogue— Viola does not resume her "maiden weeds," but remains in her boy's costume to the end of *Twelfth Night* because a change would have slowed down the action at just the moment it was speeding to a climax. Henslowe's inventory also included "a robe for to go invisible": Oberon, Puck, and Ariel must have had something similar.

As the costumes appealed to the eyes, so there was music for the ears. Comedies included many songs. Desdemona's willow song, perhaps a late addition to the text, is a rare and thus exceptionally poignant example from tragedy. Trumpets and tuckets sounded for ceremonial entrances, drums denoted an army on the march. Background music could create atmosphere, as at the beginning of *Twelfth Night*, during the lovers' dialogue near the end of *The Merchant of Venice*, when the statue seemingly comes to life in *The Winter's Tale*, and for the revival of Pericles and of Lear (in the Quarto text, but not the Folio). The haunting sound of the hautboy suggested a realm beyond the human, as when the god Hercules is imagined deserting Mark Antony. Dances symbolized the harmony of the end of a comedy—though in Shakespeare's world of mingled joy and sorrow, someone is usually left out of the circle.

The most important resource was, of course, the actors themselves. They needed many skills: in the words of one contemporary commentator, "dancing, activity, music, song, elocution, ability of body, memory, skill of weapon, pregnancy of wit." Their bodies were as significant as their voices. Hamlet tells the player to "suit the action to the word, the word to the action": moments of strong emotion, known as "passions," relied on a repertoire of dramatic gestures as well as a modulation of the voice. When Titus Andronicus has had his hand chopped off, he asks "How can I grace my talk, / Wanting a hand to give it action?" A pen portrait of "The Character of an Excellent Actor" by the dramatist John Webster is almost certainly based on his impression of Shakespeare's leading man, Richard Burbage: "By a full and significant action of body, he charms our attention: sit in a full theatre, and you will think you see so many lines drawn from the circumference of so many ears, whiles the actor is the centre . . ."

Though Burbage was admired above all others, praise was also heaped upon the apprentice players whose alto voices fitted them for the parts of women. A spectator at Oxford in 1610 records how the audience were reduced to tears by the pathos of Desdemona's death. The puritans who fumed about the biblical prohibition upon crossdressing and the encouragement to sodomy constituted by the sight of an adult male kissing a teenage boy onstage were a small minority. Little is known, however, about the characteristics of the leading apprentices in Shakespeare's company. It may perhaps be inferred that one was a lot taller than the other, since Shakespeare often wrote for a pair of female friends, one tall and fair, the other short and dark (Helena and Hermia, Rosalind and Celia, Beatrice and Hero).

We know little about Shakespeare's own acting roles—an early allusion indicates that he often took royal parts, and a venerable tradition gives him old Adam in *As You Like It* and the ghost of old King Hamlet. Save for Burbage's lead roles and the generic part of the clown, all such castings are mere speculation. We do not even know for sure whether the original Falstaff was Will Kempe or another actor who specialized in comic roles, Thomas Pope.

Kempe left the company in early 1599. Tradition has it that he fell out with Shakespeare over the matter of excessive improvisation. He was replaced by Robert Armin, who was less of a clown and more of a cerebral wit: this explains the difference between such parts as Lancelet Gobbo and Dogberry, which were written for Kempe, and the more verbally sophisticated Feste and Lear's Fool, which were written for Armin.

One thing that is clear from surviving "plots" or storyboards of plays from the period is that a degree of doubling was necessary. *2 Henry VI* has over sixty speaking parts, but more than half of the characters only appear in a single scene and most scenes have only six to eight speakers. At a stretch, the play could be performed by thirteen actors. When Thomas Platter saw *Julius Caesar* at the Globe in 1599, he noted that there were about fifteen. Why doesn't Paris go to the Capulet ball in *Romeo and Juliet*? Perhaps because he was doubled with Mercutio, who does. In *The Winter's Tale*, Mamillius might have come back as Perdita and Antigonus been doubled by Camillo, making the partnership with Paulina at the end a very neat touch. Titania and Oberon are often played by the same pair as Hippolyta and Theseus, suggesting a symbolic matching of the rulers of the worlds of night and day, but it is questionable whether there would have been time for the necessary costume changes. As so often, one is left in a realm of tantalizing speculation.

THE KING'S MAN

On Queen Elizabeth's death in 1603, the new king, James I, who had held the Scottish throne as James VI since he had been an infant, immediately took the Lord Chamberlain's Men under his direct patronage. Henceforth they would be the King's Men, and for the rest of Shakespeare's career they were favored with far more court performances than any of their rivals. There even seem to have been rumors early in the reign that Shakespeare and Burbage were being considered for knighthoods, an unprecedented honor for mere actors—and one that in the event was not accorded to a member of the profession for nearly three hundred years, when the title was bestowed upon Henry Irving, the leading Shakespearean actor of Queen Victoria's reign.

Shakespeare's productivity rate slowed in the Jacobean years, not because of age or some personal trauma, but because there were frequent outbreaks of plague, causing the theaters to be closed for long periods. The King's Men were forced to spend many months on the road. Between November 1603 and 1608, they were to be found at various towns in the south and Midlands, though Shakespeare probably did not tour with them by this time. He had bought a large house back home in Stratford and was accumulating other property. He may indeed have stopped acting soon after the new king took the throne. With the London theaters closed so much of the time and a large repertoire on the stocks, Shakespeare seems to have focused his energies on writing a few long and complex tragedies that could have been played on demand at court: *Othello*, *King Lear*, *Antony and Cleopatra*, *Coriolanus*, and *Cymbeline* are among his longest and poetically grandest plays. *Macbeth* only survives in a shorter text, which shows signs of adaptation after Shakespeare's death. The bitterly satirical *Timon of Athens*, apparently a collaboration with Thomas Middleton that may have failed on the stage, also belongs to this period. In comedy, too, he wrote longer and morally darker works than in the Elizabethan period, pushing at the very bounds of the form in *Measure for Measure* and *All's Well That Ends Well*.

From 1608 onward, when the King's Men began occupying the indoor Blackfriars playhouse (as a winter house, meaning that they used the outdoor Globe only in summer?), Shakespeare turned to a more romantic style. His company had a great success with a revived and altered version of an old pastoral play called *Mucedorus*. It even featured a bear. The younger dramatist John Fletcher, meanwhile, sometimes working in collaboration with Francis Beaumont, was pioneering a new style of tragicomedy, a mix of romance and royalism laced with intrigue and pastoral excursions. Shakespeare experimented with this idiom in *Cymbeline* and it was presumably with his blessing that Fletcher eventually took over as the King's Men's company dramatist. The two writers apparently collaborated on three plays in the years 1612–14: a lost romance called *Cardenio* (based on the love-madness of a character in Cervantes' *Don Quixote*), *Henry VIII* (originally staged with the title "All Is True"), and *The Two Noble Kinsmen*, a dramatization of Chaucer's "Knight's Tale." These were written after Shakespeare's two final solo-authored plays, *The Winter's Tale*, a self-consciously old-fashioned work dramatizing the pastoral romance of his old enemy Robert Greene, and *The Tempest*, which at one and the same time drew together multiple theatrical traditions, diverse reading, and contemporary interest in the fate of a ship that had been wrecked on the way to the New World.

The collaborations with Fletcher suggest that Shakespeare's career ended with a slow fade rather than the sudden retirement supposed by the nineteenth-century Romantic critics who read Prospero's epilogue to *The Tempest* as Shakespeare's personal farewell to his art. In the last few years of his life Shakespeare certainly spent more of his time in Stratford-upon-Avon, where he became further involved in property dealing and litigation. But his London life also continued. In 1613 he made his first major London property purchase: a freehold house in the Blackfriars district, close to his company's indoor theater. *The Two Noble Kinsmen* may have been written as late as 1614, and Shakespeare was in London on business a little over a year before he died of an unknown cause at home in Stratford-upon-Avon in 1616, probably on his fifty-second birthday.

About half the sum of his works were published in his lifetime, in texts of variable quality. A few years after his death, his fellow actors began putting together an authorized edition of his complete *Comedies, Histories and Tragedies*. It appeared in 1623, in large "Folio" format. This collection of thirty-six plays gave Shakespeare his immortality. In the words of his fellow dramatist Ben Jonson, who contributed two poems of praise at the start of the Folio, the body of his work made him "a monument without a tomb":

> And art alive still while thy book doth live
> And we have wits to read and praise to give . . .
> He was not of an age, but for all time!

SHAKESPEARE'S WORKS: A CHRONOLOGY

1589–91	*? Arden of Faversham* (possible part authorship)
1589–92	*The Taming of the Shrew*
1589–92	*? Edward the Third* (possible part authorship)
1591	*The Second Part of Henry the Sixth*, originally called *The First Part of the Contention Betwixt the Two Famous Houses of York and Lancaster* (element of coauthorship possible)
1591	*The Third Part of Henry the Sixth*, originally called *The True Tragedy of Richard Duke of York* (element of co-authorship probable)
1591–92	*The Two Gentlemen of Verona*
1591–92; perhaps revised 1594	*The Lamentable Tragedy of Titus Andronicus* (probably cowritten with, or revising an earlier version by, George Peele)
1592	*The First Part of Henry the Sixth*, probably with Thomas Nashe and others
1592/94	*King Richard the Third*
1593	*Venus and Adonis* (poem)
1593–94	*The Rape of Lucrece* (poem)
1593–1608	*Sonnets* (154 poems, published 1609 with *A Lover's Complaint*, a poem of disputed authorship)
1592–94/ 1600–03	*Sir Thomas More* (a single scene for a play originally by Anthony Munday, with other revisions by Henry Chettle, Thomas Dekker, and Thomas Heywood)
1594	*The Comedy of Errors*
1595	*Love's Labour's Lost*

1595–97	*Love's Labour's Won* (a lost play, unless the original title for another comedy)
1595–96	*A Midsummer Night's Dream*
1595–96	*The Tragedy of Romeo and Juliet*
1595–96	*King Richard the Second*
1595–97	*The Life and Death of King John* (possibly earlier)
1596–97	*The Merchant of Venice*
1596–97	*The First Part of Henry the Fourth*
1597–98	*The Second Part of Henry the Fourth*
1598	*Much Ado About Nothing*
1598–99	*The Passionate Pilgrim* (20 poems, some not by Shakespeare)
1599	*The Life of Henry the Fifth*
1599	"To the Queen" (epilogue for a court performance)
1599	*As You Like It*
1599	*The Tragedy of Julius Caesar*
1600–01	*The Tragedy of Hamlet, Prince of Denmark* (perhaps revising an earlier version)
1600–01	*The Merry Wives of Windsor* (perhaps revising version of 1597–99)
1601	"Let the Bird of Loudest Lay" (poem, known since 1807 as "The Phoenix and Turtle" [turtle-dove])
1601	*Twelfth Night, or What You Will*
1601–02	*The Tragedy of Troilus and Cressida*
1604	*The Tragedy of Othello, the Moor of Venice*
1604	*Measure for Measure*
1605	*All's Well That Ends Well*
1605	*The Life of Timon of Athens*, with Thomas Middleton
1605–06	*The Tragedy of King Lear*
1605–08	? contribution to *The Four Plays in One* (lost, except for *A Yorkshire Tragedy*, mostly by Thomas Middleton)

1606	*The Tragedy of Macbeth* (surviving text has additional scenes by Thomas Middleton)
1606–07	*The Tragedy of Antony and Cleopatra*
1608	*The Tragedy of Coriolanus*
1608	*Pericles, Prince of Tyre*, with George Wilkins
1610	*The Tragedy of Cymbeline*
1611	*The Winter's Tale*
1611	*The Tempest*
1612–13	*Cardenio*, with John Fletcher (survives only in later adaptation called *Double Falsehood* by Lewis Theobald)
1613	*Henry VIII (All Is True)*, with John Fletcher
1613–14	*The Two Noble Kinsmen*, with John Fletcher

KINGS AND QUEENS OF ENGLAND: FROM THE HISTORY PLAYS TO SHAKESPEARE'S LIFETIME

	Life span	*Reign*
Angevins:		
Henry II	1133–1189	1154–1189
Richard I	1157–1199	1189–1199
John	1166–1216	1199–1216
Henry III	1207–1272	1216–1272
Edward I	1239–1307	1272–1307
Edward II	1284–1327	1307–1327 deposed
Edward III	1312–1377	1327–1377
Richard II	1367–1400	1377–1399 deposed
Lancastrians:		
Henry IV	1367–1413	1399–1413
Henry V	1387–1422	1413–1422
Henry VI	1421–1471	1422–1461 and 1470–1471
Yorkists:		
Edward IV	1442–1483	1461–1470 and 1471–1483
Edward V	1470–1483	1483 not crowned: deposed and assassinated
Richard III	1452–1485	1483–1485
Tudors:		
Henry VII	1457–1509	1485–1509
Henry VIII	1491–1547	1509–1547
Edward VI	1537–1553	1547–1553

	Life span	*Reign*
Jane	1537–1554	1553 not crowned: deposed and executed
Mary I	1516–1558	1553–1558
Philip of Spain	1527–1598	1554–1558 co-regent with Mary
Elizabeth I	1533–1603	1558–1603

Stuart:

James I	1566–1625	1603–1625 James VI of Scotland (1567–1625)

THE HISTORY BEHIND THE HISTORIES: A CHRONOLOGY

Square brackets indicate events that happen just outside a play's timescale but are mentioned in the play.

Date	Event	Location	Play
22 May 1200	Truce between King John and Philip Augustus	Le Goulet, Normandy	*King John*
Apr 1203	Death of Arthur	Rouen	*King John*
1209	Pope Innocent III excommunicates King John		*King John*
18/19 Oct 1216	Death of King John	Swineshead, Lincolnshire	*King John*
Apr–Sep 1398	Quarrel, duel, and exile of Bullingbrook and Mowbray	Coventry	*Richard II*
3 Feb 1399	Death of John of Gaunt	Leicester	*Richard II*
Jul 1399	Bullingbrook lands in England	Ravenspur, Yorkshire	*Richard II*
Aug 1399	Richard II captured by Bullingbrook	Wales	*Richard II*
30 Sep 1399	Richard II abdicates	London	*Richard II*
13 Oct 1399	Coronation of Henry IV	London	*Richard II*
Jan–Feb 1400	Death of Richard II	Pontefract Castle	*Richard II*
22 Jun 1402	Owen Glendower captures Edmund Mortimer	Bryn Glas, Wales	*1 Henry IV*
14 Sep 1402	Henry Percy defeats Scottish army	Homildon Hill, Yorkshire	*1 Henry IV*

Date	Event	Location	Play
21 Jul 1403	Battle of Shrewsbury; death of Henry Percy (Hotspur)	Battlefield, near Shrewsbury, Shropshire	*1 & 2 Henry IV*
Feb 1405	Tripartite Indenture between Owen Glendower, Edmund Mortimer, and Northumberland (Henry Percy)	Bangor	*1 Henry IV*
May–Jun 1405	Rebellion of Archbishop of York (Richard Scroop), Earl of Norfolk (Thomas Mowbray), and Lord Bardolph	Yorkshire	*2 Henry IV*
8 Jun 1405	Trial and execution of Archbishop of York and Earl of Norfolk	York	*2 Henry IV*
20 Mar 1413	Death of Henry IV	Westminster Abbey	*2 Henry IV*
9 Apr 1413	Coronation of Henry V	Westminster Abbey	*2 Henry IV*
c.1415–16?	Death of Owen Glendower	Wales?	*2 Henry IV*
Early Aug 1415	Execution of Earl of Cambridge, Lord Scroop, and Sir Thomas Grey	Southampton	*Henry V*
14 Aug–22 Sep 1415	Siege of Harfleur	Harfleur, Normandy	*Henry V*
25 Oct 1415	Battle of Agincourt	Agincourt, Pas de Calais	*Henry V*
31 Aug 1422	Death of Henry V	Bois de Vincennes, near Paris	*1 Henry VI*
18 Jan 1425	Death of Edmund Mortimer	Ireland	*1 Henry VI*
Oct 1428–May 1429	Siege of Orléans	Orléans	*1 Henry VI*
17 Oct 1428	Death of Lord Salisbury	Orléans	*1 Henry VI*

Date	Event	Location	Play
18 Jun 1429	Capture of Lord Talbot at battle of Patay	Patay, near Orléans	*1 Henry VI*
18 Jul 1429	Coronation of Charles VII	Rheims Cathedral	*1 Henry VI*
6 Nov 1429	Coronation of Henry VI as King of England	Westminster Abbey	[*1 Henry VI*]
23 May 1430	Capture of Joan of Arc	Compiègne, near Soissons	*1 Henry VI*
30 May 1431	Execution of Joan of Arc	Saint-Ouen, near Paris	*1 Henry VI*
16 Dec 1431	Coronation of Henry VI as King of France	Notre Dame Cathedral, Paris	*1 Henry VI*
14 Sep 1435	Death of Duke of Bedford	Rouen	*1 Henry VI*
Summer–Autumn 1441	Arrest and trial of Eleanor Cobham and accomplices	London	*2 Henry VI*
20 May 1442	Lord Talbot created Earl of Shrewsbury	Paris	*1 Henry VI*
23 Apr 1445	Marriage of Henry VI and Margaret of Anjou	Titchfield, Hampshire	*2 Henry VI*
23 Feb 1447	Death of Humphrey, Duke of Gloucester	Bury St. Edmunds	*2 Henry VI*
11 Apr 1447	Death of Cardinal Beaufort	Winchester	*2 Henry VI*
2 May 1450	Death of Earl of Suffolk	English Channel	*2 Henry VI*
Jun–Jul 1450	Rebellion of Jack Cade	Kent and London	*2 Henry VI*
Spring 1452	Richard, Duke of York, marches on London	London	*2 Henry VI*
17 Jul 1453	Death of Lord Talbot at battle of Cantillon	Cantillon, Gascony	*1 Henry VI*
22 May 1455	First battle of St. Albans	St. Albans, Hertfordshire	*2 Henry VI*

Date	Event	Location	Play
10 Jul 1460	Battle of Northampton	Northampton	[*3 Henry VI*]
Oct 1460	Richard, Duke of York, holds Parliament	London	*3 Henry VI*
30 Dec 1460	Battle of Wakefield	Wakefield, Yorkshire	*3 Henry VI*
2 Feb 1461	Battle of Mortimer's Cross	Near Wigmore, Herefordshire	*3 Henry VI*
29 Mar 1461	Battle of Towton	Near Tadcaster, Yorkshire	*3 Henry VI*
28 Jun 1461	Coronation of Edward IV	Westminster Abbey	*3 Henry VI*
1 May 1464	Marriage of Edward IV and Elizabeth Woodville	Northamptonshire	*3 Henry VI*
Jul 1465	Henry VI captured	Lancashire	*3 Henry VI*
26 Jul 1469	Battle of Edgecote Moor	Near Banbury, Oxfordshire	*3 Henry VI*
Oct 1470–Apr/ May 1471	Readeption (restoration) of Henry VI	London	*3 Henry VI*
14 Apr 1471	Battle of Barnet; death of Warwick	Barnet, near London	*3 Henry VI*
4 May 1471	Battle of Tewkesbury; death of Edward, Prince of Wales	Tewkesbury, Gloucestershire	*3 Henry VI*
21 May 1471	Death of Henry VI	Tower of London	*3 Henry VI*
12 Jul 1472	Marriage of Richard, Duke of Gloucester, to Anne	Westminster Abbey	*Richard III*
18 Feb 1478	Death of Duke of Clarence	Tower of London	*Richard III*
9 Apr 1483	Death of Edward IV	Westminster	*Richard III*
Jun 1483	Death of Lord Hastings	Tower of London	*Richard III*

Date	Event	Location	Play
6 Jul 1483	Coronation of Richard III	Westminster Abbey	*Richard III*
2 Nov 1483	Death of Duke of Buckingham	Salisbury	*Richard III*
16 Mar 1485	Death of Queen Anne	Westminster	*Richard III*
22 Aug 1485	Battle of Bosworth Field	Leicestershire	*Richard III*
30 Oct 1485	Coronation of Henry VII	Westminster Abbey	[*Richard III*]
18 Jan 1486	Marriage of Henry VII and Elizabeth of York	Westminster Abbey	[*Richard III*]
Jun 1520	Meeting of Henry VIII and Francis I	"Field of the Cloth of Gold," near Calais, France	[*Henry VIII*]
17 May 1521	Death of Duke of Buckingham	Tower Hill, London	*Henry VIII*
29 Nov 1530	Death of Wolsey	Leicester	*Henry VIII*
25 Jan 1533	Marriage of Henry VIII and Anne Bullen (Boleyn)	Whitehall	*Henry VIII*
1 Jun 1533	Coronation of Anne Bullen (Boleyn)	Westminster Abbey	*Henry VIII*
7 Sep 1533	Birth of Princess Elizabeth	Greenwich Palace	*Henry VIII*
10 Sep 1533	Christening of Princess Elizabeth	Greenwich Palace	*Henry VIII*

FURTHER READING
AND VIEWING

CRITICAL APPROACHES

Barber, C. L., "Rule and Misrule in *Henry IV*," in his *Shakespeare's Festive Comedy* (1959). Superb linking to the "festive" world.

Bloom, Harold, ed., *Modern Critical Interpretations: William Shakespeare's Henry IV, Part 1* (1987). Extracts from strong twentieth-century critical approaches.

Bristol, Michael D., *Carnival and Theater: Plebeian Culture and the Structure of Authority in Renaissance England* (1985). Provocative Marxist reading.

Bulman, James, "*Henry IV, Parts 1* and *2*," in *The Cambridge Companion to Shakespeare's History Plays*, ed. Michael Hattaway (2002), pp. 158–76. Sensible overview.

Greenblatt, Stephen, "Invisible Bullets: Renaissance Authority and Its Subversion, *Henry IV and Henry V*," in *Political Shakespeare: Essays in Cultural Materialism*, ed. Jonathan Dollimore and Alan Sinfield (1985), pp. 18–47. Hugely influential "new historicist" reading. Reprinted in Greenblatt's *Shakespearean Negotiations* (1988).

Hodgdon, Barbara, *The End Crowns All: Closure and Contradiction in Shakespeare's History* (1991). Strong on structure.

Hunter, G. K., ed., *Shakespeare: Henry IV Parts I and II*, Macmillan Casebook series (1970). Invaluable selection of earlier criticism.

McAlindon, Tom, *Shakespeare's Tudor History: A Study of Henry IV Parts 1 and 2* (2000). Excellent account of critical history and cultural context, with good close reading.

McLoughlin, Cathleen T., *Shakespeare, Rabelais, and the Comical-Historical* (2000). Fascinating intertextual reading of *Henry IV* plays with Rabelais' *Gargantua and Pantagruel*.

Morgann, Maurice, *An Essay on the Dramatic Character of Sir John Falstaff* (1777, repr. 2004). Gloriously humane character criticism from the eighteenth century. Also freely available online, e.g., at www.19.5degs .com/ebook/essay-the-dramatic-character-of-sir-john-falstaff/466/ read#list

Patterson, Annabel, *Shakespeare and the Popular Voice* (1989) and *Reading*

Holinshed's Chronicles (1994). Two books that should be read as a pair.

Rackin, Phyllis, *Stages of History: Shakespeare's English Chronicles* (1990). Attentive to women and social inferiors as well as kings and nobles.

Rossiter, A. P., "Ambivalence: The Dialectic of the History Plays," in his *Angel with Horns: Fifteen Lectures on Shakespeare* (1961). Still one of the best things written on the play.

Saccio, Peter, *Shakespeare's English Kings* (1977). The best practical guide to the relationship between actual historical events in the middle ages, the Tudor chronicles, and Shakespeare's dramatic reshaping of history.

Taylor, Neil, *Henry IV Part Two* (1992). Basic guide.

Wood, Nigel, ed., *Henry IV Parts One and Two* (1995). Sophisticated collection of theoretically informed essays—not for beginners.

THE PLAY IN PERFORMANCE

Bogdanov, Michael, and Michael Pennington, *The English Shakespeare Company: The Story of the Wars of the Roses, 1986–1989* (1990). Insiders' account.

Callow, Simon, *Actors on Shakespeare: Henry IV Part 1* (2002). Takes the reader through the play "from the point of view of the practitioner"—lucid, intelligent, readable account.

Merlin, Bella, *With the Rogue's Company: Henry IV at the National Theatre* (2005). Detailed account of Nicholas Hytner's production.

Parsons, Keith, and Pamela Mason, eds., *Shakespeare in Performance* (1995). Includes a useful essay on both parts of *Henry IV* by Janet Clare—luxuriously illustrated.

Smallwood, Robert, ed., *Players of Shakespeare 6* (2004). Includes illuminating discussions by David Troughton on playing Bullingbrook/Henry IV and Desmond Barrit on Falstaff.

Wharton, T. F., *Text and Performance: Henry the Fourth Parts 1 & 2* (1983). A good basic introduction to the play and detailed discussions of three RSC productions and the BBC television version.

AVAILABLE ON DVD

Chimes at Midnight, directed by Orson Welles (1965, DVD 2000). Condenses all the Falstaff material from both parts of *Henry IV* plus *Henry V* and *The Merry Wives of Windsor*. Multi-award nominated, with a star-studded cast, as eccentric and brilliant as Welles' own performance as Falstaff. One of the all-time classic Shakespeare films.

Henry the Fourth Parts 1 and *2*, directed by David Giles (1979, DVD 2005). Somewhat pedestrian account for the BBC series. Anthony Quayle's Falstaff stands out.

Henry V, directed by Kenneth Branagh (1989, DVD 2002). Incorporated some flashback scenes from *Henry IV* with Robbie Coltrane as Falstaff.

My Own Private Idaho, directed by Gus Van Sant (1991, DVD 2005). Loosely based on the Hal-Falstaff relationship. Stars River Phoenix and Keanu Reeves as a pair of gay hustlers.

The Wars of the Roses, directed by Michael Bogdanov (1989, DVD 2005). Recording of English Shakespeare Company's eclectic and highly political stage production.

REFERENCES

1. Scott McMillin, *Shakespeare in Performance: Henry IV, Part One* (1991), p. 1.
2. A reference to *The Second Part of Henry the Fourth* or *Henry V* in Nicholas Breton's *A Post with a Packet of Mad Letters* (Part I, 1603).
3. James Wright, *Historia Historionica* (1699).
4. Colley Cibber, *An Apology for the Life of Mr Colley Cibber* (1740), p. 87.
5. Thomas Davies, *Dramatic Miscellanies* (1784, repr. 1971), pp. 124–8.
6. Davies, *Dramatic Miscellanies*, pp. 127–8.
7. Davies, *Dramatic Miscellanies*, pp. 136–41.
8. Davies, *Dramatic Miscellanies*, p. 153.
9. Laurence Selenick, *The Changing Room: Sex, Drag and Theatre* (2000), p. 270.
10. William Hazlitt, *Examiner*, 13 October 1816.
11. *The Athenaeum*, No. 902, 8 February 1845, p. 158.
12. Harold Child, "The Stage-History of *King Henry IV*," in *The First Part of the History of Henry IV*, ed. J. Dover Wilson (1946), pp. xxix–xlvi.
13. *Theatrical Journal*, Vol. 7, No. 346, 1 August 1846, pp. 243–4.
14. Henry Morley, diary entry for 14 May 1864 in *The Journal of a London Playgoer from 1851 to 1866* (1866), pp. 330–9.
15. Morley diary entry for 1 October 1864, pp. 344–5.
16. William Archer, *The Theatrical "World" of 1896* (1897, repr. 1971), pp. 141–50.
17. *The Athenaeum*, No. 3577, 16 May 1896, p. 659.
18. G. B. Shaw, *The Saturday Review*, London, Vol. 81, No. 2116, 16 May 1896, pp. 500–2.
19. William Butler Yeats, "At Stratford-upon-Avon" (1901), in his *Essays and Introductions* (1961), p. 97.
20. Herbert Farjeon, "King Henry the Fourth—Part I: Mr Robey's Falstaff," in his *The Shakespearean Scene: Dramatic Criticisms* (1949), p. 92.
21. Child, "The Stage-History of *King Henry IV*," pp. xxix–xlvi.
22. Stephen Potter, *New Statesman and Nation*, 6 October 1945, p. 227.
23. Audrey Williamson, "The New Triumvirate (1944–47)," in her *Old Vic Drama: A Twelve Years' Study of Plays and Players* (1948), pp. 172–212.
24. Anthony Quayle, in a foreword to *Shakespeare's Histories at Stratford, 1951* by J. Dover Wilson and T. C. Worsley (1970).

25. T. C. Worsley, *New Statesman and Nation*, 3 November 1951, pp. 489–90.
26. T. C. Worsley, *Shakespeare's Histories at Stratford, 1951* (1970), p. 31.
27. Worsley, *New Statesman and Nation*, 3 November 1951, pp. 489–90.
28. T. C. Worsley, *New Statesman and Nation*, 7 May 1955, p. 646.
29. Eric Keown, *Punch*, 11 May 1955, pp. 593–4.
30. Michael Bogdanov and Michael Pennington, *The English Shakespeare Company: The Story of the Wars of the Roses, 1986–1989* (1990), pp. 28–9, quoted in Barbara Hodgdon, *Shakespeare in Performance: Henry IV, Part Two* (1993), pp. 124–5.
31. Donald Malcolm, *New Yorker*, 30 April 1960, pp. 86–9.
32. Ben Brantley, *New York Times Current Events Edition*, 23 December 1993.
33. Ben Brantley, *New York Times*, 21 November 2003.
34. Paul Taylor, *Independent*, 6 May 2005.
35. Taylor, *Independent*, 6 May 2005.
36. Taylor, *Independent*, 6 May 2005.
37. McMillin, *Shakespeare in Performance*, p. 88.
38. McMillin, *Shakespeare in Performance*, p. 95.
39. McMillin, *Shakespeare in Performance*, p. 100.
40. David Troughton, "Bolingbroke in Richard II, and Henry IV," in Robert Smallwood, ed., *Players of Shakespeare 6* (2004).
41. Michael Billington, *Country Life*, 6 June 1991.
42. Janet Clare, "Henry IV Parts 1 & 2," in Keith Parsons and Pamela Mason, eds., *Shakespeare in Performance* (1995), p. 72.
43. Robert Speight, *Shakespeare Quarterly*, 15, 4 (1964).
44. London *Times*, 17 April 1964.
45. David E. Jones, *Drama Survey*, 4, 1 (Spring 1965).
46. Ronald Bryden, *New Statesman*, 24 April 1964.
47. Irving Wardle, London *Times*, 25 June 1975.
48. John Elsom, *Listener*, 3 June 1975.
49. Paul Taylor, *Independent*, 4 June 1991.
50. Taylor, *Independent*, 4 June 1991.
51. Allen Tate (1899–1979, American poet and critic), "Non Omnis Moriar."
52. John Peter, London *Sunday Times*, 2 June 1991.
53. Harold Hobson, London *Sunday Times*, 29 June 1975.
54. London *Times*, 17 April 1964.
55. Desmond Barrit, "Falstaff," in Smallwood, *Players of Shakespeare 6*.
56. *Country Life*, 6 June 1991.

57. London *Sunday Times*, 2 June 1991.
58. Charles Spencer, *Daily Telegraph*, 3 June 1991.
59. Elsom, *Listener*, 3 June 1975.
60. Hobson, *Sunday Times*, 29 June 1975.
61. Wardle, London *Times*, 25 June 1975.
62. *Hamlet*, Act 1 Scene 2.
63. John Elsom, *Listener*, 3 July 1975.
64. Troughton, "Bolingbroke in Richard II, and Henry IV."
65. Peter Thomson, *Shakespeare Survey*, 29 (1976).
66. Clare, "Henry IV Parts 1 & 2," p. 74.
67. Taylor, *Independent*, 4 June 1991.
68. Emrys James, *Theatre Quarterly*, Vol. 7, No. 27 (Autumn 1977).
69. Peter, *Sunday Times*, 2 June 1991.
70. Troughton, "Bolingbroke in Richard II, and Henry IV."
71. Benedict Nightingale, *New Statesman*, 6 February 1976.
72. Roger Warren, *Shakespeare Quarterly*, 34, 1 (Spring 1983).
73. Robert Smallwood, *Critical Quarterly*, 25, 1 (Spring 1983).
74. Barrit, "Falstaff."
75. Kate Bassett, *Daily Telegraph*, 3 July 2000.
76. London *Times*, 4 July 2000.
77. Nightingale, *New Statesman*, 6 February 1976.
78. Elsom, *Listener*, 3 July 1975.
79. Clare, "Henry IV Parts 1 & 2," p. 78.
80. Elsom, *Listener*, 3 July 1975.

ACKNOWLEDGMENTS AND PICTURE CREDITS

Preparation of *"Henry IV* in Performance" was assisted by a generous grant from the CAPITAL Centre (Creativity and Performance in Teaching and Learning) of the University of Warwick for research in the RSC archive at the Shakespeare Birthplace Trust. The Arts and Humanities Research Council (AHRC) funded a term's research leave that enabled Jonathan Bate to work on "The Director's Cut."

Picture research by Michelle Morton. Grateful acknowledgment is made to the Shakespeare Birthplace Trust for assistance with picture research (special thanks to Helen Hargest) and reproduction fees.

Images of RSC productions are supplied by the Shakespeare Centre Library and Archive, Stratford-upon-Avon. This Library, maintained by the Shakespeare Birthplace Trust, holds the most important collection of Shakespeare material in the UK, including the Royal Shakespeare Company's official archive. It is open to the public free of charge.

For more information see www.shakespeare.org.uk.

1. Herbert Beerbohm Tree (1896) Reproduced by permission of the Shakespeare Birthplace Trust
2. Ralph Richardson and Laurence Olivier (1945) John Vickers courtesy of the University of Bristol Theatre Collection
3. Directed by John Kidd and Anthony Quayle (1951) Angus McBean © Royal Shakespeare Company
4. Directed by Michael Attenborough (2000) John Haynes © Royal Shakespeare Company
5. Directed by Terry Hands (1975) Joe Cocks Studio Collection © Shakespeare Birthplace Trust
6. Directed by Michael Bogdanov (1987) © Donald Cooper/ photostage.co.uk